The Highly Civilized Man

THE HIGHLY CIVILIZED MAN

Richard Burton and the Victorian World

DANE KENNEDY

HARVARD UNIVERSITY PRESS
Cambridge, Massachusetts
London, England
2005

Library of Congress Cataloging-in-Publication Data

Kennedy, Dane Keith.
The highly civilized man :
Richard Burton and the Victorian world / Dane Kennedy.
p. cm.
Includes bibliographical references and index.
ISBN 0-674-01862-1 (hardcover : alk. paper)
1. Burton, Richard Francis, Sir, 1821–1890.
2. Great Britain—History—Victoria, 1837–1901—Biography.
3. Explorers—Great Britain—Biography.
4. Scholars—Great Britain—Biography.
I. Title.
G246.B8K46 2005
910′.92—dc22   2005040200

Contents

Illustrations

The Highly Civilized Man

Introduction

The way we view the world around us derives in large measure from notions of difference that took shape in the nineteenth century. This preoccupation with difference probably assumed its greatest urgency in the minds of those Britons we know as the Victorians, who devoted an immense amount of intellectual energy to the delineation of its traits and dimensions. The widening frontiers of trade and empire brought them into unprecedented association with peoples whose looks, speech, beliefs, and behavior differed from their own, stirring their curiosity and spurring their efforts to comprehend and classify these strangers. At the same time, their sense of themselves was destabilized by the dramatic social and economic changes sweeping through Britain, giving rise to new categories of difference at home. How the Victorians sought to make sense of these differences, to incorporate them within frames of reference meaningful to their lives, merits consideration not simply for its own sake, but because we continue to contend with the consequences of their efforts. Whether the issue is race or religion or language or sex or class, we work within or struggle against paradigms of difference the Victorians did much to determine.

This book takes as its point of entry into this Victorian world of difference the life and work of Richard Francis Burton (1821–1890). Explorer and ethnographer, polyglot and poet, consul and connoisseur of the sword, infantry officer and *enfant terrible*, this famed—and in some circles infamous—Victorian is such an over-sized figure that he seems at first sight almost *sui generis*. Biographers have tended to portray him in Nietszchean terms as a heroic, independent spirit operating outside the bounds of social conventions. Yet, for all his unusual talents and contrarian character, he was very much a man of his time, a product of nineteenth-century Britain and its imperial encounter with the world. He took part in some of the Victorians' most celebrated debates about difference—linguistic difference, racial difference, religious difference, sexual difference, and much more. Though he was not a systematic thinker, he had a restless, inquiring, and fiercely independent mind. His appetite for new experiences and curiosity about alien customs and beliefs caused him to range more widely in his inquiries into other lands and peoples than almost any figure of his generation, attaining an unrivaled familiarity with the vast array of ethical beliefs and social customs that inform human behavior. At the same time, he was capable of applying the experiences and skills he acquired abroad in appraisal of his own society, often exposing it to unsparing ethnographic scrutiny.

Burton's achievements reflect his lifelong engagement with difference. He was an exceptional linguist who claimed command of over twenty-five languages; a famed explorer and traveler whose journeys took him to India, Arabia, East Africa, West Africa, South America, North America, and elsewhere; an able ethnographer who both immersed himself in the quotidian lives of his subjects and advanced the cause of anthropology as a modern academic discipline; a prolific author who wrote over twenty travel books that give richly informed accounts of his experiences in other lands and his impressions of other peoples; and an assiduous translator who brought often unfamiliar works from Sanskrit, Arabic, Portuguese, and other languages to the notice of English readers, most famously the *Kama Sutra*. Few Victorians covered so much ground, both literally and figuratively, touching on such varied manifestations of difference in such a probing and provocative manner.

Burton's active career spanned fifty years, encompassing all but the final decade of the Victorian era, and it brought him into contact with a wide array of peoples, places, and ideas. He drew on this wealth of experience as the basis for his interventions in the various debates about difference that stirred public interest in nineteenth-century Britain. The rubric of race figured prominently in Victorians' efforts to categorize peoples, though it proved to be a highly pliable term, as its shifting usage by Burton makes readily apparent. He moved over time from a philological to a physiological to a cultural conception of racial difference. His initial understanding of the idea arose out of his experiences in the 1840s as an officer in the British East India Company's army in Sindh, where he was trained in a British Orientalist tradition that associated race with philology, stressing language acquisition as the key to ethnographic knowledge. The colonial state cultivated his exceptional linguistic talents for intelligence purposes, encouraging him to circulate in disguise among the Sindhi population. He applied this skill to the enterprise that brought him celebrity in Britain, his famous pilgrimage to Mecca in 1853 in the guise of a Sufi of Pathan origin. The boundary between impersonation and identification was a permeable one for Burton, and he acquired a deep and lasting affection for the Islamic religion and Muslim culture. They supplied important frames of reference from which he began to articulate objections to Christianity and Britain.

When Burton turned to black Africa, however, he failed to acquire a similar empathy for its peoples and practices. His inability to operate in disguise during his journey into Somalia in 1855 and his determination during the expedition to Lake Tanganyika in

1857–1859 to adopt the newly formulated role of the explorer as detached scientific observer prevented him from establishing the intimate bonds with locals that he had enjoyed in India and the Near East. Bolstered by the "scientific" racism that came to prominence in Britain and other Western countries around midcentury, Burton embraced a new view of difference, one that identified the body as its primary site and skin color and skull shape as its principal markers. By the mid-1860s he had become one of Britain's foremost proponents of the polygenist thesis that Africans constituted a distinct and inferior species of humanity. He advanced this position in a series of books about his travels in West Africa and Brazil and promulgated it as one of the founding members and leaders of the Anthropological Society of London.

Yet even as Burton positioned himself as an exponent of "scientific" racism, he also marshaled this understanding of racial difference as innate and immutable to challenge European universalist claims that its own civilization was unsurpassed and supplied a model for others to emulate. Because those claims were so closely bound up with Christianity, he deployed his knowledge of other systems of belief—not just the great traditions of Islam, Hinduism, Judaism, and Buddhism, but lesser ones such as African animist traditions and new creeds like Mormonism and Spiritualism—to demonstrate that each was embedded within its own particular historical and cultural context, precluding the possibility that any single system of religion enjoyed a monopoly on truth. This perspective served as the intellectual framework from which he wrote a subversive satire about Britain—*Stone Talk* (1865)—and a poignant plea on behalf of a freethinking agnosticism—*The Kasîdah* (1880). In both of these works his interpretation of difference took a direction that can best be described as cultural relativism.

In the final decade of his life, Burton turned his energies to the translation of works that spoke to the subject of sexuality far more frankly than most Victorians were willing to countenance. Using the Kama Shastra Society as the fictive front for his activities, he brought out a series of sexual treatises derived from classical Sanskrit and medieval Arabic texts, as well as an unexpurgated translation of the tales of the Arabian Nights, which included extended footnotes on sexual practices and a lengthy essay on pederasty. Once again he positioned his provocations within a relativist context, relying on the Orientalist expertise and frame of reference he had originally acquired in India to castigate Western attitudes toward sexuality as unenlightened and emotionally harmful. This critique and the open inquiry it initiated into the varied manifestations of sexuality brought him into collision with the moral purity forces in Britain and established him as an important harbinger of the modernist assault on Victorianism itself.

This brief summary of Burton's remarkable career barely begins to suggest the multiple levels at which he engaged with the Victorian world of difference, but it does point to the rationale for this study. Burton has already been the subject of dozens of biographies, some of them quite good.[1] Although they differ in their interpretations of his character and hence in the emphasis they give to particular aspects of his life, they share a basic premise: what makes him worthy of attention is what distinguished him from his contemporaries, what marked him as a man apart. This emphasis on exceptionalism is, of course, a truism that informs most biographies, supplying a key rationale of the genre. It carries the implicit risk, however, that the biographical subject will come to be seen as a comet blazing its own independent path, uninfluenced by those broader historical forces that shape the values and experiences of the rest of us. Burton's biographers have been especially susceptible to this notion, and the reasons are not hard to find. First, they have been too taken with the persona that

Burton himself presented to the world, one that snubbed social conventions and professed its estrangement from his homeland. Second, they have been too invested in the image of the man advanced by his Victorian admirers, who saw in him the embodiment of a heroic individualism that was out of sync with their age and hence unappreciated by it. Third, they have been too quick to assume that his peripatetic career allowed him to extricate himself from the embrace of place, interpreting his transit through so many geographical, linguistic, and ethnic zones as a *prima facie* indication of how little influence they must have had on him. Taken together, these perceptions have presented Burton as a force of nature, virtually free from the constraints that cultures and societies impose on ordinary mortals.

One impetus for this book, then, is to counter these claims of exceptionalism or, more accurately, to contextualize them, to explain how their initial promotion by Burton himself and their subsequent perpetuation by his memorialists and biographers arose out of the wider engagement with difference that preoccupied so many of the Victorians and their heirs. The first chapter opens with an examination of the most transparent of these assertions of exceptionalism—Burton as Gypsy. This serves as the point of departure for one of the main aims of the book—to demythologize and rehistoricize Burton's life. It seeks to show how Burton's natural talents were nurtured, his career options determined, and his provocative views on race, religion, and other issues informed by the broader forces—social, political, cultural, intellectual, and more—that shaped the Victorian world. I must acknowledge from the start that the difficulty in trying to articulate his life and thought with those forces derives from the sheer range and complexity of their connections: Burton's omnivorous intellectual curiosity, remarkable linguistic skills, and intimate encounters with varied peoples across the globe made available to him a vast repertoire of ideas, practices, and values. Few if any scholars possess the breadth of knowledge needed to identify all the influences that informed this polymorphous polymath. I certainly claim no comprehensiveness, but I do hope to demonstrate that we can make more sense of the man if we work harder to situate him in the multiple contexts that gave shape and direction to his life.

The second purpose of this book derives from the inverse proposition: we can gain fuller insights into the wider Victorian world through which Burton passed by giving the proper attention to his life. One of the peculiarities of the scholarship on nineteenth-century Britain, which stood at the center of a global economic and political system unprecedented in its scope and sway, is that it has long been bifurcated, consisting of two distinct historiographies that pursued quite separate agendas: a national historiography concerned with "the island story" of industrialization, class conflict, and political reform; and an imperial historiography concerned with overseas trade, migration, and conquest.[2] Until recently, historians have given little attention to the cross-pollination that occurred as a result of the constant traffic of peoples, goods, institutions, and ideas between these two spheres. (This may help to explain why Burton's biographers have neglected the larger influences on his life: they have had no historical framework within which to make sense of a man who moved so freely across the formal boundaries that the discipline has imposed on the past.) This has begun to change with the appearance of what have been termed (without much imagination) the "new British history" and the "new imperial history," which converge on the common realization that there is much to be gained from the examination of the interconnections between these hitherto separate areas of inquiry. It has become increasingly apparent, for example, that Britons' sense of their own national

identity was forged from the encounters with others that occurred as a result of commercial ventures, missionary endeavors,
imperial ambitions, and the like.[3]

At the source of this shift in historiographical practice lies the
epistemological insight that meaning is relational, arising out of
the delineation of difference. In recent years, a growing body of
research has taken up the question of how Europeans in particular constructed such categories of difference.[4] As this work has
grown more sophisticated and appreciative of the nuances of historical circumstances, it has come to understand that the efforts
by the British to establish a framework of difference that distinguished themselves from others operated in tension with an
equally compelling determination to erase difference through efforts to universalize their own norms, customs, and practices. The
result, according to several recent works, is a tension that stood at
the heart of the imperial project and, indeed, could even be traced
to the liberal foundations of Victorian thought.[5] Rather than re-
solving the contradiction between these contending views on difference, the British merely oscillated between them as circumstances warranted. Much the same tension remains with us today
in our debates about globalization, human rights, and the clash of
cultures.

An examination of Burton's career contributes to this larger
inquiry in several ways. It supplies a remarkably panoramic view
of the multiple contexts in which the British engagement with
difference played out. Burton casts light not only on the immense
geographical and ethnographic scale of this engagement, but on
the wide-ranging intellectual ferment it generated on subjects
such as race and religion and sexuality. Viewed from another perspective, Burton emerges as a man who contributed more than
most to the vast body of knowledge about other peoples and
practices that constituted the Victorians' "imperial archive."[6]

Burton's example also points to the surprising, often subversive outcomes that arose from this ferment, especially where the struggle to maintain the distinctions of difference collided with the impulse to promote universalist principles. Most of the recent scholarship on the construction of categories of difference stresses its role in the service of imperial power, showing how it sought to secure the boundaries between colonizer and colonized. Though Burton's own understanding of difference arose from this context and reflected its demands, it would be simplistic and misleading to attribute his lifelong preoccupation with this issue entirely to the instrumentalist purposes of the imperial enterprise. Difference became for Burton the basis for critical inquiry, capable of being turned in any direction, not least against Britain itself. His extended immersion in other cultures, especially those he entered by means of impersonation, gave him the experiential knowledge that made it possible for him to develop a relativist conception of difference. Once he understood that difference itself was a neutral epistemological device, a polarity that contained no inherent meaning, he began to wield it in ways that challenged the universalist claims of British society. Burton, then, remains a figure worthy of our attention not least because he embodies the transition from a Victorian to a modernist consciousness, a transition integrally connected to the encounter with the wider world of difference.

❦ I ❦

The Gypsy

A year or two after Richard Francis Burton completed his daring journey to Mecca in 1853, which brought him public renown in Britain, he sat for a photographic portrait that speaks volumes about the persona he sought to project. The identity of the photographer and the circumstances of the sitting are unknown, but the meaning of the image could not be clearer. It portrays Burton in a manner entirely at odds with conventional Victorian portraiture, which did its best to communicate the sitter's reputation and social standing through the iconography of clothing, props, and backdrop. Here we see Burton hunched over on a fabric-covered floor and framed against a blank background. His body is entirely covered by the loose, monotone folds of a blanket or *jubbah* (a long cloak or tunic worn by Muslims and Parsis) that evokes Near Eastern and North Indian custom even as its lack of definition resists cultural categorization. His face is drawn and pale as if ravaged by fever, his eyes turned to the viewer in a confrontational gaze. Nothing in the photograph gives any sign of his profession, his class, his nationality—anything, in fact, that might hint at his identity. It is the stark and unsettling image of a man who is utterly alone, who has discarded all emblems of attachment to society, who has fashioned for himself the guise of the unbound, atomistic, profoundly modern individual. At the bottom of his personal copy of the photograph, Burton supplied in

"The highly civilised man": Burton wrote those words underneath this photograph, which was taken sometime between his journey to Mecca in 1853 and his expedition to Harar in 1855. Courtesy of the Royal Geographical Society.

his distinctive handwriting a stunning caption: "the highly civilised man."[1]

What did he mean? The least likely explanation is a literal one. Although Burton was never hesitant about advertising his abilities and accomplishments, which were formidable enough to merit the admiration and even awe of many of his contemporaries, the caption's reference to such an unconventional and disquieting portrait gives it an ironic cast. This irony is directed in the first instance toward Burton himself, since his appearance so clearly contravenes the Victorian image of a civilized man. But the highly self-conscious manner in which Burton has posed against convention in the photograph points to the main target of his irony—what most educated Britons took to be the distinguishing features of civilization itself. By portraying himself as free from the familiar markers of Western cultural identity, he seems to be commenting on how such identities and the values they advance serve to define and delimit what we understand as civilization, which is itself inextricably enmeshed within these arbitrary and insular codes. Burton's expatriate youth and peripatetic career distanced him from the land of his birth and nurtured his antagonism toward the bourgeois culture that dominated Victorian Britain, a culture that associated civilized life with religious piety, sexual restraint, economic freedom, and political rights for responsible male citizens. His determination to keep his distance from that culture is apparent in the photograph, and its caption shows us how far he was prepared to go in order to fashion his claims of difference.

The subversive tenor of this self-fashioning was equally evident to others. Throughout the course of his career, Burton stirred strong feelings from his contemporaries, many of whom viewed him with suspicion. They questioned his religious convictions, his ethnic loyalties, his moral standards, his sexual proclivities, and much more. These concerns converged in a culminating doubt about whether he was, in fact, a civilized man. As *The Times* pointedly observed in its obituary of Burton, "with barbarism he had almost more sympathy than with civilisation."[2] Another posthumous assessment amplified this point: "He stands as a type of the domiciled barbarian, the natural man turned loose into nineteenth-century society. . . . Civilisation could neither redeem nor subdue him."[3] Burton both provoked these sorts of judgments with his behavior and refuted in his work their unreflecting assumption of the superiority of British society and culture.

෴෴෴

For the Victorians, Gypsies supplied a stock figure of difference, an internal other untamed by civilization. Those who knew Richard Burton best were fond of identifying him in their biographies and memoirs with those enigmatic, wayfaring people. His wife, Isabel, made repeated reference to his Gipsy-like appearance and personality, and she cited others who did the same. In the opening pages of her biography of her husband, she quoted a passage from an earlier biographical sketch of Burton by his lifelong friend Alfred Bates Richards, who speculated that the famed author and adventurer had "a drop of Oriental, perhaps gipsy, blood. By gipsy we must understand the pure Eastern."[4] Later in the book she reprinted an obituary from the *Journal of the Gypsy Lore Society*, which also suggested "a tinge of Arab or, perhaps, of Gypsy blood in Burton's race," adding that Burton was a Romany name. Though Isabel denied that her husband had any direct Gypsy lineage (a claim she seemed to contradict elsewhere in the biography), she insisted that "he showed many of [the Gypsies'] peculiarities in appearance, disposition, and speech—speaking Romany like themselves."[5] She went on to describe her own childhood encounters with the "oriental gypsies" who camped near her country home, particularly a fortune-teller auspiciously named Hagar Burton, who predicted that Isabel would marry a man bearing "the name of our tribe."[6] (In later years she would appear as "Hagar, the old gypsy matriarch" at costume balls.)[7] When she first met her future husband, she claimed that his voice left her "spellbound," much the way she felt "when I hear gypsy music." "The more I got to know of Richard," she declared, "the more his strange likeness to the gypsies struck me."[8]

These references to Richard Burton's affinities with Gypsies and their "wild and lawless life" had romantic associations for Isabel, but they carried a quite different valence for others who came in contact with him.[9] The poet Arthur Symons conceded that Burton was "a man of genius," but considered his gaze disturbing: "he was gypsy in his terrible, magnetic eyes—the sullen eyes of a stinging serpent."[10] Similarly, Wilfred Scawen Blunt, who was struck by Burton's "eyes like a wild beast's," found in his face "little of the European" and suspected "a cross in his blood, gipsy or other."[11] And Stanley Lane-Poole, a fellow Orientalist who clashed with Burton over his translation of the Arabian Nights, wrote that there were those, "including some of the Romany themselves, who saw gipsy written in his peculiar eyes as in his character, wild and resentful, essentially vagabond, intolerant of convention and restraint."[12] Each of these men saw in Burton's fierce features (accentuated by the scar across his cheek caused by a Somali spear) and hypnotic gaze (cultivated as part of his interest in mesmerism) the sinister, anarchic mark of the Gypsy.

Critics and defenders may have attached contrasting moral meanings to Burton as Gypsy, but they agreed on the appropriateness of the analogy. It spoke to those qualities that seemed to set Burton apart, to distinguish him from his countrymen, to mark him as a figure without a fixed abode or affiliation. The

Gypsy, in short, signified Burton's status as an outsider. For some of his contemporaries, this status made him a magnetic figure, for others a repellent one.

It should come as no surprise that Gypsies fascinated Burton. He sought them out during his travels to various lands and devoted a great deal of time to the study of their language, customs, and origins. In 1875 he published a brief note in *The Academy* that speculated on the Gypsies' kinship to the Jats of India, and he left at his death a longer unpublished manuscript on the subject, where he traced their migrations through Europe, the Middle East, North Africa, and the Americas.[13] He also was a founding member of the Gypsy Lore Society, which became the main institutional outlet for the late Victorian fascination with Gypsies.[14] This fascination gave expression to a deep-seated ambivalence about urban industrial civilization and the middle-class mores that informed it. The rural nomadic existence of the Gypsies, unattached to property and unregulated by authorities, evoked nostalgia for a simpler life freed from the conventions and constraints of modern English society and especially from conformity to its bourgeois moral code.[15] Burton shared the sense of dissatisfaction that underwrote this interest in Gypsies.

Gypsies possessed a more particular resonance for Burton, however: they carried the sign of "racial ambiguity."[16] Their origins were a mystery, rendered even more obscure by their nomadic ways. Yet their strange language, their peculiar customs, their odd beliefs, and their identification in the popular imagination with fortune-telling, spell-casting, and other occult practices all ensured their association with difference, with an Oriental otherness that unaccountably existed in the heart of Europe itself. As one Victorian study of the Gypsies put it, they "are the Arabs of pastoral England—the Bedouins of our commons and woodlands."[17] This analogy to Arabs—and more generally to "Orientals"—echoes the language used by Isabel and others in their remarks on Burton's affinities with Gypsies. At the same time, however, the Gypsy served the Victorians as a remnant and reminder of the ancient link between Europeans and Asians, the surviving physical evidence that they shared a common Indo-European ancestry. Hence, the mark of the Gypsy carried two seemingly contradictory meanings for Burton. First, it evoked an identity that existed outside of familiar markers of racial affiliation, providing a genealogical explanation for his ease of movement across the inbred boundaries that kept most peoples apart. Second, it established a racial association with the Oriental world, thereby accounting for his self-professed knowledge of its intimate workings without entirely undermining his affiliation as a European. By claiming a racialized identification with a group whose own racial status was ambiguous, Burton was able to reconcile these contending objectives.

Nothing made the Gypsy more emblematic of Burton's identity than the fact that Burton spent most of his life wandering from place to place. This vagabond existence began soon after his birth in Torquay, Devon, on March 19, 1821. His father, Joseph Burton, came from the lesser ranks of the Anglo-Irish landowning class, an important recruiting ground for the British army's officer corps. The third son of a County Galway squire, Joseph received a free commission by recruiting a number of tenant farmers' sons to accompany him into the army. This occurred around the time of the Irish rebellion of 1798, which may have contributed to Joseph's decision. He saw service during the Napoleonic wars in the Italian peninsula, eventually advancing to the rank of lieutenant colonel. In 1820 he married Martha Baker, who came from a well-to-do Hertfordshire family. The same year, however, saw his military career come to a premature end when he refused to testify in the notorious divorce proceedings that King George IV brought against his estranged wife, Queen Caroline, whom Joseph had met while stationed in Genoa in 1815. With political radicals rallying round the queen's cause in order to embarrass and undermine the monarchy, Joseph's decision to honor his association with the queen made him suspect to his superiors, though there are no indications that he shared the radicals' agenda. Placed on half pay, he moved his family to Tours, France, a few months after Richard's birth. They stayed there for nine years, returning to England only when the revolution of 1830 and the cholera epidemic that accompanied it drove them from France. Within a year the family was once more on the continent. Instead of returning to Tours, however, they took up a peripatetic existence, moving from one southern European town to another. Over the next nine years they resided in Blois, Lyons, Pisa, Siena, Florence, Rome, Naples, and Pau, a French town in the Pyrenees, then back again to Pisa.[18]

Each of the towns where the Burtons interrupted their march had its own tight-knit group of British expatriates. Although the "Mediterranean passion" of the British would grow more pronounced in the second half of the nineteenth century, when improvements in transportation made travel to southern France and Italy more convenient and less costly, a good many Britons of independent means had already taken up residence in the region in the 1820s and 1830s. They tended to congregate in particular towns, where they created their own close-knit communities, often complete with Anglican ministers to serve their spiritual needs.[19] Burton provides a memorable sketch of these communities in his autobiographical reflections:

At that period a host of these little colonies were scattered over the Continent . . . an oasis of Anglo-Saxondom in a desert of continentalism, somewhat like the society of English country towns as it was in 1800. . . . Knowing nothing of Mrs. Grundy, the difference of the foreign colonies was that the *weight* of English respectability appeared to be taken off them, though their lives were respectable and respected. . . . The English of these little colonies were intensely patriotic, and cared comparatively little for party politics. They stuck to their own Church because it *was* their Church, and they knew as much about the Catholics at their very door, as the average Englishman does of the Hindu. . . . They were intensely national. Any Englishman in those days who refused to fight a duel with a Frenchman was . . . bullied out of the place. English girls who flirted with foreigners, were looked upon very much as white women who permitted the addresses of a nigger, are looked upon by those English who have lived in black countries. White women who do these things lose caste.[20]

This passage is remarkable for its insight into the social dynamics that shaped these expatriate communities, which in turn contributed to the character of Burton himself. He makes it clear that these "colonies" were preoccupied by the need to maintain their sense of difference from the host populations. In this respect they were not unlike the British who congregated together in India or any other more conventional colonial setting. They drew on many of the same categories of differences, stressing their distinctive national, religious, and racial identity. They maintained these differences through social codes and strictures that required their men to defend the dignity and prestige of the community against any real or imagined challenges from local males and prohibited their women from any sort of fraternizing with those same males. These pressures to conform to a shared identity may help to explain why Joseph Burton's Irish origin was so thoroughly erased from his son's sense of self—it had no place in the fierce *English* patriotism of these communities. Ireland, strikingly, would be one of the rare lands that failed to stir any curiosity on the part of Richard, who shared the English disdain for its inhabitants.

It was, of course, the very precariousness of these expatriates' position on the continent that caused them to place so much emphasis on their English identity. Joseph sought to teach his son that it was worth risking his life whenever "his patriotism as an englishman may be in question."[21] Yet nothing did more to expose the fragility of this English identity among expatriates than the ambivalent loyalties of their children. Because children absorb local languages and customs much more easily and indiscriminately than do their parents, they are continually at risk of becoming assimilated into the host society, whether it be Italian, French, Indian, or some other foreign land. Although Joseph and Martha Burton did their best to preserve the cultural boundaries between their family and the local peoples among whom they lived, they found it difficult to maintain their children's ethnic loyalties to England and English culture: local influences were simply too pervasive and powerful. Their social counterparts in India devised an effective, if emotionally wrenching, solution to this problem by sending their children back to England after the age of five or so, where they remained until they had attained adulthood. The Burtons may have had a similar strategy in mind when they enrolled Richard, aged nine, and his younger brother Edward, aged five, in Richmond boarding schools in 1830. But the two boys hardly had time to overcome their discomfiture with their homeland's unfamiliar food, customs, and climate before the family returned again to the continent.

Thereafter the Burtons turned over the education of their children to a tutor and a governess who accompanied the family as it made its way across southern Europe. Local tutors were hired to provide supplemental instruction in mathematics, violin, painting, fencing, and other subjects. Burton probably received a far better education by these means than he later admitted. His dismissive account of his schooling, which emphasizes pranks and other forms of misbehavior, derives in large measure from his recognition that whatever intellectual merits it may have had, it left him socially disadvantaged when it came to the pursuit of his professional ambitions. Getting ahead in mid-Victorian society was heavily dependent on whom you knew, not what you knew. Many of the personal connections that would have been advantageous to Richard when he entered the public world were lost or never formed owing to his family's long residence on the continent, or so he believed. Even as the old aristocratic system of patronage began to wane in the early nineteenth century, a new old-boy's network was being forged in public schools such as Eton, Harrow, and Rugby. In retrospect, Burton became convinced that his residence and education on the continent had cut him off from those connections and even from the cultural codes in which they were grounded. He was quite explicit about the costs of this isolation in his autobiographical reflections:

> We had no idea of the disadvantages which the new kind of life would inflict on our future careers. We were too young to know. A man who brings up his family abroad, and who lives there for years, must expect to lose all the friends who could be useful to him when he wishes to start them in life. The conditions of society in England are so complicated, and so artificial, that those who would make their way in the world, especially in public careers, must be broken to it from their earliest day. The future soldiers and statesmen must be prepared by Eton and Cambridge. The more English they are, even to the cut of their hair, the better. In consequence of being brought up abroad, we never thoroughly

understood English society, nor did society understand us. And, lastly, it is a *real* advantage to belong to some parish. It is a great thing, when you have won a battle, or explored Central Africa, to be welcomed home by some little corner of the Great World, which takes a pride in your exploits, because they reflect honour upon itself. In the contrary condition you are a waif, a stray; you are a blaze of light, without a focus. Nobody outside your own fireside cares.[22]

This revealing and poignant passage moves from a complaint about the handicap his upbringing posed for him professionally to a lament over the way it left him emotionally adrift, a "stray" with no parish, no community, no sense of belonging. This estrangement from England and ambivalence about his own Englishness would become one of the dominant themes of his life. Although the experience embittered him, it also served two more productive purposes: it motivated him to prove himself to his countrymen and it ensured that he maintained a critical detachment from their smug sense of themselves as embodying a superior culture.

When Burton was sent back to England at the age of nineteen to attend Oxford University, the experience simply intensified his feeling of alienation from the land of his birth. His short-lived matriculation at Trinity College gave an early glimpse of his intellectual ambitions and interests—he declared a desire to seek first-class honors; he took independent steps to study Arabic; he attended the sermons of the Reverend John Henry Newman, whose Tractarian critique of the liberal religious and political reforms then sweeping England made him one of the most intellectually compelling figures of his day. The world of scholarship and ideas held an instinctive appeal for Burton, and it never waned, as evidenced both by his huge body of published work, much of it containing an academic armature of footnotes and appendices, and by the remarkably varied 2,700 books and pamphlets that have survived from his personal library, showing him to have been "a man endowed with extraordinary mental abilities and imbued with insatiable curiosity."[23] Unfortunately, he found Oxford emotionally alienating and socially disorienting. His lack of familiarity with the codes that governed conduct in Oxford and England more generally exposed him to criticism and ridicule. Officials humiliated him by insisting he shave off his "splendid moustache"; dons rebuked him for speaking Latin with an Italian accent; upperclassmen angered him with their cruel hazing of freshmen. He was appalled by the bad food served in the dining hall, the absence of operas or other cultural diversions in the city, and the mean dwellings that surrounded the university's grand medieval edifices. During the winter break, he pleaded to be permitted to leave Oxford and take a commission in the army. When his father ordered him to return, Richard engineered his own expulsion through a series of petty provocations against university authorities.

After that, Joseph Burton had little choice but to accede to Richard's desire to enter the military, which offered one of the few socially acceptable careers open to a young man of his class and circumstances. Richard indicated that he "preferred the Indian service, as it would show me more of the world, and give me a better chance of active service."[24] By Indian service, he meant the independent army created by the British East India Company, the quasi-private enterprise that ruled India until 1858. It cost far less to obtain a commission in the company's army than in the British one and personal accomplishments were more likely to lead to advancement. Despite Burton's complaints about the social disadvantages of being raised abroad, his father was able to draw on the personal connections needed to wrangle him an appointment. In June 1842 the Court of Directors of the British East India Company approved his application to become a cadet in its army.[25] At the age of twenty-one he prepared to sail to India.

﷽

The initial two decades of Burton's life shaped his subsequent outlook and career in several important ways. His lengthy residence in France and Italy gave him an ear for languages that he would hone over time to a remarkable level of discernment, establishing a reputation as one of the greatest linguists of his generation, reputedly fluent in twenty-five or more languages.[26] We must remember that the southern European languages Burton encountered in his youth were not as standardized as they would become with the advent of mass education in the late nineteenth century. Hence, when his family traveled from place to place, he was obliged to pick up not just the French and Italian we know today, but distinctive regional dialects such as Bernais, Provençale, and Neapolitan, as well as smatterings of Greek and Spanish. Throughout his career he relied on the receptivity to foreign tongues that he had acquired in those early years, and to the degree that his youthful ability to absorb new languages diminished with age, he developed a learning technique that compensated for the loss, systematizing its practice with such purpose that he claimed to be able to master a language after a few months of rigorous study.[27]

Another lasting effect of those early decades on Burton's life was evident in his insatiable taste for travel. His family's peregrinations across southern Europe instilled in him a lifelong compulsion to keep on the move. He spent almost his entire adulthood as a nomad, roaming restlessly through India, North Africa, Arabia, East Africa, North America, West Africa, South America, and other parts of the world. Even his long years of employment as a British consul and his bouts with gout and heart disease late in life did not keep him immobile: he always found an excuse and a means to travel. Burton was never happier than when he was on the road—or, more accurately, forging his way through territories where there were few if any roads—and never more discontented than when he was obliged to stay put.

The final residue of the expatriate existence Burton led as a youth was his profound unease in England, his discomfort with its customs, his distrust of its institutions, his disdain for its values. He made it clear that the place suffocated him and he did his best to stay away for long periods of time. And yet he also could not help recognizing that England was the ultimate arbiter of his fate, the authority that set the criteria for his ambitions and the audience that determined how his accomplishments would be received. This recognition left him torn by contending emotions, eager on the one hand to do great things to win the approbation of his countrymen and resentful on the other hand that he had to accommodate himself to their standards of value, ready at one moment to preen for the public and determined at the next to mock its pieties.

This ambivalence was voiced in his comments about "civilization," the foundational concept on which the Victorians constructed their sense of self, their faith in their own superiority, their charter to rule the world.[28] "And believe me, when once your tastes have conformed to the tranquility of such travel, you will suffer real pain in returning to the turmoil of civilisation. You will anticipate the bustle and the confusion of artificial life, its luxury and its false pleasures, with repugnance. Depressed in spirits, you will for a time after your return feel incapable of mental or bodily exertion. The air of cities will suffocate you, and the care-worn and cadaverous countenances of citizens will haunt you like a vision of judgment."[29] Burton was never entirely able to break free of his society's ethnocentric conviction that Britain stood at the apex of civilization, serving as its avatar of progress, but he struggled against it in his own unconventional fashion. Time and again he voiced objections to what he regarded as the "prison-life of civilised Europe," challenging the universalist claims it made for itself and extolling the virtues of societies that many of his contemporaries relegated to the category of the savage or the barbarous.[30] This contrarian spirit found its inspiration in India.

❧ II ❧

The Orientalist

When Richard Burton went to India in 1842, he was an impatient twenty-one-year-old, recently expelled from Oxford and eager for adventure. He arrived as a callow ensign, or *griffin,* in the East India Company's army; he left seven years later as an experienced agent of the colonial regime. Like many young men of his class and character, he was drawn to a military career in the empire by the opportunities it presented for advancement and glory. But he soon demonstrated a rare facility for languages and a consuming curiosity about other cultures, qualities that launched him on a very different trajectory from that of the average army officer. The Indian government channeled his abundant talent and ambition into the pursuit of Orientalist knowledge, cultivating the skills and habits of mind that would transform him into one of nineteenth-century Britain's most penetrating and provocative interpreters of non-Western societies.

To identify Burton with Orientalism is to thrust him in the midst of what has become a complex and contentious debate over the meaning and uses of the term. Orientalism as Burton understood it was the intellectual project associated with William Jones, Warren Hastings, and other late eighteenth-century and early nineteenth-century British officials in India whose systematic study of the languages, literatures, laws, and religious beliefs of the subcontinent's inhabitants opened up an unfamiliar body of learning to the West.[1] British Orientalism was in turn part of a wider European inquiry into the cultural traditions of peoples from the Near to the Far East, an inquiry that came to assume over time a reputation as an impartial enterprise undertaken by a venerable scholarly fraternity. This reputation has come under challenge in recent decades, most famously by Edward Said, who argues along Foucaultian lines that Orientalist knowledge operated in the service of Western power, playing a crucial role in European imperial expansion. Said redefines Orientalism as "a Western style for dominating, restructuring, and having authority over the Orient."[2] Although a great deal of controversy has swirled around Said's claims, his central insight—that knowledge and power are inextricably intertwined—has had an enduring influence on subsequent studies of Orientalism.[3] This can be attributed in part to the fact that Said resurrects a truth that was self-evident to British Orientalists such as Jones and Hastings, if not their academic heirs. These men never doubted that the colonial state would benefit from their Orientalist interests, that intellectual curiosity about India would aid their efforts to control it. Burton too appreciated the political implications of his linguistic and ethnographic inquiries. In the preface to *Sindh and the Races That Inhabit the Valley of the Indus,* his most sustained contribution to an Orientalist understanding of India, Burton summarized his purpose in terms of "the popular axiom, 'knowledge is power.'"[4]

✦✦✦✦✦

India in the early nineteenth century was a "garrison state," controlled by one of the largest standing armies in the world.[5] Two distinct forces constituted this military regime: British Crown troops, which rotated through the country on regular tours of duty, and the British East India Company's independent legions, which were divided into three armies serving the three regional administrations, or "presidencies," of Bengal, Madras, and Bombay. Each presidency army consisted in turn of separate European and Indian regiments, commanded in both cases by British officers. Burton was appointed to one of the latter regiments, the 18th Native Bombay Infantry. Although the Company's officer corps did not carry the same prestige as its British counterpart, it offered a respectable and potentially lucrative career for a person with the marginal gentlemanly status and limited financial means that Burton possessed.[6] And the overwhelmingly military cast of British India's garrison state meant that such a person enjoyed privileges and opportunities for professional advancement unavailable at home.

Nowhere in the subcontinent was the sway of the military more evident during the years Burton served in India than in Sindh, a province in the northwestern part of the subcontinent that encompassed the lower Indus valley. This region first assumed geopolitical importance for the British in the early nineteenth century as the gateway to Afghanistan, which had come to be seen as a crucial buffer against Russian expansion. The Indian government's efforts to forestall an anticipated Russian threat with a preemptive invasion of the mountain kingdom suffered a terrible setback in 1842 when the Afghans annihilated the occupying army. In the aftermath of this debacle the British sought to secure the border and recover their military prestige by conquering Sindh. General Charles Napier, who commanded the campaign, readily acknowledged it to be a bald act of aggression: "We have no right to seize Sindh, yet we shall do so and a very advantageous, useful, and humane piece of rascality it will be."[7] Burton had been in India only a few months when Sindh was annexed in February 1843, and although he and his regiment, then stationed in Baroda, took no part in the conquest, they were soon transferred to the territory as part of the occupying army.

Napier, a bold and pugnacious man who disdained the civil authorities governing the rest of British India, established a military government that ruled by decree. This aroused considerable controversy within India's colonial administration. The East India Company's governing council found Napier's Caesarean tendencies worrisome and many civil officials expressed dismay at his rough justice, which included summary executions. But Napier had his defenders as well, above all the army officers who thrived under his leadership, wielding the unrestrained powers they felt the turbulent territory required.[8] Burton, who spent the formative years of his Indian army career with Napier, was one of the general's acolytes, sharing his conviction that a "military government is the only form of legislature precisely adapted to these countries."[9] For the rest of his life, Burton would refer back to the military despotism in Sindh as a model of imperial governance, and he retained a deep admiration for its founder.[10]

Most of Burton's biographers, eager to move on to his more famous adventures in Arabia and Africa, view his years in India as significant only insofar as they offer an early indication of his penchant for the erotic promise of exotic lands and his alienation from the social constraints of colonial authority.[11] They focus on his use of opium and other drugs, his liaisons with local women, his missions in native mufti, and his investigation of homosexual brothels, offering them up as evidence of his determination to flaunt the conventions of colonial society. Georgiana Stisted, Burton's niece and one of his earliest biographers, claims that he had a tragic love affair with a Muslim princess. Edward Rice portrays him as a precursor to the hippies, smoking hemp and seeking enlightenment as a Sufi. Frank McLynn finds hints of latent homosexuality in his Indian interests and activities. Byron Farwell summarizes the standard view of Burton's Indian experience with his chapter title "Sin in Sind."[12]

Burton himself was largely responsible for this portrait. Almost every detail of the dissolute behavior cited by his biographers—the drugs, the sex, and so forth—derives from his own published accounts of his activities in India. Perhaps the most dramatic revelation concerns his knowledge of homosexual brothels in Karachi that catered to British troops. Burton claimed late in his life that he investigated the brothels at the behest of General Napier, preparing a confidential report that subsequently fell into the hands of enemies in the Bombay government, who used it to drive him out of the service. His retrospective account disclosed the range and cost of services offered in this sex trade, leaving little doubt that he possessed a personal familiarity with the subject.[13] What is in doubt, however, is whether he visited the brothels for the duteous reasons he describes and whether his career suffered the dire consequences he claims. The notorious report has never been found, nor has its existence been verified from any other sources.[14] Army service files give no indication of scandal: Burton was consistently praised in annual evaluations for exhibiting "zeal" and "attention to duties."[15] As an undisciplined and strong-willed young man, he did on occasion clash with his superior officers, as we shall see. But he retained his commission for more than a decade after leaving India to seek fame as an explorer, hardly an indication that he had become persona non grata to Bombay authorities.[16] The enigmatic Karachi incident may in fact tell us more about Burton's grievances and infatuations at the time he made his revelation in the 1880s about the brothel investigation than it does about his intentions and interests in India in the 1840s. At the very least, it gives us reason to regard his self-professed reputation as a social pariah with some skepticism.

Although Burton certainly deviated from Victorian standards of propriety by openly acknowledging the illicit temptations of

India, he was hardly exceptional in having indulged in them. It was still quite common in the 1840s for British officers stationed in outlying areas known as the *mofussil* to take drugs, cohabit with native women (or even in some instances with boys, though this would have occurred more discreetly), and otherwise seek out whatever pleasures local society had to offer. Burton himself observed when he joined his regiment that "there was hardly an officer in Baroda who was not more or less morganatically married" to an Indian woman, and an inspecting general confirmed that nearly every officer in Burton's regiment in 1845 had a concubine.[17] Colonial bourgeois constraints were still too weak and the prerogatives of military power too strong for the moral strictures that regulated behavior in settled British colonial communities like those of Calcutta and Bombay to carry much weight in Sindh.

Once we overcome the misconception that Burton's behavior placed him outside the bounds of social convention, we can begin to appreciate how hard he worked to meet the expectations of his superiors, seeking to become, in effect, a model officer. The son of a soldier, he was an eager and informed student of the art of war. As he noted in his reminiscences, "I studied military matters with all my might."[18] Evidence of the close and continued attention he gave to the subject can be found in the bayonet exercise manual he published in 1853, his sword exercise manual of 1876, and *The Book of the Sword* (1884), his antiquarian study of the use of the sword through history.[19] Burton also sought glory in battle, though this proved more difficult to achieve than might be supposed. He took part in no serious military engagements during his seven years in India. This was not unusual: most officers spent most of their days stationed in cantonments, drilling their troops and trying to relieve their boredom as best they could in what Burton called their "Castle of Indolence."[20] Yet if opportunities for combat were beyond his control, Burton understood that there were "two roads . . . to preferment," and that the second of these was within his grasp: "the study of languages."[21] British rule over India ultimately depended at least as much on knowledge of the land and its people as it did on military might, and the acquisition of local knowledge required the acquisition of local languages. By turning his formidable talents to this task, Burton turned himself in certain respects into an exemplary agent of the colonial state.

⁂

The ability to master and manipulate what Christopher Bayly has termed "the information order" of India was crucial to imperial control over the subcontinent.[22] Although indigenous intermediaries served as important cultural brokers and sources of intelligence for the colonial regime, the British were acutely aware of the risks entailed in too heavy a reliance on such persons, whose interests and loyalties often extended in directions that were detrimental to their own. In order to reduce its dependence on these intermediaries, the East India Company began to train its own agents in the linguistic and cultural skills that would allow them both to verify the information obtained from native informants and to gather intelligence on their own. The obvious candidates for such training were army officers, whose regular duties necessitated the "collection, analysis and dissemination of knowledge" about India. The officer corps would yield a remarkable array of "officer-scholars," men who managed over time to produce a vast body of knowledge about the subcontinent and its peoples.[23]

The key to this acquisition of colonial knowledge was fluency in the languages of the colonized population. Officers who commanded native regiments were under particular pressure to ac-

32

quire some facility in the tongues spoken by their troops. They were given funds to hire Indian scribes or secretaries known as *munshis* to serve as language tutors and were obliged to sit for competitive examinations that tested their proficiency, with the results published in the local press for all to see. Though most officers picked up little more than the debased or pidgin idiom they needed to issue basic commands, the Company's army offered prizes and promotions as rewards for those who attained some degree of linguistic fluency.[24] The *Bombay Times,* which urged that even more emphasis be given to mastery of languages, insisted that it was "one of the most valuable accomplishments a Company's servant can possess, and at the same time one of the strongest recommendations to official employ."[25]

Burton understood from the start that fluency in Indian languages could further his military career. He began to study Hindustani before his departure from England and continued on the voyage out to drill himself in the language with the aid of Indian servants and crew members. Soon after his arrival in Bombay he engaged the services of Dosabhai Sohrabji, a noted Parsi *munshi,* to prepare him for the government exam in Hindustani. Close and lengthy association with native speakers became the modus operandi by which he mastered a new language. In addition to the *munshi,* who was the standard source of instruction in local languages, Burton credited the contribution of the Indian concubine, often colloquially known as a "walking dictionary": "[She] connected the white stranger with the country and its people, gave him an interest in their manners and customs, and taught him thoroughly well their language."[26] Intimate relationships of this sort were an important, if often unacknowledged, source of the "affective knowledge" that Bayly suggests was vital to British intelligence about Indian society.[27]

Burton used every opportunity that presented itself to improve his skills in the vernacular, and he achieved impressive results. In March 1843 he placed first among the eleven cadets who sat for the Hindustani examination. He achieved similar success in examinations in Gujarati in October 1843, Marathi in October 1844, Persian in November 1847, and Sindhi and Punjabi in September 1848. Some hint of the ambitions behind his quick march through this series of language exams can be gleaned from the letter his father wrote to Burton's commanding officer in 1846: "I am very anxious that Richard may pass his examination in the persian language in the course of this year as it may possibly bring him into notice in Bombay."[28] Each exam qualified him as a regimental interpreter, which opened up opportunities for advancement unavailable to other officers and gave a boost to his salary (a 30-rupees-per-month increase after the Hindustani examination, for example).[29] In addition, he received 1,000-rupee bonuses for his language proficiency in 1848 and 1851.[30] Burton also studied Arabic, Armenian, Portuguese, Pushtu, Telugu, Toda, and Turkish during his years in India, and although there is no evidence that he took official examinations in Arabic or Telugu, as his wife claims in her biography, there can be little doubt that he believed his linguistic skills would improve his claims for preferment.[31]

Burton clearly possessed a rare genius for languages, a genius that laid the groundwork for almost everything he accomplished in the course of his remarkable life.[32] But it is equally apparent that the Indian government nurtured this genius, supplying the professional incentives that brought it to bloom. It enabled him to channel his ambitions and energies in a direction that was supremely suited to his talents.

Even so, Burton bridled at the bureaucratic constraints he felt prevented him from accomplishing even greater linguistic feats. In 1848 the *Bombay Times* published a series of letters critical of the established procedures for "the examination of officers in the native languages." The correspondent, who wrote under the telling pseudonym "Viator" (Latin for wayfarer or traveler), was Richard Burton. He complained that the current examination system was "useless and obsolete . . . positively mischievous in its operations" because it did not require commanders to grant junior officers the leaves they needed to be examined by the language board in Bombay.[33] He raised other objections in succeeding letters: the grammar examination was based on Latin instead of indigenous linguistic principles; the oral examination tested the candidate in conversation with his *munshi* rather than the sepoys, or native soldiers, with whom he would be expected to communicate; the *munshi* allowance was too meager for students in outlying stations; *munshis* in Arabic were hard to find. He expressed frustration with the reliance on *munshis* altogether, declaring that "the best exercise is conversing with the common people, not lying on a sofa opposite a well-shaved Pundit, whose object is rather to learn English than to teach the Sahib Maharattas." Playing on his readers' feelings of rivalry with the other presidencies, Burton concluded that Bombay's language exams were "considered mere farces" in Bengal and Madras.[34] These letters give an early glimpse of the arrogant, opinionated Burton who would become a much more visible presence in later years. In spite of his evident frustration with the existing system of language instruction and examination, however, his own ambitions and achievements offered an oblique testimony to its success in promoting the acquisition of the linguistic skills the state required, as Burton himself grudgingly acknowledged.[35]

Burton was keenly aware of the political benefits that mastery of local languages brought to the colonial regime. He would have recognized the truth of Bernard Cohn's axiom that the command of language is vital to the language of command.[36] Cohn shows that the development of lexicons, grammars, phrase books, and other reference works that regularized vernaculars and made them more accessible to outsiders was among the earliest tasks the British undertook in their efforts to consolidate colonial authority. Burton contributed to that enterprise by writing two articles in 1848 for *The Journal of the Bombay Branch of the Royal Asiatic Society,* one on the Jataki dialect of Punjabi, the other on the Pushtu language of the Afghans. In the former essay he excused the limitations of his study by explaining that "knowledge [of the Jataki dialect] must be derived from the oral instruction of half-educated Natives," indicating that this was the sort of constraint his research sought to overcome. In the latter article he alluded to the strategic significance of his seemingly parochial study, expressing dismay that "during our occupation of the country [Afghanistan] we took so little interest in what was around us, and that the first sensible work published in Pushtu should have appeared at St. Petersburg instead of at London or Calcutta."[37] This remark alluded to anxieties regarding Russian influence in Afghanistan and the potential threat it posed to British rule in India. Burton concluded one of his books on Sindh with a similar admonishment, underscoring the political benefits the Russians gained from their interest in Afghan languages and literatures and urging his countrymen to show the same attention to its Sindhi counterparts: "We are not likely to derive much amusement or improvement from the literary effusions of a semi-barbarous race, but as a means of power they are valuable weapons in our hands."[38]

Although this smug dismissal of local literature was meant to play to British prejudices, as its use of "we" signaled, it did not in fact reflect Burton's own feelings. His writings on India were replete with admiring translations of Sufi poems and fond renderings of traditional folktales and fables. He expressed genuine respect for the region's literary traditions: "In this province, as was the case throughout India generally, the poetical literature of the vernacular is . . . fresh, idiomatic, and sufficiently original, capacious, and varied in words and expressions, at the same time simple and natural."[39] Burton became acquainted in Sindh with some of the bawdy local versions of the Arabian Nights tales that Europeans knew in bowdlerized form, and his affection for them never waned, bearing fruit forty years later with his own frank and capacious translation. His interest in the region's folktales found more immediate expression in 1847 with his unpublished translation from Hindustani into English of the ancient Sanskrit tales known as Pilpay's Fables. He presented the manuscript as a primer for cadets seeking to learn Hindustani, explaining in the preface that it would "assist the young Hindustani scholar in acquiring a sufficient stock of words, idioms and phrases, together with the knowledge of Oriental manners, customs and modes of thinking, necessary to enable him to attempt other and more classical works." In a footnote, he hinted at a more practical reason for using a collection of fables to acquire mastery of the language: "In a position where a foreigner is thrown into close intercourse with natives of the East, it is absolutely necessary to study the customs of their society a little, unless he desires every day to offend by apparent neglect and incivility, and to make himself ridiculous by misplaced attention and politeness."[40]

Though these sentiments were no doubt sincere, it might well be asked whether the study of folktales was the most practical way to break through the cultural and linguistic barriers that separated the British from their Indian subjects. Underlying the practical explanations that Burton gave for his interest in indigenous literary forms were several less utilitarian considerations. Unstated but unmistakable was the influence of a particular strand of Romanticism, which invested fairy tales, folk songs, and other popular literary traditions with significance as sources of inherited wisdom. Like so many of his contemporaries, Burton admired the Waverly novels of Sir Walter Scott, which gave dramatic form to this sensibility with their imaginative reconstruction of the Scottish Highland tradition. (Scott's nephew and namesake, Walter Scott, who rose to become a general in the British Indian army, was Burton's commanding officer when he joined the Sindh Survey and became one of his closest friends in India.)[41]

A closely related but more direct inspiration for Burton's interest in local tales and literary genres was the achievements of William Jones and the British Orientalists. The wealth of knowledge they had uncovered about Bengal's literary, linguistic, legal, and religious heritage served as a model that Burton sought to emulate in Sindh. He employed similar methods, seeking out village pundits for discussion and debate, searching for obscure and half-forgotten manuscripts, analyzing the grammar and etymology of local dialects, and publishing his findings in learned journals, complete with a scholarly apparatus of footnotes, quotations, and references to other works to bolster his claims of knowledge. What these efforts and influences indicate is that even though Burton's engagement with Indian languages and literatures was informed by his appreciation of the association between knowledge and power, it was never entirely reducible to the needs of that association.

In 1848 Burton's reputation as an authority on the vernaculars of Sindh drew him into an important administrative debate about which language and script the state should adopt for elementary education and other purposes. The broader issue of whether Indians should be schooled in their own languages and literatures or in the language and literature of their rulers had already provoked the famous clash in the Indian governing council between Orientalists and Anglicists.[42] Though Thomas Macaulay and the Anglicists had won the battle at the central level in 1835, establishing the preeminence of English-language learning in colonial educational policy, the Bombay presidency retained considerable autonomy in determining policies within its own precincts. In Sindh, where most inhabitants had little or no contact with their British overlords, the Orientalist position continued to hold sway. Burton shared this view, arguing that at least for the lower grades that served the needs of most children, the Sindhi language was a suitable medium of instruction, supplying a rich literature from which an effective curriculum could be crafted.[43]

It was, however, with respect to the more technical, but no less socially and politically important, issue of which script to select as the standard for official educational use that Burton made his most lasting contribution. Vernacular Sindhi was then written in three or four different scripts, each of them loosely affiliated with a particular ethno-religious group. The two main contenders for standardization were the Devangari script, which was based on Sanskrit and popular with Hindu shopkeepers, and a Perso-Arabic script known as Naskhi, which was used by much of the Muslim population. As might be expected in light of his admiration for Sufi poetry and other literature associated with Islamic traditions, Burton preferred Naskhi, arguing that it was already widespread in Sindh and better suited to its needs. The governor of Bombay ruled in favor of Devangari, but the Court of Directors overturned his decision, endorsing Burton's position. The result was the standardization of the Sindhi language in an Arabic script that favored Muslim interests.[44] One authority on the Sindhi language observes that Burton played "a decisive role in framing the British position about Sindhi script,"[45] a contribution that in turn had profound implications for British relations with the region's contending religious communities and those communities' subsequent efforts to forge a nationalist identity.

ᘛᘚᘛᘚᘛᘚᘛ

Both for Burton and the regime he served, fluency in Hindustani and other vernaculars was regarded as crucial to the acquisition of knowledge about conquered peoples. It was not long before Burton's linguistic talents brought him to the attention of Lieutenant Colonel Walter Scott, a military engineer who was seeking able young officers to serve in the newly formed Sindh Survey Canal Department. He tried in August 1844 to second Burton to the Survey, but his request was initially rejected for reasons that give us a glimpse of the restiveness toward authority that would trouble Burton throughout his career. Scott was informed that Burton was "under a cloud. . . . He has been behaving rather bumptiously to his Commanding Officer, and the matter is not yet settled. . . . It is a great pity, for he evidently would be very useful to you. Perhaps it may all come right in time."[46] It did. A few months later Burton was appointed assistant surveyor in the Canal Department.

Much of Sindh was still *terra incognita* to the British, and one of the foremost tasks they faced as the territory's new rulers was to map its dimensions and identify its resources, much as they had done elsewhere in India. The most ambitious and important of these colonial surveys was the Great Trigonometrical Survey, which managed over time to map the whole of the subcontinent. It has been described as motivated by the desire to create "a legitimating conception of empire, of political and territorial hegemony, mapped out in a scientistic and rational construction of space."[47] Although the Sindh Survey would eventually contribute to this larger mapping enterprise, its tasks were more modest in the early years when Burton served on its staff. It was charged with surveying waterways and forest tracts and clearing and repairing the canals that supplied the lifeblood of the peasant economy throughout much of the region.[48]

Scott observed in his report on the Survey's activities that the ideal surveyor would possess a familiarity with hydrology, surveying, engineering, and accounting, as well as being a "good linguist; there can be no certainty of knowing what the people want, or giving them satisfaction, if their language is not understood."[49] Few of the officers seconded to his unit, he complained, had the full complement of skills needed to competently carry out the work of the Survey. This may well have been true, but it is equally evident that Scott sought out men whose ambitions and abilities far surpassed those of the average officer. As Napier observed, Scott placed "demands upon the brains of the rising generation of Griffins."[50] Burton thus quite rightly regarded the appointment as a mark of approbation. It brought him to the notice of superiors, boosted his salary, and freed him from the monotony of regimental life. Above all, it opened up an opportunity for this adventurous and intellectually omnivorous young man to immerse himself in the everyday lives of the Sindhi people, honing his language skills in exchanges with landlords and peasants and collecting ethnographic information that both satisfied his own curiosity and served the intelligence needs of the colonial state.

Burton's initial task with the Sindh Survey was to map and "level" some of the canals that sustained agriculture in the lower Indus valley. Soon, however, his superiors appear to have recognized his unusual talents, sanctioning his desire to conduct a far more sweeping investigation of the region. Burton began to gather information on Sindh's geography, climate, natural resources, land usage, and agricultural products, as well as on its inhabitants' speech, dress, dwellings, ceremonies, religious beliefs, social ranks, and much more. The Bombay government subsequently published two of Burton's intelligence reports, the titles of which offer a glimpse into the range of subjects that interested the colonial state: "Notes Relative to the Population of Sind; and the Customs, Language, and Literature of the People" and "Brief Notes Relative to the Division of Time, and Articles of Cultivation in Sind."[51] A much fuller record of Burton's intelligence-gathering activities can be found in the books he subsequently wrote about Sindh. These were *Scinde; or, The Unhappy Valley* (1851), which reappeared in a much revised form as *Sind Revisited* (1877); *Falconry in the Valley of the Indus* (1852), which closed with a revealing autobiographical postscript; and *Sindh, and the Races that Inhabit the Valley of the Indus* (1851), the most ethnographically informative of his studies of the region. Burton sought in these works, especially the last, to give an encyclopedic account of the territory and its inhabitants, touching on all manner of topics, including terrain, crops, land holdings, taxes, languages, literatures, education, medicine, intoxicants, religions, customs, and ceremonies such as marriages and funerals. Much of the material from the two published reports appears in his books, and it is likely that their pages recycled other unpublished reports as well. *Sindh* in particular was a quasi-official work, with Burton dedicating the book to the British East India Company, which purchased 150 copies—and required the suppression of certain passages it considered offensive.[52] Even so, Burton felt obliged to caution readers in the book's preface that they might find its "descriptions of the manners and customs of a barbarous or semi-civilized race" disturbing. The intended audience, he indicated, was "the linguist and the ethnographer," by which he meant those officials whose task it was to make the inhabitants of Sindh more transparent to the Company and amenable to its designs.[53]

Because of the dangers this newly conquered province posed for the British, Burton was obliged at first to carry out his surveying duties accompanied by another officer and a contingent of sepoys. He also relied on *munshis* and other native informants and intermediaries to gain his social and political bearings, though he was acutely aware of their divided loyalties and frustrated by his own dependence on them. "The fellow may be, and ten to one is, a spy: he repeats to you all the scandal he can collect. . . . He is in all men's secrets, according to his own account; everything, court intrigue, political events, and private 'gap' [gossip], he knows."[54] Despite these general reservations, Burton graciously acknowledged the assistance he received from his Hindustani *munshi* Dosabhai Sohrabji, his Persian *munshis* Mirza Mohammed Hosayn and Mirza Daud, and Napier's principal *munshi,* Mirza Ali Akbar Khan, a close friend whom Burton eulogized in *Sind Revisited.* Another Indian who figures prominently in Burton's account of his Sindhian years is Ibrahim Khan Talpoor, a local notable who introduced him to the sport of falconry. Burton introduces him in *Falconry in the Valley of the Indus* as "my friend,"[55] and portrays their relationship in the familiar terms of Victorian male bonding, replete with accounts of easy banter and high adventure.

Still, Burton was impatient for unmediated access to the common people of Sindh. As he grew more confident in his physical security and linguistic skills, he began to tour the region on his own, often dressed in local garb. This decision was not at first intended to deceive; rather, he simply determined that "there is nothing so intrinsically comfortable or comely in the European costume, that we should wear it in the face of every disadvantage." By adopting the dress of the region, he found that "peasants will not run away from us as we ride through the fields, nor will the village girls shrink into their huts as we near them."[56] Soon, however, Burton realized that he could gain fuller access to Sindhi society and insight into its lineaments by deliberately disguising his own identity. "The European official in India," he explained, "seldom, if ever sees anything in its real light, so dense is the veil which the fearfulness, the duplicity, the prejudice and the superstitions of the natives hang before his eyes. And the white man lives a life so distinct from the black, that hundreds of the former serve . . . without once being present at a circumcision feast, a wedding, or a funeral."[57] The run-of-the-mill British officer might well have asked why anyone would want to attend a circumcision feast, but its importance to the people of Sindh made it a matter of interest to Burton. His curiosity, moreover, was sharpened by the challenge that confronted any outsider who sought to infiltrate an endogamous community. Despite his facility for languages, Burton never underestimated the difficulty of this task. It took some time for him to determine through trial and error which disguises generated the least suspicion. Eventually he settled on the persona of Mirza Abdullah, a traveling salesman whose odd accent could be attributed to his origins as "a half Arab, half Iranian."[58]

Burton was certainly not the first Briton in India to assume the identity of a "native," nor would he be the last. William Moorcroft, Alexander Burnes, and other agents of the Raj had ventured into Afghanistan and neighboring territories in disguise in the early nineteenth century.[59] Burton himself is often identified as the model for Rudyard Kipling's memorable character Strickland, the police detective who went undercover as an Indian to collect intelligence, although a recent study suggests that the more likely inspiration was a policeman named John Paul Warburton, a contemporary of Kipling's who was reputed to be a master of the art of disguise. In the late nineteenth and early twentieth centuries, various British intelligence officers assumed Indian guises in order to infiltrate revolutionary nationalist groups, though their efforts were often farcically inept.[60]

It is impossible to know if Burton was as successful at disguising his real identity from the people he investigated as he claimed to be. There can be little doubt, though, that his efforts brought him into much closer contact with their communities than the average colonial officer could or would have contemplated. His claim to ethnographic authority rested in the final analysis on the intimacy of his association with the inhabitants of this unfamiliar land. His position in this regard was not unlike that advocated by current practitioners of cultural anthropology, a discipline that still generally regards fieldwork as the foundational practice that opens the way to an understanding of other societies. Modern anthropologists have, to be sure, jettisoned many of the ethnocentric assumptions that Burton brought to his own fieldwork in Sindh, not to mention the dissimulation that disguised his intentions from his subjects. But they share his conviction that ethnographic knowledge must in the end derive from the intimate, unmediated encounter between the observer and the peoples being observed. And for all the interference and distortion that personal subjectivity invariably imposes on that encounter, much of its epistemological value lies in the unpredictable effects it has on the observer, as expectations collide with realities and certainties come undone.

For Burton, these destabilizing effects are evident in the tension that appears in his books on Sindh between his determination to classify its peoples in categories familiar to his contemporaries and his desire to describe their lives, customs, and beliefs in all their varied complexity. Although he makes occasional reference to "true Orientals" as a generic type,[61] his detailed account of the multiple layers of identity and experience that shape the social fabric of Sindh makes it apparent that his use of the phrase is little more than a rhetorical convention. Although he endorses the classic imperialist stratagem of divide and rule in dealings with Hindus and Muslims,[62] his own analysis of the relations between these two religious communities continually blurs the distinctions between the two faiths, stressing instead the syncretic dimensions of their beliefs while noting their internal doctrinal divisions. He notes, for example, that "the Hindoo's religion has, like the Moslem's, been contaminated by contact with strangers," and although his frustration at this fact is coded in his use of the word "contaminated," he repeatedly resists the temptation to describe them in stark, binary terms.[63] He acquires a keen and appreciative awareness of the powerful role that Sufism and Sufi saints play in the spiritual lives of the majority Muslim population in Sindh, devoting considerable attention to its beliefs, practices, and poetry.[64] He also takes note of the presence of Sikhs, Jains, and other minority religious groups. Similarly, Burton shows a keen eye for the ethnic, linguistic, caste, and other distinctions that differentiate the region's inhabitants from one another. And though this sort of ethnographic mapping obviously serves the interests of the colonial state, Burton traces its contours in such meticulous detail that it seems in some respects to exist for its own sake.

This seemingly indiscriminate deluge of information was troubling to contemporaries, who perhaps sensed that it evinced a curiosity that could not so easily be contained within the boundaries of social convention and political purpose. One of the complaints raised in the *Athenaeum*'s review of *Goa, and the Blue Mountains* (1851), a book Burton wrote about his travels through western India, was indicative of a more general objection to his writings: the book was "a curious piece of patchwork, made up of the most heterogeneous materials," presented in a tone "which borders on the offensive."[65] And, indeed, Burton's frank discussion of drugs and intoxicants, nautch dancers and courtesans, polygamy and polyandry, female infanticide and abortion must have shocked many readers. It is not merely the fact that he addresses these topics that causes offense. More troubling is the absence of any moralizing judgments in his remarks. He expresses unmasked enthusiasm for nautch dances and opium. Rather than condemn polygamy and female infanticide, he explains the social forces that motivate these practices. He offers various comparisons intended to make this unfamiliar culture more comprehensible to his readers. He equates the division between Sunnis and Shiites to the one between Catholics and Protestants. He draws an analogy between Indian nautch dances and ancient Greek dances. He alludes to the cultural relativity that informs standards of modesty by reference to Malabar's bare-breasted women. He indicates the depth of poverty in Sindh by describing it as "an Eastern Ireland on a large scale."[66] On occasion he turns these comparisons against his readers in much the same manner as modern anthropologists have used their knowledge of other cultures to critique their own.[67] He contrasts the leniency of domestic servitude in India to the brutality of chattel slavery in the West. And he finds Sindhi child-rearing practices far more humane and loving than the negligent behavior of British parents.[68]

In other respects, however, Burton adopts entirely conventional attitudes toward the various peoples with whom he comes in contact. He often measures them against the standards set by his own society, issuing sweeping statements that praise or condemn with blithe abandon. Like most of his contemporaries in India, for example, he prefers highland warriors to lowland farmers. The latter he characterizes as lazy, cringing louts, while the former are "manly races" that exhibit "morality, hospitality, simplicity, strong affections, fidelity, [and] stubborn courage."[69] These differences are inscribed in their physical appearance: "the dark complexion of the Sindhi [peasant] points him out as an instance of arrested development," while the Afghan is "the handsomest race we have yet seen."[70] Burton also shares the widespread concern among colonial officials about the village moneylender's corrosive effects on agrarian society. He depicts this despised figure in the stock imagery of anti-Semitism, describing him as a "Shylock" with "hooked nose, thin lips, and cheeks of crumpled parchment."[71] These moneylenders are Hindus, however, not Jews. Another Hindu-dominated profession he paints in anti-Semitic colors is that of the *amil,* the official who administered the traditional ruling emirs' states. He is portrayed as a corrupt, conniving figure, skilled in fraud and deceit.[72] If the Hindu assumes the attributes of the anti-Semite's Jew, then analogy suggests that the Muslim he victimizes must take on the role of the Christian. Though Burton never draws this unsettling correspondence directly, he does declare where his sympathies lie: the Persians, who brought Islam to Sindh, are "probably the most perfect specimen of the Caucasian type," while Hindus are "the most imperfect."[73]

Informing these sweeping appraisals is a rough-hewn effort to establish some sort of schema for differentiating among the varied inhabitants of this newly conquered dominion, identifying them with particular moral, cultural, and physical attributes. "Race" is the word most often used to signify this imperial effort to rank and sort peoples. In this pre-Darwinian era, however, it remains a vague, ill-defined term, associated to varying degrees with language, religion, culture, nation, climate, caste, class, and physical appearance. The way in which Burton deploys the term is indicative of this indiscriminate usage: it appears in the title of *Sindh* in reference to various forms of social differentiation.

Even so, race as a marker of identity is in this period more than a mere catchall category; it is a signifier whose signification is open to debate, with contending parties claiming it for different purposes. The signs of this struggle are apparent in Burton's unsettled approach to the subject. In certain respects he shares the Orientalist view that races should be classified in terms of their linguistic affinities, a definition that places Indians and Europeans in racial kinship as Indo-Europeans.[74] He marked his copy of James Prichard's influential *Natural History of Man* with a number of marginal notes (most likely written in the late 1840s or early 1850s) that associate race with language, including an approving reference to William Jones's assertion of an Indo-European language family, as well as a statement that "language [is] the most direct . . . & lasting impression of the whole national mind."[75] Evidence that Burton retained late into his life some remnants of this Orientalist understanding of race include his fascination with Gypsies as a genealogical bridge between Europeans and Indians and his conviction that an intellectual lineage could be traced from ancient Sanskrit fables through the medieval tales of the Arabian Nights to modern European literature.[76]

It is clear, however, that Burton is pondering other understandings of race as well. The classificatory schema of the natural sciences intrigues him. The annotations in his copies of Prichard's *Natural History* and George Cuvier's *Animal Kingdom* show an interest in race as a set of physical attributes such as skin color and skull shape.[77] He may have been thinking along these lines when he associated the "arrested development" of the Sindhi peasantry with their dark skins. Yet his most sustained comments on race as a physical or biological category appear in his reflections on the Portuguese in India. Burton visited the Portuguese colony of Goa, on the west coast of India south of Bombay, while on sick leave in 1847. He gives a lengthy account of his impressions of the place in his first book, *Goa, and the Blue Mountains.* The question that preoccupies him in this account is why the Portuguese have fallen so precipitously from their former imperial greatness. His answer is "the short-sighted policy of the Portuguese in intermarrying and identifying themselves with Hindoos of the lowest castes." The mestizo population that derived from this policy has brought torpor and decay to the Portuguese imperial project. He deplores their character and considers their appearance repellent: "It would be, we believe, difficult to find in Asia an uglier or more degraded looking race than that which we are now describing." It is not merely intermarriage, however, that has degraded the Portuguese population. Even the "pure blooded" children of Portuguese colonists have deteriorated, because their parents have failed to send them back to Portugal for their education. Burton endorses a view widely shared by the British in India that persons of European stock will "degenerate after the second generation" if measures are not taken to provide respite from "the deleterious effects of a hot and dry climate."[78] There are obvious inconsistencies between this climatic understanding of race and the argument associating it with breeding, but Burton does nothing to reconcile the two.[79] His analysis is focused instead on the imperial lessons to be learned from the Portuguese: "Heaven preserve our rulers from following their example!" Any effort on the part of the British to reduce the distance between the "races" through miscegenation or assimilation through permanent settlement is a "delusive and treacherous political day dream." Britons and Indians must remain apart if imperial rule is to prevail.[80]

What is most striking about Burton's comments on the Portuguese is the way his remarks on race are so integrally connected to his concerns about imperial power. Race, in effect, becomes a marker of biological difference insofar as it serves to sustain the system of hierarchy that Burton believes essential to the maintenance of British rule in India. Where the issue of power is not applicable, the notion of race as biological destiny does not arise. Thus it is not a prominent consideration in Burton's analysis of the various strata within Sindhi society, where he goes into great detail about religious, linguistic, economic, and other divisions without suggesting that these differences are derived from any innate racial characteristics. Nor does he deploy this understanding of race with regard to Europeans in Europe itself. On the contrary, he rejects the very idea that Europeans constitute a distinct racial type: "In the most civilized European countries there has been such a mixture of blood and breed that now an almost infinite variety of features and complexions, shapes and forms, has been grafted upon the original stock which each region grew."[81] If Europeans are already racially interbred, then the objections he raises to miscegenation between Europeans and Indians cannot be understood as meant to protect some putative racial purity, but rather must be construed as an effort to maintain a situational sense of self that is constituted in response to the political demands of the colonial situation.

So where did this leave Burton himself? How did he reconcile this insistence on the maintenance of racial boundaries with his own delight in transgressing the rules that restricted transactions between Britons and Indians. He could only do so by crafting a persona that placed him at the interstices of the great cultural divide, claiming a liminal status exempt from the codes and conventions that separated ruler from ruled. To operate as a free radical in this colonial orbit must have been emotionally exhilarating for Burton, and it certainly caused him to stand apart, opening up a promising path to celebrity. But it also carried the risk of condemnation by his peers, who were always alert to any signs that one of their own might be "going native."

The disparaging phrase "white nigger" gives vivid expression to the objections that some of Burton's colleagues evidently lodged against his life on the margins. In his reminiscences about his Indian years he mentions two occasions when this epithet was flung at him. The first occurred early on, when Burton and his regiment were still stationed in Baroda. Although baptized and raised as an Anglican, Burton started attending services at a Catholic chapel, where a Goan priest presided over a congregation that consisted mainly of Goan mestizos and Indian converts. Burton never offers an explanation for this strange decision, which seems so much at odds with the antagonism he expressed in *Goa* toward the mixed-race progeny of the Portuguese. But it is easy to understand why other officers in his garrison might have found his conduct objectionable. This was a doubly deviant act, a rejection of his religious heritage and a betrayal of his communal-cum-national loyalties, which took conformity of faith as a constituent element of the status accorded the British ruling elite. The second time Burton mentions being called a "white nigger" comes in the context of his friendship with two *munshis,* Mirza Ali Akhbar Kahn and Mirza Daud. Once again his behavior cut against the grain of social norms among Anglo-Indians, who distrusted any association with native informants that blurred the boundaries between professional and personal relations.[82]

Though Burton's behavior undoubtedly caused consternation among some of his peers, biographers have been too quick to take these taunts as proof that he came to be regarded as a social pariah by officials. We have already seen that much of the conduct offered up as evidence of his alienation was in fact fairly typical of fellow officers. (It is worth noting in this context that neither of the incidents that provoked the insult "white nigger" was related to his cohabitation with native women, which indicates how little social opprobrium was attached to this practice.) We also know that his efforts to achieve knowledge of native peoples by establishing intimate associations with them were sanctioned and rewarded by the colonial state. If some tarred him with the epithet "white nigger," others applauded his enterprise and rewarded his expertise. To fully appreciate what the charge of "white nigger" tells us about Burton's relationship to other Britons in India, it is important to give closer scrutiny to his own stance and intentions. First, we need to recognize that he drew a distinction between his professional and his social position in the colonial scheme of things. Second, we need to understand why he chose to publicly reveal an accusation that was intended to humiliate him.

Insofar as Burton felt alienated from fellow Britons during his years in India, this feeling did not derive for the most part from his professional activities, which quite clearly brought him much satisfaction and a certain degree of success. True, Burton fell afoul of Napier at one point, much as he had fallen afoul of his previous commander. In 1846 Napier removed him from the Survey for disobeying orders: although we know little of the particulars about his offense, Joseph Burton suggested in an exculpatory letter that it was the result of his son's overzealous desire to "distinguish himself in action."[83] Whatever the cause, the incident left no lasting scars on his military career, nor did it diminish his admiration for Napier. Though Burton's headstrong personality occasionally got him into trouble with commanding officers, he was estranged not from the army itself but rather from the social life in those towns and cantonments where the British in India gathered in large numbers, creating their own closed and strictly regulated communities. Most of his Indian career was conducted on the colonial frontier, where the codes and conventions of these communities were loosely enforced at best. On those occasions when he was obliged to circulate in what was known as "society" among his countrymen in India, he invariably felt ill at ease, just as he had when living in Britain itself. He heartily disliked his visits to Bombay, describing the social environment he found there as follows: "Essentially a middle class society, like that of a small county town in England, it was suddenly raised to the top of a tree, and lost its head accordingly."[84] He voiced similar objections to the British in Ootacumund, the hill station in southern India where he went to recuperate from illness in 1847. As he later recalled, it was "a very rotten hole full of middle-class, respectably-pious and water-swilling Mules."[85] His antipathy for the rituals and hierarchies that shaped social life at the hill station was palpable in the account he gave in *Goa.* "You dress like an Englishman, and lead a quiet gentlemanly life—doing nothing"—a comment that seems especially revealing in light of what we know about his activities in Sindh.[86] Subtle shifts of language in *Goa* signaled his disdain: his choice of pronoun changed from the warm and collusive "we" employed in the chapters on Goa and Malabar to a cool and disaffiliated "you" in the chapters on Ootacamund. Although he had been granted a two-year medical leave at the sanitarium to recover his health, he scarcely had the patience to remain there a few months before fleeing back to Sindh.[87]

This sense of social unease does not help us understand, however, why Burton would let it be known that he was called a "white nigger." Although this revelation comes in reminiscences dictated late in his life, it simply gives more highly charged expression to a self-characterization that can be traced back to some of Burton's earliest published accounts of his Indian experiences. Almost everything we know about his apparent transgressions—the indulgence in drugs and sex, the defense of deviant customs, the curiosity about rival faiths—derives from his own writings. He is in fact consciously engaged in creating a persona, an image of himself that flirted with scandal. As Parama Roy has noted, "Burton desired not simply to pass for a native in the east, but also to have it suspected in England that he has actually gone native."[88]

This self-fashioning is evident in everything Burton wrote about his Indian experiences. Even though he spent much of his army career in close association with fellow officers, he invariably portrays himself as a solitary sojourner in an alien land, associating exclusively with its indigenous inhabitants. In *Falconry*, for example, his hunting companions are without exception Indians. He scarcely mentions in his published works the various Britons with whom he established deep and lasting friendships. Any expressions of emotional engagement with others occur in contexts that transgress social conventions. In *Goa* he tells several tales of forbidden love: one about a British officer who abandons his career to live with the nautch girl he adores; another about a Hindu corporal who takes a vow of poverty after failing to rescue the object of his affection, a Brahmin widow, from her husband's funeral pyre.[89] He also recounts his own infatuation with a Persian woman in *Scinde*.[90]

Perhaps the clearest demonstration of Burton's efforts to fashion his image in opposition to the typical Briton can be found in *Scinde; or, The Unhappy Valley*. Here he revisits much of the same ground covered in his other major book on Sindh, but this time he does so in a manner meant to be more lively and accessible to the average British reader. The first line of the book makes clear its intent: "Step in, Mr. Bull,—after you, sir!" Burton seeks to engage his reader by presenting John Bull, the symbolic national everyman, as the narrator's imaginary interlocutor. The narrator himself, however, stands in stark contrast to the respectable Mr. Bull.[91] He is a self-described "semi-Oriental," who dons native dress, smokes bhang and drinks opium, and romances local ladies. He teases his readers with his own willingness to stray beyond the bounds of propriety, and then mocks their presumed disapproval. Consider the way his account of a nautch dance shifts from its erotic appeal to Mr. Bull to the reproof he can expect from overrefined women at home: "At this rate you will be falling in love . . .—I tremble to think of the spirit in which your lapse would be received by the bonneted, well curled, be-mantled, straight-laced, be-petticoated partner of your bosom." By representing himself as an outsider, he is able to turn some of the acumen and acerbity he displays in his examination of Sindhi society back on British society. It is revealing that the book ends with Mr. Bull departing for England, while the narrator "remain[s] upon this sultry shore." Burton has created a persona that cannot return to England.[92]

Nor, for that matter, could the real Burton. Suffering from a debilitating and persistent eye infection, he received an extended furlough from the Bombay Medical Board in 1849. It was assumed that he would recuperate in Britain, but he had scarcely arrived there when he left for Boulogne, one of those French towns that had attracted a large British expatriate population. Here he found lodging with his mother and sister, settling down to write about his Indian experiences. The remarkable result of this effort was the publication of three books in 1851 and a fourth in 1852, a burst of productivity that gave the first full indication of the intellectual energy and ambition of the man. It was in the midst of this intense period of self-reflection that Burton most likely came to acquire a more mature apprehension of his own subjectivity, a sharper insight into the person he meant to be and the career he meant to pursue. There is little doubt that this sense of self was ambivalently situated vis-à-vis England. Burton sought the recognition of his countrymen, but saw little prospect of attaining it through conventional avenues. Instead, he began to conceive for himself a more audacious path to glory, one more consistent with his emotional appetites, intellectual abilities, and social limitations. He embraced his own sense of difference, claiming a position outside the boundaries of class and custom, fashioning a public persona that obeyed no authority but its own critical intelligence. This assertion of independence hinged on his willingness to wander the edges of the earth, to investigate strange societies and explain their unfamiliar ways, to speak uncomfortable truths even at the risk of being labeled a "white nigger."

ᴋᴙ III ᴂ

The Impersonator

Richard Burton burst onto the British public scene in the early 1850s. His decision to enter Mecca in the guise of a Muslim pilgrim in 1853 was carefully calculated to attract the attention of his countrymen, and it succeeded beyond his wildest expectations, bringing him the renown his flurry of books about India had failed to produce. The enterprise was couched in earnest terms as a disinterested inquiry into knowledge of another land and its people, but it tapped into a far more complex array of enthusiasms and emotions on the part of his Victorian audience. Their Christian piety fed a fascination with the Holy Lands and harbored a fear of Islam; their Indian empire and East Asian trade made the Arabian region a focus of strategic interest; their affinity for the theater and its world of fictive identities nurtured a fondness for cross-cultural role playing. Burton's adventure was perfectly fashioned to appeal to these interests, and it succeeded in bringing him into the national spotlight.

The pilgrimage to Mecca was not without its risks, however. It required a high-stakes masquerade that was vulnerable to exposure at different levels by different parties. On the one hand, Burton ran the risk that his disguise would fail to deceive the Muslim peoples he encountered on his journey. On the other hand, he ran an equally serious risk of failing to persuade the British public that his embrace of Islam was nothing more than a performance. The pilgrimage was not an unqualified triumph in either regard.

There is some evidence, for example, that he was less successful in hiding his English identity from his fellow pilgrims than his audience at home was led to believe. By the same token, some Christian critics wondered whether his Muslim persona really was the sham he made it out to be. In the final analysis, these doubts were traceable to his own reluctance to commit to a stable and readily identifiable identity, a reluctance rooted in the emotional and intellectual satisfaction he received from transcending the conventional boundaries of religion and race.

⁂

With his medical furlough drawing to a close in 1852, Richard Burton had little desire to return to his regiment. A military career in the Bombay presidency offered him far less freedom to operate as he pleased now that his patron Napier had departed and the administration of Sindh had become more bureaucratized. In April he managed to delay his departure for six months by claiming his health remained fragile. Soon thereafter he hit on an expedient that offered a more intriguing means of escape from his regular duties, one that also promised to put the linguistic skills and ethnographic expertise he had acquired in India to good use. The Royal Geographical Society was offering £200 to anyone who would explore the interior regions of Arabia. Burton leaped at the opportunity, thereby launching himself on an adventure that offered the personal liberty and public attention he craved.

Burton initially proposed to travel across southern Arabia from Aden, the British protectorate at the mouth of the Red Sea, to Muscat, the Omani port near the entrance to the Persian Gulf. In his letter requesting approval from the India Office, he detailed his qualifications: "I have devoted eight years to the study of Oriental manners customs & literature, I served nearly four years in the Scinde Survey, can sketch & model, speak the Arabic language and have a superficial knowledge of medicine, besides which I possess the bodily strength and activity necessary for a traveler in wild countries." He also explained how he intended to make his way through a region that was well known for its dangers to outsiders, especially non-Muslims. "I propose to pass for a petty trader & physician, the safest character that can be assumed in those regions. Moreover, I doubt not that by virtue of my knowledge of the Muslim Faith and personal appearance, I should be mistaken for an Arab even in the midst of Mecca."[1] Burton, in effect, was proposing to turn the skills he had developed in Sindh to use in Arabia.

The itinerary that Burton mapped out was intended to appeal both to the Royal Geographical Society, which wanted to fill in the blank spaces on its maps of the region, and the British East India Company, which had a strategic interest in the sealanes around the Arabian peninsula. But the Company's Court of Directors turned down Burton's request for a two-year leave of absence to carry out the journey, citing its inordinate risk. It did, however, grant him one year of leave, ostensibly to spend time in Egypt and Arabia improving his Arabic. Burton reassessed his plans accordingly, deciding that he would use his knowledge of Islam and talent for disguise to undertake the pilgrimage from Cairo via the Red Sea to the Muslim holy city of Mecca.[2]

This decision was an inspired one. From a political standpoint, it played on the British preoccupation with the strategic corridor that ran from the Nile Delta through the Gulf of Suez and the Red Sea to the Gulf of Aden. This region was increasingly viewed as a chokepoint in trade and communications between Britain and its Asian possessions. In 1839 the British proclaimed Aden a protectorate, thereby establishing a naval presence at the mouth of the Red Sea. In 1841 the Peninsular and Oriental Steam

Navigation Company acquired a concession at the port of Suez, instituting a regular route to Bombay that cut months off the standard voyage around the South African cape. Though passengers had to cross the isthmus by land, there was growing talk of a canal being cut between Suez and Port Said. In 1854, the year after Burton's pilgrimage to Mecca and just before the publication of his *Personal Narrative*, Ferdinand de Lesseps obtained his concession to build the Suez Canal. All of these developments heightened the public interest in Burton's adventures and observations.

Burton also tapped into a fascination with the Near East that was deeply rooted in Victorian culture. It derived above all from the Bible and the images it conjured up of Christianity's birthplace. It also entered the popular imagination through the tales of the Arabian Nights, a staple of British children's literature in that period. From the late eighteenth century onward, many British intellectuals made reference to the region and its inhabitants as a counterpoint to their critiques of Western society. Enlightenment figures such as William Jones and Edward Gibbon looked upon the Bedouin of Arabia as savage savants who possessed a natural instinct for political liberty. Lord Byron, Percy Shelley, and other Romantic writers regarded the Near East both as a region oppressed by Ottoman despotism and a site associated with heightened feeling, a realm where Romantic sensibilities could find free reign. For Victorian sages such as Thomas Carlyle, the desert domain of the Arabs harbored an innate spirituality, a view that Benjamin Disraeli racialized in his novel *Tancred* (1847), with its claims that Semitic peoples possessed a heightened religious sensibility.[3] Among the many readers enthralled by Disraeli's mystical evocation of the region was Richard Burton's future wife, Isabel Arundell.[4]

By the early nineteenth century, a small but steady stream of

Britons had begun to venture into Egypt, Palestine, and surrounding territories, publishing accounts of their travels that fascinated the reading public at home.[5] Perhaps the most successful
example was Alexander Kinglake's *Eothan* (1844), a charming account of his journey through the region in 1835. David Roberts's
paintings of Egypt and Palestine, which he toured in the late
1830s, were greeted with similar enthusiasm. Regular steamship
service was instituted between Marseilles and Alexandria in the
1830s and between Southampton and Alexandria in the 1850s.
Travelers to Egypt could follow a standard tour route that took
them from Alexandria to Cairo, then up the Nile to view the
ancient ruins at Thebes. An array of prominent Britons made
this journey, among them Florence Nightingale, Francis Galton,
Harriet Martineau, and Richard Monckton Milnes. Writing
from Cairo after his return from Mecca, Burton noted the numerous tourists on the streets and observed sarcastically: "No end
of gents who keep journals & will doubtless commemorate their
Nile boats & Dragoman in mortal prose."[6] Not all of the British
in Egypt were transient sightseers, however. Some of them took
up extended residency in Cairo, adopting the dress and lifestyle
of the Turkish ruling elite and immersing themselves in local
Egyptian culture. The most noteworthy of these figures were
Gardner Wilkinson, an early Egyptologist who published the
Manners and Customs of the Ancient Egyptians (1827), and Edward
Lane, who adopted the alias Mansur Effendi to aid him in his research into the *Manners and Customs of the Modern Egyptians*
(1836). Lane also produced the first English translation from Arabic manuscript sources of the tales of the Arabian Nights. In ad-
dition, cultural brokers such as Osman Effendi, a Scottish soldier
who had converted to Islam after his capture and enslavement by
Muhammed Ali's forces in 1807, operated on the fringes of this
British Egyptian community.[7]

The Victorian image of the Middle East was intimately bound up with its impressions of Islam, the dominant influence on the region's social and cultural character. As Christendom's historic rival, Islam remained a strange and menacing faith to most Britons, known mainly in terms of Orientalist stereotypes about polygamy, harems, and other exotic practices. Its mysteries were magnified by the prohibition against the entry of non-Muslims to Mecca, Islam's center of worship. For all the European tourist traffic through Egypt and other parts of the Middle East, Mecca remained for the most part free from the prying eyes of unbelievers. Burton saw an opportunity to tap into this rich vein of curiosity by undertaking the pilgrimage to Mecca and exposing the city and its Muslim faithful to the scrutiny of his Christian countrymen.

Burton was not the first European to make the pilgrimage to Mecca. Various others had done so over the centuries, and at least half a dozen had published first-hand accounts of the journey and the holy city at its terminus.[8] Burton carefully studied what his predecessors had written in preparation for his own trip, later including generous selections from some of their works as appendices to his *Personal Narrative of a Pilgrimage to Al-Medinah and Meccah* (1855). The most recent and informed of his precursors was Johann Ludwig Burckhardt, the Swiss-born explorer who traveled through Syria, Palestine, Egypt, and the Nile valley on behalf of the British-based African Association between 1812 and 1817. Disguised as an Indian Muslim merchant, he managed to enter Mecca in 1814–15 (accompanied by Osman Effendi), and although he died before he could return to Europe, his journals describing the journey were published posthumously in 1829 as *Travels in Arabia.* Burton, though duly appreciative of Burckhardt's accomplishment, praising his audacity and knowledge, also took pains to point out instances where his own efforts and observations surpassed those of the great Swiss adventurer. He was acutely conscious of the need to demonstrate that he had seen and done things unmatched by his predecessors and peers, understanding that this was the currency that would buy him fame.

From the perspective of a practicing Muslim, of course, there was nothing remarkable about the journey he prepared to undertake. Tens if not hundreds of thousands of pilgrims made their way to Mecca every year, many of them from far greater distances and with far fewer resources than Burton. Even though Islam's holiest city remained shrouded in mystery to most Europeans, it was at the center of a global community of believers, the *umma*, who shared a common faith, law, and language. The pilgrimage itself strengthened that *umma*, supplying those who undertook the journey with a richer, more cosmopolitan view of the *dar al-Islam* (the world of Islam). For Muslims, in other words, the pilgrimage to Mecca carried a completely different meaning than it did for non-Muslims.[9] Burton could scarcely have dared to launch such a risky undertaking were it not for the fact that the hajj attracted pilgrims from such varied corners of the *dar al-Islam*, making variations of speech, dress, and customs the norm, not the exception.

It must be understood, however, that Burton's decision to undertake the hajj in an "Oriental" disguise was directed as much at a British audience as it was at the Muslims with whom he associated during the journey. His subterfuge was not in fact necessary to gain entry to Mecca: he could have gone there freely and openly had he simply proclaimed his conversion to Islam, which was in any case the sine qua non for the disguise he adopted. As one Arab commentator later observed, "On the pilgrimage to

Mecca, Burton would be known as a devout British Muhammedan just as easily as we recognise an Arab convert on a missionary platform."[10] Why Burton chose instead to carry out his elaborate deception says something about the complex array of professional ambitions and social pressures that influenced his judgment. First, he still harbored a desire to go from Mecca into Arabia's Empty Quarter, which would have been difficult to do as an Englishman, even one who had sincerely converted to Islam. Second, he believed that an "Oriental" persona would give him greater access to the intimate world of the peoples who inhabited the region, much as it had done in Sindh. Third, he understood that his adventure would be measured against the achievement of Burckhardt, who had entered Mecca and Medina in disguise. He could do no less.

There was one further consideration that made any thought of undertaking the pilgrimage as a self-professed English convert to Islam impossible: it would invalidate his accomplishment and destroy his reputation in the eyes of the British public. A genuine conversion would place him beyond the pale of respectable society, extinguishing any prospect of making a name for himself as a national hero.[11] Even a sham conversion would be seen as an act of abasement to an inferior faith and culture if carried out while he maintained his identity as an Englishman. Indeed, for some Victorians, any sort of masquerade was regarded as socially deceitful and morally repugnant. It carried associations with sexual license and libertinism, which derived from the notorious aristocratic masquerades in the eighteenth century and persisted in the nineteenth-century theater's reputation as a haven for prostitution and pornography.[12] Evangelicals in particular objected to any form of impersonation, viewing it as a vehicle for escaping personal moral responsibility.[13] It made no difference to these devout Christians that Burton's acts of obeisance to an alien faith were

Burton in Arab dress. His impersonation of a Muslim pilgrim brought him fame and played a central role in his persona.From Richard F. Burton, *Personal Narrative of a Pilgrimage to Al-Madinah and Meccah*, Memorial Edition (London: Tylston and Edwards, 1893). This lithograph reproduces an original oil painting (ca. 1853–54) by Borgo Cassatti, now in the collection of the Orleans House Gallery, Twinkenham, England.

carried out in his role as an "Oriental": he remained an Englishman whose actions were seen as sullying himself, his country, and—a presumptive element of his national character—his Christian faith. "There is something indescribably revolting to our feelings," railed the *Edinburgh Review,* "in the position of an English officer . . . crawling among a crowd of unbelievers, around the objects of their wretched superstition."[14] The Arabian traveler and evangelical Christian Charles Doughty shared this opinion: he refused to read the *Personal Narrative,* despite its potential value in preparing for his own journey into the region, because of his moral objections to Burton's masquerade as a Muslim.[15]

For most of his countrymen, however, the decision by Burton to pass himself off as an "Oriental" made all the difference in the world. It transformed him into an actor, and the theater held such a prominent, if contested, place in Victorian life that most of the public was culturally conditioned to draw the distinction between the person and the performance, and to applaud the latter when carried off with aplomb.[16] Burton enjoyed socializing with prominent actors such as Henry Irving and Ellen Terry, and he possessed an instinctive flair for the theatrical, as many of those who met him over the years observed. His doctor, Grenfell Baker, noted "his lifelong obsession for assuming poses."[17] His journey to Mecca and Medina was staged in effect as a performance, a demonstration of his skills at impersonation. And, as such, it elicited an enthusiastic reception from a significant portion of his British audience. They admired the audacity of his undertaking and the ingenuity that allowed him to pull it off. The prospect that he might have been exposed as an imposter gave his performance dramatic tension, the frisson of danger that kept his audience on the edges of their seats. The fact that he was able to deceive the guardians of Islam's holiest shrines and gain access to

their inner sanctums supplied the story with its triumphant resolution, its proof of his thespian talents. Not only did it generate
admiration for the quasi-magical powers exhibited by the successful actor; but it also inspired a chauvinistic sense of pride, a
feeling that the ability to assume the external attributes of the native demonstrated the superiority of the English character.

The role that impersonation played in Burton's pilgrimage has
attracted renewed attention in recent years. Though biographers
have generally taken his effort to pass as a Muslim pilgrim at face
value, accepting his explanation that it was necessary to gain
entrée to a world he could not otherwise have come to know
so intimately, other scholars, particularly specialists in literature
and literary theory, have evaluated his adventure in very different
terms, raising intriguing questions about its implications for self-
representation and identity. Informing these questions are several
related theoretical presuppositions—a postmodernist understanding of the self as a shifting, contingent category and a postcolonial preoccupation with mimicry and hybridity as manifestations of this unfixed self. Much of this scholarship, following the
lead of Homi Bhabha, has referred to mimicry as a strategic ma-
neuver by the colonized to subvert the authority of the colonizer,
while hybridity is taken to be the preeminent expression of the
postcolonial disintegration of colonial categories.[18] What, then, is
one to make of Burton's use of mimicry and hybridity? Here we
have the problematic case of an agent of imperialism wielding
what are widely regarded as the weapons of the weak. This poses
the question of what ends are being served by this appropriation.
The answer most frequently proposed by postcolonial critics is
the one Anne McClintock gives in her analysis of Rudyard Kipling's *Kim,* the famous novel about an Anglo-Irish youth who
passes as an Indian in order to gather intelligence for the British
Raj. Kim, she states, used "mimicry and cross-dressing as a tech-

nique not of colonial subversion, but of surveillance."[19] This interpretation can certainly be applied to Burton. We have already seen that he conducted surveillance missions for the colonial regime in Sindh, and his pilgrimage to Mecca promised to contribute valuable intelligence on a region that held considerable strategic interest for British authorities. Moreover, Burton himself affirmed the political value of his observations, which were punctuated by editorial remarks of the following sort: "Egypt is the most tempting prize which the East holds out to the ambition of Europe."[20]

Still, we would do well to distinguish between the justifications that Burton supplied for his masquerades and the motivations that actually inspired them: the latter were shot through with ambiguities. The problem, as Kaja Silverman has noted in reference to T. E. Lawrence, another Englishman who reveled in his ability to impersonate an Arab, is that "imitation . . . veers over into identification."[21] The line between the one and the other is especially difficult to delineate in the case of Burton. Edward Said, for example, credits Burton, almost alone among his countrymen, with being "able to become an Oriental . . . to penetrate to the heart of Islam," an accomplishment that he attributes to Burton's "having successfully absorbed its systems of information and behavior" and "shaken himself loose of his European origins."[22] Parama Roy is more critical in her assessment of his intentions, which she believes were inextricably associated with imperial designs, but even she concedes his "heterogeneous affiliations."[23] Burton's contemporary critics wondered with some justice where his real loyalties resided. Whatever success he attained in his efforts to pass himself off as a born-and-bred "Oriental" derived from his determination to go beyond the surface markers of identity, the signifiers exemplified by dress and speech. It is clear that he found Islamic faith and culture appealing at a deeply emotional level, and he immersed himself in this worldview. At the same time, he maintained his ideological attachment to the British empire, to the imperatives of power and the opportunities it presented for personal advancement. In this regard, as in so many others over the course of his long and eventful career, he staked out a position so rich in ambiguities, so riven with contradictory commitments, that contemporaries found it difficult to identify exactly where he stood or, more to the point, who he really was. This determination to resist definition, to keep his own identity in continuous play, is in fact what makes him such a profoundly modern figure.

Burton left his British self behind when he boarded a ship bound for Egypt in April 1853. It had been at least four years since his previous effort to pass as an "Oriental," and his skills in Arabic and instincts for dissimulation were rusty. He tried out several different personas before he hit upon one that seemed to suit his needs. The first experiment in otherness came during the voyage from Southampton to Alexandria, when he disguised himself as a "Persian Prince" traveling in the company of his friend, Captain Henry Grindlay, a Bengal Army officer. Although he never explains what motivated this choice of identity, the shipboard segregation of passengers along economic and ethnic lines was almost certainly a consideration. As a "prince" with a British officer to vouch for him, Burton could book a first-class berth, which was desirable not only because of its comforts, but because it was much easier for him to maintain his masquerade among the fellow Europeans who traveled first class than it would have been among non-Europeans, most of whom were pressed together in steerage. The two-week voyage allowed him to get "into the train of Oriental manners" without worrying overmuch about the threat of exposure. Even so, his disguise was far from foolproof: a Turkish acquaintance traveling on the same ship recognized Burton.[24]

When he arrived in Egypt, Burton spent five weeks in Alexandria, rooming in the garden guesthouse of a friend, John Larking, who himself "lived in half-Oriental style."[25] Here he dropped the princely masquerade and took up a new identity as Shaykh Abdullah, a Sufi from Persia who dispensed medical advice and tonics.[26] Acting as a nostrum-peddler appealed to him because it provided access to the intimate lives of those who came to him for cures, and he thought that he could do no more harm than British army surgeons, especially to "uncivilized peoples" who in his view tended to suffer uncomplicated ills. Adopting the role of a Sufi also had its attractions: "No character in the Moslem world is so proper for disguise as that of the Darwaysh [Sufis]," he declared, equating them to "Oriental Freemasons," whose bonds of fellowship extended across territorial and cultural boundaries. Furthermore, their wandering ways and reputations as eccentric mystics made any anomalies of behavior by Burton less likely to arouse suspicion, and if suspicion should arise, "he had only to become a maniac, and he is safe." He was well versed in Sufi beliefs and poetry from his days in Sindh, and, indeed, claimed that he had been initiated in the Kadiriyah order while he was there, offering as proof a diploma that pronounced his attainment of "the proud position of a Murshid, or Master."[27]

Burton worked to refine this identity during his initial immersion in local life, first in Alexandria, then in Cairo, where he spent an additional six weeks improving his fluency in Arabic by conversing with the patrons of coffeehouses and bath houses and his knowledge of the Qur'an through study with imams in local mosques. He made several friends, the most important of whom was Haji Wali, a Russian-born merchant in Alexandria, with whom he fasted during Ramadan and shared a fondness for hash-ish. Wali soon saw through Burton's disguise, but instead of ex-pressing shock at the deception, he offered advice on how to im-prove it. He urged Burton to abandon his pretense of Persian origin, which was too risky given the prevalence of Persian pil-grims and the antagonism their Shiite beliefs stirred in the Sunni majority. Burton was encouraged instead to adopt a more compli-cated heritage that better accounted for his oddities of accent and experience. Henceforth, Burton became a wandering Sufi of Pathan origin, born to Afghan parents in India but educated in Rangoon: this pedigree was meant to account for his passable, but by no means native-spoken, Persian, Hindustani, and Arabic.

This third and final iteration of his "Oriental" identity took hybridity about as far as it could go. Its very heterogeneity is what made it such an attractive alias for Burton—it defied efforts to trace it to an essential, irreducible core. At the same time, it pre-sented a paradox for his claims of authenticity. As Parama Roy has observed, the "marginality" of Burton's position made him "an outsider who can pass as an 'Oriental' because of his unknow-ability rather than his familiarity or, more properly, an unknow-able familiarity."[28] He could succeed in this paradoxical role be-cause it was carried out in an environment where the traditional forces that bound person to place were undermined both by the destabilizing effects of British imperialism and by the cosmopoli-tan influence of the Muslim pilgrimage itself.[29]

However well suited to his circumstances, Burton's disguise was by no means impenetrable. Several times in the course of the journey he found himself at risk of exposure. Once he crossed paths with a Pathan pilgrim who showed an unwelcome curios-ity about his origins. On another occasion, his covert efforts to sketch scenes along the pilgrimage route were observed, arousing suspicion. The most serious threat to his subterfuge, however, came from the Meccan youth Mohammed el-Basyuni, a member of his traveling party who "suspected me from the first of being at least a heretic"—meaning a Shiite. Early in the journey, Mohammed discovered among Burton's belongings a sextant, a scientific instrument that he rightly regarded as signifying a secret identity and purpose. Unbeknownst to Burton, Mohammed denounced him to the other members of the party as "one of the Infidels from India," but after some discussion they dismissed his charge as unfounded. Burton claims that he learned of the incident after he had returned from the hajj to Cairo, where he had a chance encounter with one of his erstwhile travel companions, Omar Effendi.[30]

What makes this incident so intriguing is what it leaves unexplained. Did Burton's fellow pilgrims decline to act on the Meccan youth's accusation because they found it implausible *or* because they found it inconvenient? Is it possible that they already suspected or even knew his true identity? Naturally, Burton insists that his knowledge of Muslim theology and other demonstrations of authenticity overwhelmed any doubts raised by Mohammed. To suggest otherwise could have caused his readers to question the entire premise of his adventure, which presumed that it was both necessary and possible to pass as an "Oriental." In a footnote, however, Burton concedes that Effendi "must have suspected me" at the time. He also notes that he had made loans to Effendi and the other members of the party, causing them to be "affectionate and eloquent in my praise" and supplying a plausible motive for rejecting his accuser's charges. If he was subsidizing their journey, what incentive did they have to see him exposed? The absence of evidence from any sources other than Burton himself makes it impossible to confirm that his companions knew more about his deception than he appreciated at the time or acknowledged after the fact. But it seems reasonable to entertain the possibility that the other members of Burton's travel party conspired to keep their suspicions about his identity to themselves, engaging in effect in their own deception vis-à-vis the person who sought to deceive them.[31]

⌘⌘⌘⌘⌘

Burton began his journey to the heartland of Islam in early July 1853, some three months after he had first arrived in Egypt. His itinerary was a common one for pilgrims from North Africa. He and his traveling companions rode camels from Cairo to Suez, the port town at the northern end of the Red Sea, where they boarded a vessel overcrowded with pilgrims for a twelve-day voyage to Yanbu', the main point to entry to Medina from the west. Here they joined a large party of pilgrims for the treacherous trek inland. Burton lingered at the second city of Islam for a month, visiting local shrines and regaining his strength. When a large caravan from Damascus set off on the ten-day journey from Medina to Mecca, he attached himself to it. His arrival in Islam's holiest city in early September marked the culmination of his high-stakes journey, and after fulfilling his obligations as a pilgrim— and making observations as an outsider—he left for the port of Jeddah, where he obtained passage back to Egypt.[32]

Although Burton faces various hardships and dangers over the course of the journey, including intense heat and dehydration, a seriously infected foot, and attacks by Bedouin bandits, he clearly considers the experience an exhilarating one. He glories in the openness of the desert and the sense of freedom it inspires: "Your *morale* improves; you become frank and cordial, hospitable and single-minded: the hypocritical politeness and the slavery of civilization are left behind you in the city. Your senses are quickened: they require no stimulants but air and exercise . . . There is a keen enjoyment in mere animal existence." He finds the Arabs an at-

74

tractive, congenial people: "they are of a more affectionate nature than the Persians, and their manners are far more demonstrative than those of the Indians." Like many of his countrymen, he voices particular enthusiasm for the Bedouin, "a truly noble compound of determination, gentleness, and generosity." He compares the Bedouin favorably to the American Indian, often regarded by Europeans as the archetypal noble savage, claiming they share similar characteristics, including "the same wild chivalry, the same fiery sense of honour, and the same boundless hospitality," while insisting that the Arab ranks higher "on account of his treatment of women, his superior development of intellect, and the glorious pages of history which he has filled."[33]

Burton attempts to break through his Western readers' ingrained prejudices against the Islamic world by pointing out that many of the criticisms lodged against it can be turned with equal effect against the West. He insists, for example, that Muslims are no more susceptible to superstition than Christians: "Europe, the civilized, the enlightened, the skeptical, dotes over clairvoyance and table-turning . . .—I must hold the men of Al-Madinah to be as wise and their superstitions to be as respectable, as that of others." To those who dismiss the rituals associated with the pilgrimage as crude exhibitions of idolatry, he responds: "What are the English mistletoe, the Irish wake, the Pardon of Brittany, the Carnival, and the Worship of Iserna? Better far to consider the Meccan Pilgrimage rites in the light of Evil-worship turned into lessons of Good than to philosophize about their strangeness." He defends the education offered in mosques against its Western critics by asking, "Would not a superficial, hasty, and somewhat prejudiced Egyptian or Persian say exactly the same thing about the systems of Christ Church and Trinity College?" And he counters objections to Muslim attitudes toward women by observing: "Certain 'Fathers of the Church,' it must be remembered, did not believe that women have souls. The Moslems never went so far."[34]

How Muslims treat women is in fact one of the defining issues that sets Burton at odds with his countrymen. The Victorians held that the level of civilization attained by a society could be measured in terms of the status it accorded women.[35] Burton shares the evolutionary assumptions that underwrite this evaluation,[36] but he disputes its derogation of the Muslim world as inferior to the West because of the sanction it gives to polygamy, veiling, and other practices that seem to subordinate women. The notion "that women in Muslim countries want liberty," he sighs, "seems burned into the European brain, but it is simply absurd, the effect of misrepresentation and a most superficial study."[37] He insists that Muslim customs support stable, loving relationships and provide women with satisfactions and freedoms unrealized by their Western sisters. He tries to demystify polygamy and harems, claiming that "jealousy and quarrels about the sex are the exception and not the rule of life" in polygamous households and suggesting that the harem "often resembles a European home composed of a man, his wife, and his mother." He challenges his readers to identify any European literature that can match the depth of feeling for women expressed in Arab love poetry. He praises the veil as "the most coquettish article of woman's attire." Even the objections he raises to certain features of gender relations in the Muslim world undermine prevailing Western assumptions. For example, he laments the fact that Egyptian women can obtain government protection from abusive husbands, fearing it has made them "unruly."[38]

The position that Burton stakes out with regard to women in Muslim societies can be interpreted as a reactionary defense of patriarchal authority, which was beginning to come under challenge in England from feminists. Rana Kabbani makes a forceful case for this view, arguing that Burton constructed a myth of the Orient that derived from his desire for a "master-slave relationship" between the sexes, with women serving as "chattel and sexual convenience."[39] Scattered comments in Burton's corpus of writings lend some support to this analysis. To dismiss Burton as a male chauvinist, however, is to neglect the subversive undercurrents that course through his opinions on relations between the sexes, losing sight of their unsettling effects on his British readers. In the books and articles that follow *Personal Pilgrimage,* Burton returns repeatedly to the issue of polygamy and other gender practices in Muslim societies, challenging his countrymen's conviction that their effects on women are oppressive. Polygamy, he insists, does not derive from the lust of men, as European critics claim, but from the social and economic interests of both sexes. Commenting on its practice in West Africa, he concedes that a "multitude of wives ministers to the great man's pride and influence, as well as to his pleasures and to his efficiency," but argues that the wives benefit too: "after feeding their husbands, what remains out of the fruits of their labours is their own, wholly out of his reach—a boon not always granted by civilization." Hence, "polygamy here has not rendered the women . . . a down-trodden moiety of society; on the contrary, their position is comparatively high."[40]

Burton's interest in polygamy drew him in 1860 to the newly established Mormon settlement at Salt Lake City, which he referred to as the "young Meccah in the West."[41] In *The City of the Saints,* his account of this visit, he makes his most sustained case for polygamous marriage, which in this instance has been adopted by persons of European ethnicity, including a considerable number of English converts. Once again he stresses its benefits to women, suggesting that it lightens the burdens of domestic labor for individual wives and reduces their sexual obligations to their husband, thereby promoting harmony within the household, though diminishing romantic sentiments. It is not clear, however, how he reconciles what seems his rather conventional Victorian notion that wives want less sexual attention from their husbands with the argument he makes at other times that women are more highly sexed than men. Similarly, his concession that amatory feelings are less pronounced in polygamous marriages seems inconsistent with his earlier praise of Arabic love poetry. Burton's main purpose, however, is to refute the European charge that polygamy is a license for licentiousness: he stresses that a strict Mosaic code against adultery and emphasis on female modesty and celibacy by single males operate both in Mormon and in Muslim societies. He also tries to place polygamy beyond the reach of Western moral censure by sketching out a social-scientific interpretation of its intent, suggesting that among peoples in thinly populated regions it is the most effective strategy for producing progeny. By contrast, he suggests, the densely populated, purportedly monogamous societies of Europe keep their numbers under control through widespread resort to prostitution, which he argues is in effect a polyandrous practice far more degrading to women than polygamy.[42]

Burton presses his case in favor of Muslims' treatment of women in still another area—that of legal safeguards. He gleefully notes that women under Islamic law enjoy rights denied their Western counterparts. "Nowhere," he asserts, "do women hold a higher position, or enjoy such true liberty, as in Moslem lands; and it is curious to hear the assertion made in England, where by statute a man may beat his wife moderately, force her by law to submit to his loathed companionship, and dispose of her property as well as her person."[43] In another work he again points out "the superior liberty of the sex amongst Moslem races. . . . She has immense advantages in the management of children, property, and servants, and in real freedom, despite apparent seclusion, which in modest women is always voluntary."[44] Nor can he resist observing that Parliament's passage of the Married Women's Property Act in 1882 granted modern British women rights to property and inheritance that the Qur'an had made available to Muslim women centuries earlier.[45]

By defending Islam against what its Western critics see as its most vulnerable feature—the status it accords to women—Burton makes clear his sympathies for the faith. No one can read the *Personal Narrative* without recognizing that its author has great respect for the doctines and rituals of Islam. Here is how he describes his feelings when he arrives at the sacred heart of Mecca, the Ka'bah: "I may truly say that . . . none felt for the moment a deeper emotion than did the Haji from the far-north. It was as if the poetical legends of the Arab spoke truth, and that the waving wings of angels . . . were agitating and swelling the black covering of the shrine." After attending a prayer service at a mosque, he declares: "I have seen the religious ceremonies of many lands, but never—nowhere—aught so solemn, so impressive as this." And in the preface to the third edition of the *Personal Narrative,* which appeared in 1879, he declares in bitter defiance of his critics that "the Moslem may be more tolerant, more enlightened, more charitable, than many societies of self-styled Christians."[46] Thus while Burton remains a relentlessly gimlet-eyed observer who readily heaps abuse on particular individuals and practices, he never directs his scorn toward Islam itself.

His affinity for the Islamic faith carries through to his subsequent writings as well. In *First Footsteps in East Africa* (1856), the account of his journey to the Ethiopian city of Harar, he recalls the sense of peace that came over him when he again heard the call of the muezzin: "no evening bell can compare with it for solemnity and beauty. . . . I fell asleep, feeling once more at home."[47]

In *The Guide-Book: A Pictorial Pilgrimage to Mecca and Medina* (1865), a pamphlet he wrote to accompany an exhibition about the journey that had made his name, he sought to demystify Islam for the British public, giving a respectful account of its origins, doctrines, and rituals. At the same time, he indicated his own sympathies for the faith, most notably in a passage that mirrored the one in *Personal Narrative* about his visit to the Ka'bah.[48] In a lecture he gave to an audience of Brazilian Catholic dignitaries on his pilgrimage to Mecca, he insisted that Islam is "a creed remarkable for common sense."[49] Perhaps his most outspoken defense of Islam, however, came in a review essay he wrote in response to a German work of anthropology that had criticized the influence of Islam. His frustration welling to the surface, he declared that "nowhere in El Islam appear the disgraceful excesses of Christendom." Islam is in fact "the first and greatest reformation of the corrupted faith called Christianity; and its effects have endured till this day." Those who adhere to its doctrines are superior to Christians "in morality and manly dignity," not to mention "in industry and honesty."[50] Though Burton toned down his rhetoric in later years, he continued to express his admiration for Islam. Among his posthumous publications is an essay on Islam that reiterates earlier arguments in its favor, praising Mohammed as a sincere prophet who "bequeathed to the world a Law and a Faith . . . whose wide prevalence—wider indeed than that of any other creed—alone suffices to prove its extrinsic value to the human family."[51]

It is hardly surprising that critics often accused him of being a convert to Islam. During a heated Anthropological Society debate about the missionary endeavor in Africa, one antagonist characterized him as one who "stands up for Mohammedanism in opposition to the Christian faith." (Burton interrupted: "This is personal.")[52] Reviewers of his books often expressed outrage at his opinions on Islam and the practices associated with it, most notably polygamy. In its review of *Abeokuta and the Cameroons Mountains* (1863), the *London Review* indicated its dismay at "so zealous an advocacy—or rather an apology—of polygamy," and wondered what Burton's wife thought of his views. Isabel made her feelings publicly known several years later when she appended a personal preface to Richard's latest book, *Explorations of the Highlands of the Brazil* (1869), which he had left her to shepherd through the publication process while he took up his new posting in Damascus. Deeply offended by his defense of polygamy and criticisms of her own faith, Roman Catholicism, she announced that she "protest[s] vehemently against his religious and moral sentiments." Her public objections had no discernible effect, however, on his determination to voice controversial views. A year later, *The Echo* observed that Burton "seems more convinced than ever that the happiness of future generations depends in great measure on the spread of polygamic principles." *The Spectator* excoriated *Two Trips to Gorilla Land* (1876) for its "bad taste" and anti-Christian views, complaining that Burton's "tone is so aggressive against decency that one has hardly patience to seek for his facts." The *Saturday Review* described Burton as "an orthodox Haji and Dervish" in its review of his *Gold Mines of Midian* (1878). And a lengthy, unidentified review essay on two of Burton's books about West Africa concluded that his "coarse vein of sensuality and indecorum," his "proclivities in favour of polygamy," and his defiance of "all notions of Christian decency" demonstrated that he must be a Muslim: "Captain Burton would have acted more openly and honestly towards his readers, if he had added to all the other titles that trail along after his name, the words, 'An English Gentleman, converted long ago to El Islam.'"[53]

Was it true? Had Burton converted to Islam? The answer has

to be "no" if conversion is understood in terms of strict obser-
vance of prayer and other demonstrations of faith. If, on the other
hand, it is understood as a way of life, a set of values that informs
one's outlook on the world, then Burton may very well have
viewed himself as a Muslim—at least for a period of time. He
clearly found Islam's ethical doctrines and codes of conduct more
edifying and socially purposeful than any of its rivals', though
there is little evidence that he personally abided by them. He also
felt a genuine affinity for the sentiments expressed in Sufi poetry
and practice, though this association raises questions of its own
about the depth of his commitment to Islam. The British Orientalists who originally encountered Sufism in India in the late
eighteenth century—and, indeed, coined the term—believed that
it had "no intrinsic relation with the faith of Islam," viewing it instead as an Eastern form of freethinking.[54] Burton saw it in a similar light, adopting a Sufi perspective, persona, and poetic style
for his own freethinking manifesto, *The Kasîdah* (1880).

What this suggests is that Burton's feelings toward Islam must
be framed in the context of his attitudes toward Christianity. He
was drawn to Islam because it gave him a vantage point from
which to point out the limitations of his own European Christian
heritage, not because it possessed in his mind any unqualified
truths or virtues. He was most fervent in his advocacy of Islamic
beliefs and Muslim practices during the decade—the late 1850s to
the late 1860s—when he was most actively engaged in a polemical
campaign against the universalist claims of evangelical Christianity. His dismay at what he regarded as the destructive effects of
Christian missionary activity among the West African peoples
with whom he came in contact during his years as British consul
in Fernando Po (1861–1864) made him especially outspoken in his
praise of Islam. Not only did he argue in his books on the region
that Islam was better suited to the needs of Africans than Chris-

tianity, but he also referred to himself as a Muslim in private communications and conversations. In letters from West Africa to his friend Monckton Milnes, he wrote that he was taking "'sweet counsel' together" with his "Moslem brethren" and wishing "for a little of the 'Higher Law' (viz that of Mohammed)."[55] Soon after his return from West Africa to England, he spent a weekend at the country home of Lord John Russell, where his hostess reported in her diary that he "calls himself openly a Musselman." His host, however, qualified Burton's provocative affirmation of faith, noting that he "believes in no particular religion, though calling himself a Musselman."[56] This gets us closer to what Islam meant for Burton—not an expression of faith in its own right, but a means of challenging the unquestioning faith of his countrymen.

Burton exhibited an intellectual curiosity in religions of all sorts, but this curiosity never carried over into the unquestioning commitment of the devout believer. While in India he was intrigued not only by Islam, but by Roman Catholicism, choosing its services over those of the Anglican chapel while he was stationed in Baroda, and by Hinduism, claiming that his intensive study of the faith had been rewarded by the privilege of wearing "the *Janeo* (Brahminical thread)."[57] He gave a sympathetic hearing to the doctrines of Mormonism during his visit to Salt Lake City, concluding that Mormon theocracy was "the perfection of government."[58] He even had something good to say about what he termed the "fetish" beliefs of West Africans, which avoided the objectionable "anthropomorphism" that afflicted Christianity. "The Negro Deity, if disassociated from physical objects, would almost represent the idea of the philosopher," by which he meant "a pure theism."[59] Late in life he became interested in the claims of Spiritualism, finding in its eclectic "mix of rationalism, experimentation, and anti-Christian secularism" a perspective much to his liking.[60] Ironically, what motivated this catholicity of interest was his deep skepticism about any religion's claims to absolute truth. Ever the ethnographer, he understood that every theological system provided its believers with a set of codes for governing behavior, and he appreciated this social purpose. He also admired the philosophical insight and elegance of different religious doctrines, though he ranked some much higher in this regard than others. But he was unable to embrace any of them with the unquestioning devotion they demanded. A question he posed regarding Catholicism pointed to his dilemma: "is there any middle term between the God-like gift of reason or the un-reason of Rome?"[61] Much of his intellectual life was spent in search of that "middle term." His wife, Isabel, whose desperate desire to convert him to Catholicism caused tensions in their marriage and controversy after his death, probably understood better than anyone the impetus that drove him on his religious odyssey. After she had arranged for his burial in a Catholic cemetery by claiming his death-bed conversion to the Roman faith, she acknowledged that he had "tried religions all round. . . . In each religion he found something good, and much that disappointed him; then he took the good out of that religion, and went away. He was sincere with the Mohammedans, and found more in that religion than in *most*."[62]

After his return from Mecca, Burton lingered in Cairo as long as his leave would allow. His professed purpose was to squirrel himself away so he could write an account of his journey while it remained fresh in his mind. Some of the *Personal Narrative* was drafted during those uninterrupted months in Cairo, though he did not complete the manuscript until after his return to India.

But he remained in Cairo for another, more personal reason: he was reluctant to divest himself of his "Oriental" identity, which gave him a kind of freedom—not least with regard to sexual conduct—that he never could have enjoyed as a British officer in Egypt. In a series of letters to Norton Shaw of the Royal Geographical Society, he described his continued masquerade in terms that appear especially telling in light of the later accusation in his reminiscences that his fellow officers in India had referred to him as a "white nigger." "I was quite a *nigger* in Cairo & saw no English," he wrote in October 1853. A month later he reported that he was "still dressed Nigger fashion and called the Haji." He boasted that he inhabited "a precious scene of depravity; showing what Cairo can do at a pinch & beating the Arabian Nights all to chalks! That too when the Pacha has positively forbidden fornication." This letter was signed "Shaykh Abdullah."[63]

Burton was already campaigning to undertake another mission. This time he set his sights southward, inspired in part by reports from the German missionary Johann Krapf of snow-capped peaks in the East African highlands. Krapf, he proclaimed with conscious irony, was "my John the Baptist."[64] Burton proposed that he launch a probe into the interior of the continent from Somalia or Zanzibar, both of which were still within the Islamic sphere he knew best, albeit on its margins. He also broached the idea of a journey across equatorial Africa to the Atlantic, an ambition that had attracted the interest of other explorers.[65] His Arabian achievement gave him the ear of East India Company officials, who had their own economic and geopolitical reasons for supporting British probes into the East African hinterland. He accompanied Lord Elphinstone, the governor of Bombay, on a visit to the pyramids and found a patron in James Grant Lumsden, a member of that presidency's governing council, who provided him with accommodations in his Bombay home while Burton was completing his book on the pilgrimage to Mecca. The Company soon granted approval for an expedition intended to carry out a reconnaissance of Somalia, a territory that interested Bombay officials because of its strategic location near the Red Sea's southern entrance, a choke point for seaborne traffic passing to and from India.

For the first time, Burton found himself in sole command of other Europeans. His party consisted of William Stroyan, an officer in the Indian navy and old friend from the Sindh Survey; G. E. Herne, another acquaintance from the Survey and a lieutenant in the 1st Bombay European Infantry; and John Speke, a Bengal army lieutenant who was brought on board at the last minute after the unexpected death of another member of the party. Burton, however, was temperamentally unsuited for his role as supervisor of the expedition. He immediately broke up his party, sending Stroyan and Herne to report on commerce and the slave trade in the area around the market town of Berbera, dispatching the newcomer Speke to investigate reports of gold and other natural resources in a region known as the Wadi Nogal, and reserving for himself a daring scheme to gain entry to the mysterious walled city of Harar, supposedly closed to non-Muslims, which was located in the highlands of what is now Ethiopia. Interest in this land had recently been stirred by the publication of Mansfield Parkyns's *Life in Abyssinia* (1853), which described the years he spent living among the Ethiopians. Burton saw an opportunity to replicate the achievement that had made his Arabian adventure such a success, intending once again to use his skills at deception to seek entry to a forbidden city. This was nothing less than another bid for personal fame: he cared little about the activities carried out by the other members of his party, and the

East India Company cared little about Harar, an obscure, enfeebled, land-locked city-state. Even at the purely personal level, however, Burton badly misjudged the benefits that might accrue to him from the adventure. In Britain, everyone had heard of Mecca; no one had heard of Harar. Whatever the risks entailed in seeking entry to the city, it simply did not evoke the same interest from the British public as had the pilgrimage to Mecca.

Perhaps the most significant outcome of the Harar episode was that it demonstrated to Burton that nature had placed limits on his ability to pass as a "native." He began his journey in the familiar guise of Haji Abdullah, now a Muslim merchant. He also ordered Stroyan, Herne, and Speke to dress as Arab traders. Speke, who believed Burton wanted them to "appear as his disciples," sloughed off his turban and robes almost as soon as his commanding officer was out of sight, finding them uncomfortable and unbefitting an English gentleman.[66] Stroyan and Herne probably did the same. And Burton's own disguise as the trader Abdullah quickly unraveled. It was impossible to conceal his identity from his own Somali travel party, which consisted of twenty armed guards and two female cooks, and their knowledge of his identity was bound to spread to peoples along the way. But Burton faced a more fundamental problem: his white skin attracted the sort of notice he had never encountered before. Rumors swept the region about this white stranger and his ominous intentions. Some locals ran screaming in fear when they laid eyes on him. Others no doubt understood that "the jocose idea of crowning me king of the country," which Burton and his major-domo acted out in a mock ritual at one point in the journey, gave nascent expression to British imperial designs on their country.[67]

Burton soon began to receive warnings that "they will spoil that white skin of thine at Harar!" By the time he reached the outskirts of the city, he knew the game was up. He discarded his disguise and entered Harar as a British officer. He claimed that his decision was motivated by two factors: the belief among local peoples that hiding one's origins in the face of danger was cowardice and the concern that his light skin might cause him to be mistaken for an agent from Turkey, "a nation more hated and suspected than any Europeans, without our *prestige*."[68] These considerations cannot be discounted: Burton certainly would have sought to resist any imputation of cowardice and he is correct in claiming that local peoples regarded the Turks (and Egyptians) as a more serious threat to their interests than the British.[69] But even if we accept Burton's assertion that he abandoned his masquerade of his own free will, the fact remains that his action amounted to a concession that its purpose had failed. He had discovered that his white skin left him an outsider, reducing the matter to the choice of whether he wished to be mistaken for a Turkish outsider or acknowledged as a British one.

Just as Burton had feared, his white skin did place him in danger, though not in Harar itself, which proved disappointingly drab and torpid. He spent ten uneventful days in the "forbidden city" before reconnoitering on the coast with the other members of his party. They had gathered at Berbera to launch a further probe into the country when Somali tribesmen launched a surprise night raid on their camp. The attack most likely came in retaliation for Burton's decision to arrest an *Abban*, or tribal official, whom Speke had accused of obstreperous behavior when he was his guide to the Wadi Nogal. Stroyan was killed in the assault, Speke was seriously wounded, and Burton had a javelin thrust through his face, entering his left cheek and exiting the right. The desperate survivors fled to the British base at Aden for medical treatment.[70] An official investigation of the incident charged Burton as commanding officer with negligence in his preparations for the camp's defense, a humiliating reprimand for a man who prided himself on his military skills.[71]

❧❧❧

The strategy Burton had used in India, Egypt, and Arabia to gain entrée to the intimate lives of other peoples had failed him in Somalia and the implications of that failure extended across sub-Saharan Africa. However much he might have supposed black skin to be a "garb"—the term he uses to describe it in the early pages of *First Footsteps*—it was not possible for him to don it as a disguise.[72] His pale appearance exposed him unmistakably and irrevocably as an outsider. For a man whose understanding of others derived from his ability to pass as one of them, this obstacle presented a formidable challenge, compelling a reconsideration of the meaning of race itself. In the aftermath of this journey, physical traits began to assume the sort of significance for Burton's understanding of race previously held by cultural traits such as language, religion, and custom. When he launched his next expedition into the lake region of central Africa in 1857, he did so as a British officer, knowing full well that any effort to assume a "native" persona was doomed to failure.

Only when Burton returned to the Near East as British consul at Damascus in 1869 did he again have an opportunity to indulge his penchant for disguise. Six months after his arrival, he wrote to a friend that he intended to "dress as a Bedouin . . . & ride right off to Nejd—a part not yet visited by any European."[73] The British ambassador at Constantinople received word later that year that Burton had been seen in a hotel in "the costume of an Arab Moslem Sheikh."[74] Isabel Burton states that she and her husband would sometimes don Arab dress to wander through the streets of Damascus or make excursions through the desert. Did they do so merely for the thrill of dressing up or with some ulterior pur-

89

pose in mind? Isabel claims that she went to the bazaar or the mosque dressed "like a Moslemah . . . that I might hear all the gossip, and enter something into their [Muslim women's] lives."[75] It is difficult to believe that a woman who spoke little Arabic and who was married to one of the city's most prominent public figures could pass herself off as a local resident, her duplicity undetected by those around her. Much the same skepticism applies to Richard as well. An Arab who knew him in Damascus reports that "his attempts to pose as a native were a constant source of amusement to all with whom he came in contact," mainly because his accent was so unmistakably foreign.[76] Once again, we are left to wonder, as we did in the case of the relationship between Burton and the other members of his pilgrimage party, who was deceiving whom.

In the end, this valedictory excursion into the alternative self that masquerade made possible has to be understood in terms of the psychic satisfaction it gave Burton and his wife. Isabel says that when she and her husband went out in the desert together, she often dressed in male clothes. Though donning men's apparel was not uncommon for Western women traveling in the Near East, it took a strange turn for the Burtons, who maintained the pretense that Isabel was Richard's son.[77] We cannot possibly plum the psychological depths that inspired such role playing. All we can do is observe that the Burtons were hardly alone in their affinity for cross-dressing, a practice that was deeply engrained in British culture. Here again we return to the intriguing connection between the Burtons' enthusiasm for "Oriental" disguises and their fellow Victorians' fascination with theatricality. What they shared was that sense of freedom that derives from the adoption of a different identity, an invented self. Whether the British penchant for disguise and cross-dressing took public form in pantomimes and other theatrical performances or found private

This mausoleum, a full-sized stone replica of a desert tent, was designed by Isabel Burton to memorialize her husband's love of travel. It holds the remains of Richard and Isabel in the Catholic cemetery at Mortlake, west of London. From Isabel Burton, *The Life of Captain Sir Richard F. Burton* (London: Chapman and Hall, 1893).

expression in dress, demeanor, or sexual preferences, it gave expression to what was viewed by conventional standards as transgressive behavior.[78] There is little doubt that Burton too was attracted to impersonation precisely because it provided a way of transgressing against the codes and conventions that governed society, challenging the psychic shackles imposed by civilization.

For Burton, the desert became the primary locus of this freedom, the place where he could escape "the hypocritical politeness and the slavery of civilisation."[79] He, perhaps more than any other person in British letters, was responsible for romanticizing the desert, portraying it as a place of purity where the constraints of civilization could be sloughed off like soiled clothes, where "Nature" could be experienced "in her noblest and most admirable form—the Nude."[80] The power of this eroticized trope drew to the Arabian desert a distinguished parade of British travelers who wrote with memorable feeling about the exhilaration they felt in this harsh landscape: Charles Doughty, William Gifford Palgrave, T. E. Lawrence, Gertrude Bell, Harry St. John Philby, Freya Stark, Wilfred Thesiger, and others. All of these individuals shared Burton's ambivalence about Western society and his sense that the desert offered a return to a more pristine existence, cleansed of what they considered the polluting effects of civilization.[81] When Burton died, his widow designed a tomb that evoked these Romantic longings in a wonderfully evocative fashion. She had his body interred in a dazzling white, full-scale stone replica of the tent that served as their home on their desert travels, a string of camel bells strung across its interior.

✣ IV ✣

The Explorer

In the mid-nineteenth century, the British public became enthralled by the exploits of a new breed of celebrity-hero, the African explorer. This figure came to embody those qualities the Victorians regarded as emblematic of all that was best about themselves as a people—manly courage, moral virtue, individual enterprise, patriotic spirit, and scientific curiosity. By testing himself against the deprivations, dangers, and delirium of Africa's uncharted interior, the explorer laid claim to the status of national hero, an avatar of progress, reason, empire, and civilization.[1] Burton seemed in many respects ideally suited for carrying out the exploration of Africa. He possessed the requisite physical stamina and mental strength of will, the linguistic and mapping skills, the ethnographic curiosity about other peoples, and the craving for public recognition and reward. Moreover, his earlier adventures had prepared him as well as anyone to pursue the holy grail of midcentury exploration—discovery of the source of the White Nile, rumored to be hidden amid great lakes and snow-capped peaks. What remained uncertain, however, was whether he was capable of exhibiting those qualities of character that the British expected of their heroes.

No aspect of Burton's career has attracted more interest than his expedition into the lake region of East Africa in 1857–1859. It has inspired a historical novel and a Hollywood film, figured prominently in narrative accounts of African exploration, and served as the dramatic centerpiece for countless Burton biographies.[2] Naturally, attention has focused on the dramatic dispute between Burton and his travel companion John Hanning Speke, both strong and ambitious personalities. When at the end of their journey into the East African interior Speke returned to England several weeks ahead of Burton and proclaimed that he had discovered the lake from which the White Nile issued, the stage was set for a clash between the two men that would cause public shame and private tragedy. But the preoccupation with Burton and Speke's personal conflict has obscured the larger social and intellectual forces that informed their dispute and that, in turn, led Burton to adopt a new and disturbing understanding of difference.

The 1857–1859 expedition into East Africa marked an important shift in the object of Burton's inquiry as an explorer and the strategies he used to achieve it. The goal of this journey was a physical manifestation of nature—the great lakes of the region—and a fetishized geographical abstraction—the source of the Nile. This was a far cry from the purpose of his previous expeditions, which had been driven by curiosity about the cultural geography created by human hands, as evidenced in the cities of Mecca and Harar. With his turn from the human to the natural world, Burton also turned to new methods of investigation. He abandoned the use of impersonation and the ambivalent intimacy it entailed, adopting instead the aloof stance of the outside observer. Although the motivation for this decision came in part from his failure in Somalia to stay in disguise, it also was driven by the demands of his sponsor, the Royal Geographical Society, which was determined to give greater legitimacy to exploration as a scientific enterprise. Engaging in an act of self-fashioning once again, Burton sought to recast himself as a man of science whose enterprise conformed to a well-defined set of professional protocols, entailing "objective" observation and precise measurement of the natural world. The claims of science were integral to a series of controversial stances that Burton took in the aftermath of his East African expedition. Not only did his quarrel with Speke about the source of the Nile hinge on the issue of scientific observation and verification, but his contentious views on Africans, whom he regarded as an inferior race, were framed in terms of the higher truths of science. Moreover, his subsequent journeys across the globe would continue to be informed in important ways by the scientific practices and principles that he adopted in this pivotal period.

꧁ꕥ꧂

Burton contemplated plans for a more ambitious expedition into East Africa even as he recuperated from the wound he incurred in the Somali attack at Berbera. His attention was temporarily diverted by the Crimean War, which broke out in 1854. Although he obtained a staff appointment in 1855 with Beatson's Horse, an irregular Turkish cavalry unit, any hopes he had of achieving military glory were frustrated once again. Beatson's Horse never saw combat and it soon collapsed as a result of internal bickering and the antagonism of the British high command. By late 1856, his Crimean interlude was over and he renewed his efforts to launch a new expedition into the East African interior.

The journey that Burton prepared to undertake at this time was unlike anything he had ever attempted before. Although its Somali precursor had involved more of his fellow countrymen than the upcoming enterprise would, Burton had dispersed them in ill-defined pursuits while focusing his attention on the purely personal goal of entering Harar. The East African expedition had its share of heroic narcissism as well, but it was harnessed in unprecedented ways to an institutionally imposed set of objectives and procedures. Burton's sponsor, the Royal Geographical Society, presented him with a list of the tasks he was expected to fulfill. His goal was the great lake or lakes that unsubstantiated reports had placed in the East African highlands. During the course of the journey, he was instructed to obtain geographical data on the region, to identify potential products for commercial export, and to gather intelligence on the indigenous populations. His letter of instruction from the Society cautioned him that "the test of an accomplished traveler will always be measured by the accuracy with which his progress is marked by a detailed topography and satisfactory delineation of his positions."[3] He was expected to record his longitude, latitude, and altitude, to calculate the height of mountains, the width of rivers, and the dimensions of lakes, and to keep track of temperature, wind patterns, and rainfall. He was also charged with the collection of geological samples, botanical specimens, and ethnographic information about the products, customs, and languages of local peoples. He was subordinated, in short, to the disciplinary designs of Victorian natural science, which was driven by the expansive, all-encompassing empiricism that Mary Louise Pratt has aptly termed a "planetary consciousness."[4]

The Royal Geographical Society had become by the mid-nineteenth century the principal institutional agent of this planetary consciousness. Under the shrewd leadership of the geologist Sir Roderick Murchison, it had supplanted the Admiralty as "Britain's quasi-official directorate of exploration."[5] This role was perfectly consistent with its aims as a scientific society, which stressed the tireless collection of data, specimens, and other information concerning the physical environment. Its encyclopedic empiricism fostered a descriptive understanding of science, centering on observation and measurement.[6] The legitimacy of geography as a new scientific discipline hinged on its ability to establish a set of protocols that would standardize its descriptive methods. These protocols were directed toward merchants, missionaries, soldiers, and others who contributed to geographical knowledge through reports on unfamiliar territories, but they placed a particular obligation on men like Burton, who took up the pursuit of geographical knowledge as a professional opportunity. It was their alliance with the Royal Geographical Society and acquiescence to its scientific requirements that transformed the traveler into the explorer.

The protocols of geographical observation and measurement were worked out in a series of midcentury how-to books written for those who journeyed into "wild countries"—a phrase that came from the subtitle to the most successful of these works, Sir Francis Galton's *Art of Travel*.[7] Galton was one of the Royal Geographical Society's most active and powerful members, heading the Expeditions Committee that approved Burton's East African expedition and drafting its letter of instruction.[8] In 1854 he wrote an essay titled "Hints for Travellers" for a special edition of the *Journal of the Royal Geographical Society*. Its success, which generated a series of expanded editions issued as books, inspired Galton to write *The Art of Travel* for a broader audience. Drawn largely from his own experiences trekking through Namibia in 1850–1852, this work offered practical advice on how to cope and what to record in the wilderness. It went through eight editions between 1855 and 1893.[9] Burton owned a heavily annotated copy of the second edition and judged it an "excellent book." He also admired the tellingly titled *What to Observe; or, the Traveller's Reminiscencer* by Colonel J. R. Jackson, one-time secretary of the Royal Geographical Society, later revised and reissued by Jackson's successor (and Burton's friend), Norton Shaw. It included chapters on hydrography, meteorology, geology, metallurgy, zoology, peoples, habitations, agriculture, industry, commerce, religion, government, science, literature, the military, instruments, and collecting. Another popular reference work, edited by Sir John F. W. Herschel, was *A Manual of Scientific Enquiry,* a book originally prepared for naval officers sailing into unfamiliar realms. It contained essays by leading scientists on astronomy, magnetism, hydrography, tides, geography, geology, earthquakes, mineralogy, meteorology, atmospheric waves, zoology, botany, ethnology, medicine, and statistics. Like his copy of Galton's book, Burton's copy of Herschel's was heavily annotated.[10]

Burton took the Galton and Jackson books with him on the journey into the East African interior, along with James Prichard's *Natural History of Man,* George Cuvier's *Animal Kingdom,* Ludwig Krapf's grammar of the Swahili language, and technical manuals on lunar tables and surveying techniques, all of them evidence of his determination to conduct the expedition in accord with the Society's expectations regarding scientific observation and measurement.[11] He also received advice from Galton on the scientific equipment that would be required for the journey. The expedition set off with six thermometers, five compasses, two chronometers, two sextants, two artificial horizons, one mountain barometer, a pocket pedometer, a telescope, a sundial, a rain gauge, and various other devices for mapping and measuring the natural world.[12] It was an impressive collection of scientific instruments, though most of them proved too fragile for the journey. All of the chronometers failed before the party had made much progress into the interior; most of the thermometers broke over time; other instruments were lost, stolen, or stopped working owing to rough handling or harsh conditions.[13] As a result, readings of longitude, latitude, and altitude were often little more than educated guesses, marred by errors that the geographical fraternity in Britain would be quick to expose. What must be stressed, however, is the determination with which Burton and

Speke carried out their scientific tasks. Speke, the member of the expedition who assumed primary responsibility for surveying and mapping their route, did so with considerable care and accuracy given the crude conditions under which he worked. Burton, in turn, "was a prodigious note-taker," whose notebooks "astonished" Galton for the detailed and varied information they contained on the region's flora, fauna, and, above all, peoples.[14] The two men also kept records of rainfall levels, barometric pressure, and other meteorological data, and gathered geological samples, botanical specimens, and human artifacts. Upon their return to England, they submitted their field books and maps to the Royal Geographical Society, shipped their collection of rocks and soils to the School of Mines, and supplied shell, snake, insect, and plant specimens to Kew Gardens and the British Museum. They also gave a range of artifacts to the Bombay Geographical Society in appreciation for the scientific instruments that the Society had supplied to the expedition.[15] These donations were intended to provide the material evidence of the expedition's contributions to science.

None of this scientific activity would have been possible if Burton had sought to replicate his previous modus operandi by traveling incognito. The possession and use of scientific instruments signified a cultural identity just as readily as did speech or dress, as Burton had learned to his peril when he attempted to take a sextant on the pilgrimage to Mecca. In the report he made to the Royal Geographical Society about his journey to Harar, Burton expressed the apologetic hope that the scientific value of his endeavor would not be judged "unacceptable," even though he had been "reduced by hard necessity to use nature's instruments—his eyes and ears."[16] Although he had briefly toyed with the idea of traveling into East Africa "disguised as an Arab merchant," he soon came to realize that his penchant for disguise would prevent him from working within the new scientific protocols that the Society was seeking to impose on the profession of exploration.[17] It also was inconsistent with the Society's efforts to portray the explorer as a national hero, who hardly seemed heroic when engaged in the furtive impersonation of barbarians or savages. Burton was an agent of his country, whose national honor he was obliged to uphold. In his lengthy report to the Society upon completion of the expedition into East Africa, he reassured his sponsors that he had been conscientious in keeping to the role they expected him to play: "Knowing that every Englishman who appears in the outer East, either with or without the sanction of his Government, is looked upon practically as the representative of his nation, I traveled without disguise. . . . We adhered in all points to the manners and customs of our country."[18] The fact that he had little choice in the matter made this declaration in some respects a moot point: it was physically impossible for him to represent himself as a black African and politically impossible for him to do so as an Arab, given Arab involvement in the region's slave trade. The presence of Speke, who adamantly objected to any effort to disguise his English identity, posed an additional constraint. For all these reasons, Burton understood that his commitment to an expedition that sought to advance the prestige of his country entailed a commitment to represent himself as an Englishman.

Burton, then, was a willing accomplice in the Society's efforts to validate exploration as an emblematic expression of the Victorian pursuit of scientific knowledge and national honor. Here was an opportunity to establish himself as one of the foremost representatives of Britain's forward march across the globe in its self-conceived pursuit of knowledge and progress.[19] His ego was attracted to the prospect of personal fame while his intellect was absorbed in the scientific quest to comprehend the natural laws that governed human affairs.

࿐࿐࿐

Burton would later express reservations about the obligations that the new geographical science imposed on the explorer. He lamented the loss of the bold independence of action that characterized the late eighteenth- and early nineteenth-century expeditions in Africa by James Bruce, Mungo Park, and René-Auguste Caillié, not to mention the fifteenth- and sixteenth-century adventures of the Portuguese in Africa and Asia. These ranked in his mind as "the ages of heroism."[20] (His fascination with the Portuguese led him to translate Camoes's epic chronicle of their endeavors, *The Lusiads,* and to write an admiring biography of the author and his work.)[21] Burton also grumbled about the onerous technical demands that science placed on the modern explorer:

> Formerly the reading public was satisfied with dry details of mere discovery. . . . Of late . . . the standard has been raised. Whilst marching so many miles per diem . . . the traveler . . . is expected to survey and observe, to record meteorology and trigonometry, to shoot and stuff birds and beasts, to collect geological specimens and theories, to gather political and commercial information, beginning, of course, with cotton; to advance the infant study of anthropology; to seek accounts, to sketch, to indite a copious, legible journal—notes are now not deemed sufficient—and to forward long reports which shall prevent the Royal Geographical Society napping through its evenings.[22]

This concluding dig at the Royal Geographical Society alludes to another source of irritation for Burton. He objected as much to the efforts by "armchair" or "theoretical" geographers at home to appropriate the information and evidence he collected as he did to the actual burden of collecting it. His resentment was indicative of the tension that coursed through the mid-Victorian geographical fraternity regarding claims of authority over geographical knowledge.[23] The upper-middle-class gentlemen who oversaw the affairs of the Royal Geographical Society viewed themselves as the discipline's intellectual guardians, an elite who had the educational background and breadth of vision to bring order and meaning to the mass of information that colonial officials, missionaries, traders, and others were transmitting to London from the four corners of the globe. Although the Society's leaders were responsible for transforming a select few of these informants into scientific explorers and promoting their expeditions as heroic national endeavors, they simultaneously sought to restrict these field agents to the role of mere data collectors, reserving the analysis and interpretation of the data to themselves. This was made abundantly clear in the snide letter Francis Galton sent to James Grant, Speke's companion on his second expedition into East Africa:

> I should earnestly recommend your not burning your fingers with meteorological theorizings. Poor Speke's notions on these things were so crude and ignorant, that his frequent allusions to them did great harm to his reputation. What he could have done, and what you can do, is state accurately what you *saw*, leaving it to stay-at-home men of science to collate the data of very many travelers, in order to form a theory. All that you two saw is a mere strip of land in the Equatorial Zone. The circumference of the Equ. Zone is 24,000 miles,—you have seen & are otherwise assured of a breadth, say, of 100 miles at the utmost, or 1/240 the part of the whole. How is it possible to theorize on this?[24]

The intellectual arrogance and social snobbery of the armchair geographers were deeply resented by the explorers they sponsored. Speke referred scornfully to "geographers . . . who sit in carpet slippers, and criticise those who labour in the field." Henry Morton Stanley condemned the leaders of the Royal Geographical Society for "their insolence, their prurient curiosity, and their sneers."[25] And Burton complained in a posthumously published passage about "the cabinet savant, who is ever appearing . . . to snatch from the explorer's hand the meed of originality. The former borrows from his books a dozen different theories; and when one happens to be proved true by the labours of the man of action, he straightway sets himself up as the 'theoretical discoverer' of the sources of the Nile, or of any other matter which engages popular attention." In his preface to *The Lake Regions of Central Africa,* Burton pointedly objected to the notion that he was "to see and not to think."[26] To the contrary, he was convinced that his direct experience in the field placed him in a privileged position to analyze and interpret geographical evidence.

The dispute that arose between Burton and W. D. Cooley aptly illustrates this tension between the explorer and the armchair geographer. Cooley, a long-standing Fellow of the Royal Geographical Society, enjoyed a reputation as a leading authority on the geography of Africa, despite the fact that he had never set foot in the continent. In the 1850s he had scoffed at reports of snow-capped mountains in the East African interior while forcefully espousing the view that the region was home to a single vast lake. When Burton returned from his expedition with evidence that contradicted both of these convictions, he pointed out Cooley's errors.[27] In response, Cooley published a pamphlet suggesting that Burton, in effect, had no idea what he was talking about, having been led astray by his ignorance of local languages.

According to Cooley, Burton could not have communicated with Africans in the interior by means of Swahili, as he claimed, because Swahili was unknown beyond the coast.[28] This was rather rich coming from someone ensconced in his London study; it also was wrong. But the confidence with which Cooley made his assertion was indicative of the armchair geographer's belief that his ability to analyze and interpret information from varied sources trumped the direct observation and experience of the explorer.

Class played a crucial role in this clash between the explorer and his metropolitan sponsors. The social chasm that stood between most of the leaders of the Royal Geographical Society and most of the explorers—a chasm perhaps best characterized by the phrase "gentlemen and players"—profoundly affected their relations. When Burton returned from his East African ordeal to learn that the Society had abandoned him in favor of Speke, who was rewarded for his discovery of Lake Nyanza with funding for a follow-up expedition to confirm the source of the Nile, there can be little doubt that class played a role in the decision: Speke was the golden-haired boy of good gentry stock and modest manner, while Burton was the swarthy striver whose unconventional behavior and beliefs made him socially suspect.[29] Those suspicions were reinforced by nasty rumors Speke spread about Burton, rumors of cowardice, sexual deviancy, and other behavioral flaws that showed him to be unequal to the standards expected of an English gentleman.[30]

What did the most damage to Burton's reputation, however, was his refusal at the end of the expedition to give various African members of his party their expected compensation. He argued that they had been paid an advance and deserved no additional reward because their mutinous behavior had placed the expedition in jeopardy; in any case, he had already incurred nearly £1,400 in out-of-pocket expenses (in part because the East India Company had reneged on its promise of £1,000 to support the expedition) and believed that any further obligations should be met by the British and Zanzibar governments. Whatever the extenuating circumstances, this was certainly not one of Burton's finer moments. It revealed a streak of meanness—both financial and emotional—that runs through his dealings with servants and other social inferiors throughout his career. Moreover, it opened him to criticism by Speke and another antagonist, Christopher Rigby, the new British consul at Zanzibar, whose vigorous campaign on behalf of the aggrieved porters and soldiers left Burton looking like a cad. His actions came under investigation by the East India Company and his stock with the Society fell accordingly, while Speke looked even more clearly the right sort.[31]

A decade later, Burton would witness another case of a prominent explorer falling out of favor with the Society for reasons associated with class and character. Upon his arrival in England in 1872 after finding the sainted David Livingstone on the shores of Lake Tanganyika, Henry Morton Stanley became the target of a vicious campaign by Francis Galton and other leaders of the Royal Geographical Society, who sought to humiliate him by exposing his illegitimate origins.[32] Burton sympathized with Stanley and raged against Galton, whom he had come to see as the personification of the Royal Geographical Society's arrogance and determination to keep men like himself in their place: "The R.G.S. has, as usual, put its foot into the wrong hole, but what can you expect of a body who owns as one of its heads, Mr. Galton? . . . He hates with a small and possessive . . . hatred. . . . For years he inflected his corvine voice before evening meetings simply for the same petty vanity."[33] Remarks such as these—and the events that provoked them—indicate how seriously the relationship between explorer and armchair geographer was scarred by struggles over class and status.

⁕⁕⁕⁕⁕

Most of Burton's biographers portray his expedition with Speke to the lake region of East Africa in much the same manner as the Victorian public viewed it—as a remarkable feat of endurance and bravery that was marred by the petty ambitions and character flaws of its main protagonists. This emphasis on individual heroism and tragedy distorts our understanding of the expedition and its significance in several important ways. First, it leaves the misleading impression that Burton and Speke operated in an entirely unfamiliar and unforgiving environment without respite or resources other than their own formidable strength of will. They in fact relied on a well-established system of intelligence and assistance to carry out their endeavor. Second, it presents the rift between the two men in purely temperamental terms, as the product of stress, suspicion, and envy. This obscures what was at the heart of their dispute—two profoundly different conceptions of what constituted valid geographical knowledge.

Burton and Speke were by no means entering into terra incognita when they launched their venture into the East African interior in June 1856. They were in fact following a caravan route used regularly by African and Arab merchants, one of several heavily traveled arteries in the region that carried ivory and slaves to the coast in exchange for textiles and other manufactured goods.[34] Arab traders associated with the Sultanate of Zanzibar had established an aggressive presence in the interior, and Burton, who was much at ease in their company, relied heavily on their advice and support for the success of the expedition. They were his main informants about the territory the caravan intended to pass through and the peoples it was likely to encounter. The Arab trading station at Kazeh (now Tabora) provided a crucial refreshment stop where Burton and Speke were able to recover their strength and replenish their supplies both on their way to the lake region and on their return. When they reached Lake Tanganyika, it was another Arab trading station, Ujiji, which served as their base of operations as they reconnoitered the lake. (Speke tried unsuccessfully to rent a dhow owned by an Arab merchant who traded along its shores.) By the same token, when they ran into trouble with Africans, it was often related to their associations with the Arab merchants, whose incursions into a trade previously dominated by the Nyamwezi in the highlands and the Swahili on the coast had provoked deep-seated rivalries, making it difficult, for example, to recruit new porters along the way. They also had trouble paying the heavy *hongo,* or transit fees, that local chiefs demanded from passing caravans. Burton and Speke, in short, had entered a realm with its own complex network of institutions and allegiances, a region already connected by trade and other forces to the wider world.

The small army of porters, soldiers, and hangers-on that Burton and Speke led into the interior of East Africa itself was indistinguishable in crucial respects from Arab trade caravans. An Afro-Arab named Said bin Salim was appointed the expedition's guide on the recommendation of the sultan of Zanzibar, who also contributed a dozen soldiers to protect the party. These soldiers, referred to as Beluchis, were reflective of the wide reach of *dar al-Islam,* deriving either directly or by way of their ancestors from Beluchistan, a mountainous region northwest of Sindh that supplied mercenaries for Zanzibar and other Muslim states.[35] Another indication of the connections between East Africa and the greater Indian Ocean region is that Burton received letters of recommendation and credit from the sultan's Indian collector of customs. These letters guaranteed the expedition assistance from the network of merchants and chiefs who supported the caravan trade in the interior. Most of the porters hired for the journey were recruited from the peoples who specialized in this sort of work for Arab traders. As was customary for these caravans, a retinue of women, children, and slaves accompanied the porters, soldiers, and other paid staff. The result is that the caravan had nearly double the number of its eighty-odd official members.[36]

When Burton had first begun to contemplate the East African expedition several years before, he had looked forward to the prospect of leading a large, well-armed force: "This time we [will] march as masters with 20 guns & horses etc, so that by day we need not fear a host." In retrospect, he was less sanguine about the size of his party: "African explorations are campaigns on a small scale, wherein the traveler . . . has to overcome all the troubles, hardships, and perils of savage warfare."[37] But, unlike Henry Morton Stanley, who would stir widespread criticism in Britain for organizing a heavily armed expedition in 1887–1889 that acted like an invading army,[38] Burton did not so much clash with indigenous peoples as he did with the members of his own caravan. He struggled to control his men, raging against what he saw as their insolence, indolence, and assorted other misdemeanors. His porters deserted in droves, provoked at least in part by the verbal and physical abuse he heaped on them. Although violence was by no means uncommon on caravans—and desertions were equally routine—Burton seemed inordinately troubled in his relations with the porters and guards. Perhaps as a military man he expected unquestioning obedience, failing to recognize that he lacked the institutional means to enforce his authority. What the situation required was an ability to recognize when to compromise and when to stand firm, something he never learned. When considered in conjunction with his harsh and ill-judged decision to deny many of his staff full payment for their services at the end of the journey, this expedition suggests once again that Burton was emotionally unsuited to supervising other men.

Even so, the expedition carried on for more than two full years, attaining its main goal and returning to the coast with scarcely any loss of life. It seems in retrospect something of a miracle. Both Burton and Speke suffered through stupefying bouts of fever and other illnesses that reduced them to varying degrees of helplessness during the journey. Unable at various times to walk, to see, to hear, or even to talk, they returned to England emaciated shells of their former selves. Illness obviously compromised their ability to carry out the scientific tasks they had been assigned by the Royal Geographical Society, and it may have had even more profound effects on their perceptions and personalities. In a fascinating study of Belgian and German explorers in Central Africa, Johannes Fabian argues that the fevers they endured and the alcohol, opiates, and quinine they consumed to treat their symptoms worked together to undermine their sense of objectivity and rationality, producing instead altered states of mind, a kind of madness he terms "ecstasis."[39] Burton's observations about his own bouts with fever support this argument. He notes that during one attack he experienced "a queer conviction of divided identity, never ceasing to be two persons that generally thwarted and opposed each other."[40] As an aficionado of opium, hashish, and other mind-altering drugs, he found the psychotropic effects of fever intriguing and even exhilarating: "There is nothing unpleasant in these attacks; rather the contrary. The excitement of the nerves is like the intoxication produced by a plentiful supply of strong tea; the brain becomes uncommonly active, peopled with a host of visions, and the imagination is raised almost to Parnassus." And again: "It is . . . a highly intellectual complaint; it heightens all the faculties; the memory becomes most acute; visions of past things flit before the mental eye with startling vivacity; flattering hopes of the future bubble from the brain."[41] A fevered brain also figured prominently in the rift between Burton and Speke. Speke was in the throes of a malarial-induced delirium when he first voiced the deep-seated resentments he harbored against his companion, speaking emotional truths he had kept suppressed while in control of his faculties.

The rupture in relations between Burton and Speke had tragic consequences for both men. The issues that divided the two went much deeper than clashing ambitions and incompatible temperaments, though these were by no means negligible sources of conflict. They held fundamentally different views on the nature of exploration and the role of the explorer. Like Burton, Speke was an officer in the Indian army with a taste for travel, and they might have been expected to share similar interests and values. Burton no doubt assumed so when he invited Speke to join him on the East African expedition. (His failure to learn otherwise in Somalia can be attributed to the fact that he sent Speke out on an independent reconnaissance, giving himself no opportunity to get the measure of the man while on trek.) Once they were thrown together in East Africa, they found they had little in common. Speke had an almost pathological interest in shooting wild animals and saw the expedition as an opportunity to add to his trophies; Burton could be induced to kill game only to supply meat for his men. Burton had an insatiable curiosity about the customs and languages of the peoples he encountered; Speke could have cared less about the human inhabitants of the lands he passed through. The two men were entirely at odds about the purposes and significance of their enterprise.

Burton was dismayed by Speke's lack of intellectual curiosity. He described him as "unimaginative," "incurious," and afflicted by a "vagueness of thought [that] necessarily extended to his language."[42] Nothing spoke more tellingly against him for Burton than his linguistic deficiencies.[43] Burton made repeated references to the fact that, apart from a smattering of "debased Anglo-Indian jargon," Speke knew no Asian or African languages.[44] This was more than a personal flaw; it was a professional handicap, seriously inhibiting Speke's ability to contribute to the expedition. In stressing this point, Burton continued to exhibit the influence of his Orientalist training: language remained for him the primary avenue of knowledge about unfamiliar territory, the essential tool required to gain information and cooperation from local inhabitants. His ability to speak Arabic made it possible for the expedition to obtain invaluable advice and assistance from the Arab merchants who operated in the region; the phrase "according to the Arabs" pervades his account of the journey in *The Lake Regions.* He also put to good use the Swahili he had acquired in Zanzibar, discovering that "almost every inland tribe has some vagrant man who can speak it" and serve as a translator.[45] Even as he recuperated in Kazeh from the ordeal involved in the journey to and from Lake Tanganyika, he took the time to gather vocabularies and other information on local languages and dialects from resident slaves, convinced that his efforts would bring dividends down the road.

It was while Burton was recovering his strength at Kazeh that Speke made his independent journey to investigate Arab reports of another great lake to the north. He returned to announce not only that he had discovered Lake Nyanza, but that he had become convinced it was the source of the White Nile. Burton's surprise soon turned to skepticism, then outright scorn. His critique of Speke's claim centered in large measure on the latter's linguistic limitations. Speke, who had only reached the southern edge of Lake Nyanza, rested his case that the Nile flowed from its northern shore in part on the testimony of native informants.

Burton did not question the veracity of the informants themselves; he too relied on such sources. Instead, he questioned whether they actually had said what Speke believed they had said. He observed that exchanges between Speke and his informants had passed through several layers of translation, creating plenty of opportunities for misunderstanding. The only person with whom Speke could communicate during his independent journey from Kazeh to Lake Nyanza was the expedition's factotum, Sidi Mubarak Bombay.[46] Since Speke did not understand Swahili and Bombay did not understand English, the two conversed entirely in a simplified form of Hindustani, a pidgin tongue otherwise known as Anglo-Indian Hindustani. When Speke sought to interrogate the locals about their knowledge of a river flowing from the northern end of the lake, he had to pose his questions in this debased Hindustani to Bombay, who translated them into Swahili for an intermediary, who then translated them into the language of the person being questioned. Answers wended their way through the same laborious and shaky series of translations.[47] Under these circumstances, Burton had good reason to wonder whether his erstwhile companion had grasped what his informants had said.[48] The problem could be summed up thus: Speke could not speak, and hence could not know.

Speke had a very different view of the role of the explorer and the epistemological standards he was obliged to meet. For him, linguistic knowledge was entirely subordinate to visual knowledge: terra incognita could only truly come uncloaked through direct observation by the explorer. To put it another way, to see was to know. The expedition's arrival at Lake Tanganyika had been a "bitter disappointment" for Speke because he was at the time suffering from an inflammation of the eyes that rendered him virtually blind. His inability to actually *see* the lake diminished the significance of the achievement in his own mind.[49] By the same token, Speke had personally gazed on Lake Nyanza, while Burton had not: this fundamental fact trumped any objections Burton could raise against his conviction that he had found the source of the Nile. True, he had not actually seen the great river flow from the lake, a deficiency that demanded a second expedition. But it is not surprising that the Royal Geographical Society selected Speke rather than Burton to lead the expedition that would confirm his discovery. Quite apart from other considerations, Speke had demonstrated that he shared to a far greater extent than Burton the Society's foundational premise that the explorer's scientific role was to gather information through direct observation.[50]

This emphasis on experiential knowledge was married, as Burton recognized, to an intense anti-intellectualism. "I hate writing," Speke confessed to his editor as he struggled to draft an account of his journey to Lake Nyanza.[51] Speke's evident discomfort with words made him distrustful of Burton's linguistic and literary abilities and the purposes to which he put them. In several telling turns of phrase, he complained that Burton "did not come out here to open up the country, but to make a book and astonish the world with his prowess." Speke added: "He never learnt observing," by which he meant the practical field skills connected with hunting that he prided himself on possessing.[52] On another occasion, Speke claimed that Burton "had not shown himself capable of doing anything but making ethnological remarks," writing "notes at the dictation of the Arabs" (note the imputation of subordination and passivity) while Speke shouldered the practical burdens of the expedition.[53] Burton believed that his companion's resentments arose from his limitations, asserting that Speke "was at such a disadvantage from want of language . . . [that] this made him . . . a little sour."[54] But Burton had misread his man. Speke simply did not share his own views on

*words vs
eyes*

the value of knowledge derived from words, whether spoken or written.

These deeply rooted differences between the two men affected their attitudes toward indigenous peoples, though not in readily predictable ways. For Speke, it did not really much matter whether he had gotten the words of his informants quite right, since he never believed that the resolution of the mystery of the Nile rested on their words. It depended in the end on his own eyes: this was the unspoken conviction that informed his approach to exploration. He had no curiosity about local peoples and their languages because he had no real use for them—they could never substitute for the direct observation and experience of the explorer.[55] Although he resided at the court of the king of Buganda for four and a half months during his second expedition, he never made the slightest effort to learn the language of his hosts, relying throughout his stay on interpreters.[56] This aloofness also was motivated by his determination to maintain racial boundaries. He saw no reason to degrade himself, as he thought Burton did, by studying the language of an inferior people. When he required information from the Arabs at Kazeh, he "asked Snay [bin Amir], through Captain Burton," who became by this account an instrument of his own higher purposes, serving, in effect, as the counterpart to his Lake Nyanza translator, Sidi Bombay. Tellingly, Speke also made it clear to Snay and his Arab colleagues when they recommended that he don Arab dress in order to ease his passage to Lake Nyanza that he would not "lower himself to their position."[57]

Speke's stout sense of racial aloofness made him in some respects more at ease with the peoples he encountered on the journey through East Africa than was the case with Burton. Speke was not much bothered, for example, by the unremitting stares he received from Africans who had never before seen white men.

Although gawkers in one instance crowded around him in such numbers that he had to use a stick to clear his path, he remarked: "Poor creatures! They said they had come a long way to see, and now must have a good long stare; for where was there ever a Mzungu [white person] here before?" On another occasion he described the admiring attention he received from a female member of an African royal court: "Next my hands and fingers were mumbled, and declared to be as soft as a child's, and my hair was likened to a lion's mane."[58] Lacking so little in the way of ethnographic curiosity himself, he viewed their curiosity about him with tolerant bemusement.

Burton, by contrast, found Africans' stares a disconcerting "infliction." He was so acutely aware of the many African eyes fixed on him that he believed he could detect in them different motives and meanings: he categorized them as "the stare furtive," "the stare open," "the stare curious," "the stare stupid," "the stare discreet," "the stare indiscreet," "the stare flattering," "the stare contemptuous," "the stare greedy," "the stare peremptory," "the stare drunken," "the stare fierce," and, last, "the stare cannibal."[59] The intensity of Burton's reaction was a reflection of his discomfort at being the object of the ethnographic gaze.[60] It cut against the grain of his instincts for dissimulation. It stood in stark contrast to his previous position as the observer who went unobserved. It left him feeling exposed and vulnerable. Nothing made his sense of discomfort more transparent than that final category, "the stare cannibal."

It is difficult to escape the conclusion that this troubling shift in his own position vis-à-vis the peoples he sought to study contributed to an equally troubling shift in his understanding of difference. Burton returned from East Africa with a much more pronounced sensitivity to the body as the marker of race, and race in turn as the marker of difference. His ethnographic descriptions of the Africans he encountered on the expedition are replete with references to their physical features—the color of their skin, the texture of their hair, the shape of their skulls. He describes their odor as rank, their appearance as animalistic. He is often overcome by feelings of revulsion, as in this description of some villagers near Mombasa: "The faces were hideous to look upon, with black, coarse skin, scarred and seamed by small-pox; huge mouths, and rolling eyes."[61] In seeking to understand why he gives such pathological attention to the African body, we should not ignore the impact that *the Africans'* attention to *his* body has on this preoccupation. Because he could not pass as an African, he could not experience the sense of affinity that he derived from his previous associations with the peoples of Sindh and Arabia, nor could he exult in the sense of invulnerability that came from his success in impersonating other peoples. He was now entering a new realm of race.

The Royal Geographical Society's decision to endorse Speke's proposal to organize a follow-up expedition to confirm that the Nile had its source in Lake Nyanza was a devastating blow to Burton's ambitions as an explorer. What the British geographical fraternity viewed as the greatest prize of mid-nineteenth-century exploration was now within the grasp of the man whom he believed had betrayed him, while he was left with his reputation sullied and his future in question. Eager to escape from an England that must have seemed even more stifling and hostile than usual, he set off in early 1860 for the United States, hoping to improve his "health & spirits."[62]

Burton had a vague idea of traveling through the "wild" West. Here was another realm where the imperial imagination reigned unfettered. He hoped to "enjoy a little Indian fighting," though once again his bellicose instincts found no outlet.[63] Most of the Indians he came across on his stagecoach trip from St. Joseph, Missouri, to San Francisco seemed far too demoralized and dependent on drink to put up much of a fight. Even though he was, as he put it, "liquored up" much of the time himself, his descriptive powers and keen eye for ethnographic details did not desert him. They found expression in *The City of the Saints and across the Rocky Mountains to California* (1862), an informed and discerning book that provides a richly detailed account of the American West at this time, taking meticulous note of its topography and natural resources, its native inhabitants and white invaders, and especially its newly established Mormon "Mecca" of Salt Lake City. Although the journey itself was hardly in a league with the adventures Burton had undertaken through the 1850s, his account of the experience has supplied historians of the American West with a wealth of information.[64]

One byproduct of his American escapade was a revised edition of *The Prairie Traveler,* a handbook written by Randolph B. Marcy, a U.S. army officer who had done survey work in the West, which Burton edited and annotated for publication in Britain.[65] Here was another example of that new genre, the scientific guide to travel in unfamiliar territory, a counterpart of sorts to Francis Galton's *Art of Travel.* Drawing on his own experiences, Burton appended notes to the original text on topics ranging from firearms to health precautions. The most intriguing of his contributions was an extended analysis of Indian sign language. He prepared a vocabulary of some one hundred "word-signs," which he recommended for use by explorers when confronted with peoples whose speech they did not know.[66] A year later he tested his word-signs on Africans during an expedition into the Cameroon Mountains, claiming he had some success in using them as the basis for communication. He insisted, improbably enough, that a "hundred words easily learned in a week, 200 signs, and a little facility in sketching, would enable, I believe, a traveler to make his way through any country, even China, a few days after arrival."[67] What makes this curious inquiry into sign language noteworthy is that it shows once again how determinedly Burton sought to overcome the linguistic limitations that so often prevented explorers from communicating with and collecting information from local peoples.[68]

Burton's edition of *The Prairie Traveler* gave proof that he remained very much committed to the disciplinary ethos and protocols of the new geographical science. This commitment persisted even as his role and reputation as an explorer waned. Other men took center stage in the long-running melodrama that exposed "darkest" Africa to an enthralled British audience: Speke and his travel companion James Grant, Samuel Baker, Henry Morton Stanley, and, of course, the greatest idol of them all, David Livingstone. Burton, meanwhile, made two decisions in the early 1860s—one personal, the other professional—that markedly diminished the prospect of his regaining his previous eminence as a celebrity-explorer. On January 22, 1861, he married Isabel Arundell; a few months later, he accepted an appointment as British consul at Fernando Po.

The life of the explorer presented numerous disincentives to marriage: the income was too uncertain, the periods of separation too lengthy, the risk of death too great. By taking a wife, Burton implicitly acknowledged that the career path he had pursued for the past decade had come to an end. His choice of partner has puzzled many, who cannot understand what attracted a religious skeptic to a devout Catholic.[69] Burton, however, would have been hard pressed to find someone who shared his own contrarian views on Christianity. Furthermore, Catholicism carried its own mark of estrangement in mid-Victorian England, where anti-Popish sentiments were still widespread. Isabel was not, in any case, constrained by her faith to conform to the stereotypical obligations of the Victorian lady. An intelligent, independent, outspoken woman, she was determined to live her life on her own terms, and those terms entailed a fierce desire to travel and seek adventure.[70] She married Richard against the wishes of her mother and proved in many respects a fine match for her restless, unconventional husband. She also brought to the marriage invaluable social connections. She was related through her father to one of the most distinguished of England's Catholic aristocratic families, the Arundells of Wardour, and through her mother to the Gerards, another aristocratic lineage. Isabel had spent much of her youth at the Arundell country estate in Wiltshire, rubbing shoulders with the landed elite of England. When she wed she received a coveted invitation to the court of Queen Victoria. She showed no hesitation about using her personal contacts to advance her husband's career. Richard might never have gained entry to the British Consular Service, which occurred only a few months after his marriage, if not for Isabel's pleas on his behalf to Lord John Russell, then foreign secretary and a family acquaintance.

With his appointment as a British consul, Burton obtained the respectable employment and steady income that his newly married status required. He would remain in the consular service for the rest of life, taking up postings in Fernando Po (1861–1864), Santos, Brazil (1864–1868), Damascus (1869–1871), and Trieste (1873–1890). Although Burton used each of these consular posts as launching pads for exploratory probes into neighboring hinterlands, his travels rarely opened up territory entirely unknown to or untouched by Europeans. His obligations as a public servant

The wedding portrait of Isabel Burton (née Arundell), who married Richard Burton in 1861. A strong personality in her own right, she gave her husband unwavering support while tempering his excesses. A painting by Louis Desanges. Courtesy of the Orleans House Gallery, Twickenham.

prevented him from ever again organizing the kinds of high-profile expeditions that carried the sanction and cachet of the Royal Geographical Society.

Despite his altered personal and professional circumstances, Burton remained deeply engaged in the pursuit of geographical knowledge and committed to its scientific practices. He continued to keep a meticulous record of his observations and experiences in daily journals whenever he took to the road, and his later travel books appear to have been transcribed from these journals with little in the way of embellishment for the benefit of his readers. Too often the results were monotonous narratives told in turgid prose, as even he occasionally acknowledged: "this stage was dull riding, and consequently, I fear, it will be dull reading as well as writing."[71] Whatever their literary weaknesses, however, these works were testaments to his scientific empiricism, offering close and detailed accounts of what Burton observed and learned on his journeys.

Another aspect of the scientific explorer's protocol that Burton continued to practice was the systematic collection of climatological data, geological samples, human artifacts, and botanical and animal specimens. He sent 490 plant cuttings to Kew Gardens' experts after one of his trips through West Africa. At the end of another, he shipped stuffed birds, stone implements, and other items he had collected to the British Museum.[72] During his travels through the Syrian desert in 1870, funded in part by the Palestine Exploration Fund, he used an aneroid barometer and thermometer to take daily readings of altitude and temperature.[73] He also gathered plant specimens, skulls and other human remains, coins, pottery fragments, and mortuary lamps, and he copied inscriptions from tombs and other stone ruins. He did much the same during his two trips to northwestern Arabia in 1877 and

1878. He never lost interest in the scientific measurement and classification of the natural world, nor did he doubt that this endeavor might bring to light some product of economic importance or artifact of historical significance.[74]

Burton also kept well informed about the latest developments in African exploration. He carefully followed newspaper reports about the progress of Livingstone and other explorers and took an active part in the debates among geographers regarding the significance of their discoveries. He came to the defense of Paul du Chaillu when others questioned his claim in 1861 that he had found a giant new species of ape, the gorilla, in Gabon, West Africa. He cultivated friendships with various African explorers, including du Chaillu, Winwood Reade, Verney Lovett Cameron, and Henry Morton Stanley.

The outcome of Speke's second expedition into East Africa held particular interest for Burton. When Speke emerged from the upper reaches of the White Nile in 1863 to announce that he had traced its source to Lake Nyanza, he became a national hero in England. Soon, however, his star began to wane, especially within the geographical fraternity. Speke's savage attack on the reputation of John Petherick, the British consul in the Sudan whom he unfairly accused of failing to fulfill his commitment to the expedition, exposed the vindictive side of his character, and his ill-considered decision to publish his story in *Blackwood's Magazine* without first presenting a report to his sponsor, the Royal Geographical Society, antagonized its influential leaders. Once his account of the journey appeared in print, critics were quick to pounce, pointing out various surveying errors (such as altitude readings that suggested the Nile ran uphill for some distance), gaps in evidence (due to the failure to follow the river for large stretches), and questions of judgment (particularly concerning praise for the ruler of Buganda).[75] These criticisms began to undermine confidence in Speke's claim that he had in fact solved the riddle of the Nile.

Meanwhile, Burton had begun to make a case for Lake Tanganyika as the true source of the Nile, suggesting that the river intersected other bodies of water to the north, such as Lake Nyanza, as it wended its way to Egypt and the Mediterranean. His self-serving argument was almost entirely speculative and seemed inspired in large measure by spite, but it attracted the interest of Murchison, Livingstone, and others because it bolstered their growing doubts about Speke and kept the question of the Nile open for further investigation. As a result, Burton was able to restore his reputation in geographical circles, setting the stage for a fateful confrontation with Speke.

In 1864 Murchison invited Burton and Speke to present their contending views on the Nile's source to the annual meeting of the British Association for the Advancement of Science, which was to take place in Bath in September. The Royal Geographical Society's impresario saw this debate as a perfect opportunity to keep the organization and the activities it sponsored in the public eye. As Burton later observed: "These were the days when the Society in question could not afford to lack its annual lion, whose roar was chiefly to please the ladies and push the institution."[76] Interest in the event was high, with ticket sales far exceeding the numbers from past meetings of the Association.[77] On the morning before the debate was scheduled to take place, Speke and Burton glimpsed each other in the meeting hall, their first physical encounter since their joint expedition in East Africa. Soon thereafter Speke left for his uncle's nearby estate, where later in the afternoon he died of a self-inflicted gunshot wound while out hunting. Although the coroner ruled the death an accident, many contemporaries understandably suspected suicide and the suspicion has lingered to the present day.[78]

This violent climax to the long-festering conflict between Speke and Burton was a personal tragedy, to be sure, but it carried another message as well. It spoke to the high stakes that surrounded the exploration of Africa and the intense pressures that the accompanying cult of personality placed on the explorers themselves. *The Times* spoke to this point in its editorial commentary on Speke's death: "This unfortunate accident will put an end to the controversy which was to have amused the Geographers at Bath. Captain Speke and Captain Burton can no longer be pitted against each other for a gladiatorial exhibition."[79]

The Times was correct in characterizing the event as a "gladiatorial exhibition," but wrong in assuming that the death of Speke would bring the controversy to a close. Though Burton was genuinely shocked and saddened by the premature death of his erstwhile companion, he refused to allow sentiment to force him into any concession regarding the substance of their disagreement. Within days of the tragedy, Burton wrote *The Times* to challenge its assertion that Speke had discovered the source of the Nile.[80] Several months later Burton published the paper discrediting Speke's claims that he had intended to give at the meeting in Bath. It appeared in *The Nile Basin*, a book that also reprinted a series of articles from the *Morning Advertiser* by one of Speke's most relentless critics, James Macqueen, a vocal figure in geographical circles.[81] This collaboration was rich in irony: Macqueen was an armchair geographer who had never been to Africa, exactly the sort of figure Burton might have raged against in other circumstances. Moreover, their joint publication made Burton an accomplice in Macqueen's insinuation that Speke had fathered half-caste children during his lengthy stay in Buganda, a scurrilous charge in the opinion of many reviewers. Speke's family and friends never forgave Burton.[82] For leading members of the geographical fraternity, however, the book's insistence that the source of the Nile remained unsettled echoed their own doubts. It took Stanley's circumnavigation of Lake Nyanza in 1875 to finally lay the matter to rest, confirming Speke's discovery.[83]

Though personal egos and public attention tended to focus on the race to discover the source of the Nile, which in the end was little more than a geographical abstraction fetishized as a token of the European quest to bring the world under its dominion, the exploration of Africa and other lands was intended above all else to advance the material interests that motivated this quest. Explorers were engaged in a global search for the natural resources needed to sustain the European-centered capitalist economy. The resources most eagerly sought were precious metals and other minerals. The spread of industrialization across Western Europe in the second half of the nineteenth century set off a fierce scramble to discover and exploit the world's untapped minerals. Railway lines, iron-hulled steamships, and other industrial marvels generated a voracious demand for iron ore and other metals that could only be met by the discovery of new deposits. The series of gold rushes that occurred in various parts of the world in this period supplied the bullion that made it possible for Britain to maintain the gold standard, which in turn regulated the international financial system.[84] Sir Roderick Murchison, the man who guided the Royal Geographical Society to its mid-Victorian prominence, was first and foremost a geologist who saw exploration as a way to scout out the likeliest locations where soils and rocks harbored valuable mineral resources. Burton shared this interest in the discovery of minerals in uncharted territory, not least because he saw it as a way to make his fortune.

Most of the later travels that Burton undertook were inspired to one degree or another by the search for precious stones and metals. The main motive for his journey into the highlands of Brazil in 1867 was to visit the gold mine of Morro Velho. He gave a detailed account of its operations, and even had himself lowered down one of the shafts to inspect the mine face. Later in this trip he also toured a diamond-digging area. Brazil, he proclaimed, was a "land of boundless mineral wealth," its potential scarcely tapped.[85] He speculated in the Brazilian mining industry and even floated his own lead mining company on the London Stock Exchange, an enterprise that brought a rebuke from the Foreign Office.[86] In 1872 and again in 1875 he visited Iceland, where he surveyed its sulfur reserves on behalf of a British entrepreneur.[87] During his valedictory visit to India in 1876 he took time out to determine whether its old diamond pits had been "prematurely abandoned," concluding optimistically that they had.[88] He also plumped for the mining potential of Midian, the region of Arabia located along the upper end of the Red Sea that was reputed to have been the site of ancient gold workings. In 1877 he conducted a three-week reconnaissance of the area, persuading the khedive of Egypt to sponsor the much larger and better-equipped geological survey he organized the following year. This expedition attracted a great deal of hopeful attention from the British press, but the mineralogical samples collected during the four-month journey showed only traces of gold, squashing his hopes of making a fortune from a mining concession.[89] Finally, Burton and another African explorer, Verney Lovett Cameron, went in search of gold in the Gold Coast of West Africa in 1881, acting as the agents of the Liverpool merchant and mining speculator James Irvine. Burton was by now too old and weak to endure the region's climate and fevers; he soon fell ill and cut short his itinerary. This did not prevent him, however, from coauthoring a book that put the gold-mining potential of the Gold Coast in the best possible light. He also wrote a stream of letters to *Mining World*, the *Athenaeum,* and other publications about the underground riches he believed were waiting to be found in West Africa and elsewhere.[90]

Because of his fame as an explorer and his indiscriminate enthusiasm for untapped mineral wealth, he was an attractive shill for unscrupulous floggers of mining stock. And there were plenty of these people around: the late nineteenth century saw a frenzy of speculative investment in mining syndicates. The businessman who hired Burton to survey the sulfur deposits in Iceland did so because "the testimony of a well known explorer like Captn. Burton would be far more convincing to the public" than that of a trained mining engineer.[91] Burton served as the front man for an Austrian lead- and cinnabar- mining venture that came to an unhappy end when its founder embezzled the investors' funds.[92] Isabel, who tended to be far shrewder than her husband when it came to financial matters, observed: "I was always sorry when [Richard] got on the mine track, because he always ended up in one way. Shady people, partially or wholly dishonest, would praise up his knowledge to the skies," then take advantage of him.[93] Burton, however, was a willing, if naive, accomplice. He accepted shares and positions on the boards of several of the Gold Coast mining companies created by James Irvine, whose activities one historian has described as "a classic case of stock watering . . . a scam for the benefit of promoters" that amounted to "legalized embezzlement." In a delicious irony, Irvine and Burton were themselves "hoodwinked" by local Africans who sold them concessions that they knew to be worthless.[94]

This sorry denouement speaks at a personal level to Burton's poor judgment and questionable ethics, but it also tells us something more profound about the transformation that occurred in Europe's relationship with Africa and other underdeveloped parts of the globe in the late nineteenth century. By this point there were very few uncharted regions remaining to be explored.[95] With European states now scrambling to claim African and other territories and investors eager to profit from the land and mineral resources that this scramble opened up, explorers increasingly became the direct emissaries of imperial expansion and commercial exploitation. Burton was hardly the only explorer of his stature to engage in this feverish enterprise. Henry Morton Stanley, for example, sold his services to King Leopold of Belgium, leading an expedition up the Congo River that made it possible for the king to claim this huge swath of central African territory as his personal domain—with disastrous consequences for the indigenous inhabitants.[96] There is no doubt that the earlier explorations of Burton, Stanley, and their counterparts had been the opening wedges in this process, but their own roles were reshaped as a new, more aggressive era of imperial conquest took hold. They could no longer portray themselves as heroic individuals engaged in the disinterested pursuit of scientific truths: they were now the direct agents of capitalist enterprises and imperial states, their own independence subordinated to and diminished by these larger forces.

The high Victorian moment that saw the explorer enshrined as a public hero passed for another important reason—the rise of mass tourism. Many of those places that had been inaccessible to the British bourgeois public in the mid-nineteenth century came within its orbit in later decades as a result of improvements in the speed and comfort of transportation, new medical advances to combat tropical diseases, and the establishment of bureaucratic colonial regimes that assured greater security. As an inveterate traveler, Burton was acutely aware of these developments and understood their implications for his own hard-won status. Time and again in his later books he made dismissive remarks about modern tourism, expressing disdain for Cook's prepackaged tours

The caption to this *Punch* cartoon reads: "Captain Burton: Our Un-Commercial Traveller." It portrays Burton as an independent, Orientalized figure who was the trailblazer of modern travel. From *Punch,* May 13, 1882.

and taking delight in detailing the errors and questioning the value of the popular Murray and Baedeker guidebooks that catered to tourists.[97] In 1882, the humor magazine *Punch* published a cartoon that showed Burton dressed in Oriental garb, an exotic and imposing presence, while in his shadow stood two booklike figures identified as the Murray and Baedeker guides, one of whom remarks to the other, "A bit ahead of us, my boy."[98] It was a flattering commentary, one that celebrated Burton for blazing the trails that modern tourists now traveled. But the cartoon also carried an undercurrent of nostalgia, an implicit acknowledgement that there were no more trails to be blazed. Burton's antagonism toward the tourist industry was fueled by his regret at the passing of the age of exploration.

V

The Racist

In the 1860s Burton came to be known as one of the most fierce and vocal advocates of the view that black Africans constitute a distinct and inferior species of humankind. Drawing on observations and experiences from his extensive travels through Africa and the Americas, Burton presented himself as an expert on the African "race" and a witness to its innate barbarity. He promoted his provocative views with relentless determination, advancing them in papers to learned societies, in magazine articles and missives to newspapers, and, above all, in the dozen or so books he wrote about his travels through East and West Africa, the United States, and Brazil. He also took a leading role in the establishment of the Anthropological Society of London, which provided an institutionalized forum for the "scientific" study of racial difference.

Burton adopted his controversial stance at a time when the British political and intellectual climate was saturated with talk about race as a determining force in world affairs. This was in part the result of British involvement in a traumatic series of racially charged clashes around the globe, starting with the Indian mutiny and rebellion of 1857–58, continuing with the Maori wars of the early 1860s in New Zealand, and climaxing with the Morant Bay uprising in Jamaica in 1865. The American Civil War of 1861–1865 also brought the issue of race to greater prominence for the British as they confronted the question of whether to support the South's secession.[1] More obliquely, race figured in the decade's growing domestic political debate about extending the franchise to working-class males, who, opponents of reform argued by analogy to Africans and other nonwhite peoples, were incapable of governing themselves.[2] Finally, the subject assumed a new importance as a result of the intellectual revolution wrought by the publication of Charles Darwin's *Origins of Species* (1859), which caused many readers to view race as a category and concept indispensable to the understanding of human evolution.[3]

Burton's racism has been downplayed by most of his chroniclers, who have paid little attention to its influence on his worldview or its contribution to the public debate about race in British society.[4] Many historians of Africa, by contrast, view him as a poster boy for mid-Victorian racism, helping to lay the ideological foundations for the imperial conquest of Africa.[5] Neither perspective does justice to the curious mixture of cruel animosity and subversive radicalism that characterized Burton's opinions about black Africans, nor does either give us any insight into how those opinions found their counterintuitive way into a relativist conception of culture.

꙳꙳꙳꙳꙳

Burton's first sustained statement asserting the innate inferiority of Africans appeared in the concluding chapter of *The Lake Regions of Central Africa* (1860), titled "The Character and Religion of the East Africans; their Government, and Slavery." Here he sketched out many of the themes he would reiterate and refine through the course of the decade. The East African, he declared, is a "barbarian . . . the slave of impulse, passion, and instinct." His religious beliefs fail to rise above a fetishistic "propitiation of natural objects"; he recognizes "neither god, nor angel, nor devil." His "stagnation of mind, indolence of body, moral deficiency, superstition, and childish passion" condemn him to an "apparent incapacity for improvement": "Still he has stopped short at the threshold of progress; he shows no signs of development; no higher and more varied orders of intellect can be called into being. Even the simple truths of El Islam have failed to fix the thoughts of men who can think, but who, absorbed in providing for their bodily wants, hate the trouble of thinking. His mind, limited to the object seen, heard, and felt, will not, and apparently can not escape from the circle of sense, nor will it occupy itself with aught but the present. Thus he is cut off from the pleasures of memory, and the world of fancy is altogether unknown to him."[6]

Burton would modify these views somewhat as a result of his experiences as a British consul in West Africa. He found societies there that seemed more politically and economically advanced than those he had encountered in East Africa, eliciting his grudging respect. He had the opportunity to acquire a deeper appreciation for their religious beliefs and cultural traditions than he had been able to do during his arduous journey through East Africa. As a result, Burton conceded that the "superior degeneracy of the eastern tribes" was explicable in part by "the prevalence of the slave trade," which he had earlier dismissed as secondary to the innate brutishness of the people.[7] Still, he held in the main to an uncompromising racist line: the differences between East and West Africans were measurable merely in their degree of "degeneracy."

Burton deployed many of the standard tropes of racists to demean Africans. He gave venomous descriptions of their appearance, referring to them as "hideous" and "bestial." He drew metaphorical associations between Africans and apes, referring to their "chimpanzee-like fingers," portraying them as "gesticulating like excited baboons," and asserting "the quasi-gorillahood of the real 'nigger.'"[8] He complained that they had a "rank" smell and expressed the racist's characteristic revulsion against physical contact with them, complaining that they left behind an oily residue that "infects every part of the body with which it comes in contact."[9] He insisted that their primitive instincts frequently found expression in a sadistic delight in torturing animals and fellow humans, which he attributed to a perversion of sensual pleasure.[10]

The half-dozen books Burton wrote about his West African experiences were the principal outlets for his racist opinions, none more so than *Wanderings in West Africa* (1863). The views he expressed there were so harsh and controversial, especially coming from a consular official, that the book was originally published anonymously (its author identified simply as an "F.R.G.S." —Fellow of the Royal Geographical Society). It was only with the second edition, released after he had been posted to Brazil two years later, that his name appeared on the title page. In the book he used the analogy of the human body to indicate the African's place in the world racial order: "I believe the European to be the brains, the Asiatic the heart, the American and African the arms, and the Australian the feet, of the man-figure." The African's "intellect [is] weak," he insisted, his "morale deficient, amiability strong, temperament enduring, destructiveness highly developed, and sensibility to pain comparatively blunt." Hence it was understandable that Europeans would come to believe that "this race had been cursed to be 'servants of servants.'"[11]

Burton did more than merely give vent to his racist views in writing; he propagated them by institutional means as well. While on furlough from his African consular duties in 1863, he helped to found the Anthropological Society of London and shape its reputation as the leading forum for scientific racism in Britain. This organization emerged from a schism within the

Ethnological Society, which had held sway since its own founding two decades earlier as the main arena for the scientific study
of humankind. Burton was one of the leaders of the dissident fac-
tion that objected to some of the Ethnological Society's governing policies and premises. The dissidents objected first and foremost to the Society's admission of women, arguing that their
presence in meetings inhibited frank discussion of all facets of
human behavior, including sexuality. They also objected to the
philological view of race associated with the Society's founder,
James Prichard, arguing instead for a physiological approach that
involved craniometry and other measurements of physical difference. Finally, and most important, they objected to the society's
endorsement of the Christian-derived doctrine of monogenesis,
challenging its presumption of the essential unity of humankind
and arguing instead that racial variations required consideration
of separate origins, known as polygenesis.[12]

Burton, the first vice president of the Anthropological Society,
saw it as a "refuge to destitute truth," a place where the science
of humankind could find a forum unconstrained by social conventions and religious mores.[13] By excluding women, it allowed
members to give frank attention to the varieties of sexual customs
found in other societies. This was a subject of special interest to
Burton, and he had long been frustrated by the moral censorship
that inhibited its study.[14] The Anthropological Society provided
him with an opportunity to share his esoteric knowledge with
like-minded men. His first paper to the Society was devoted to
"certain peculiar customs" among the people of Dahomey, notably polygamy, phallic worship, the fostering of eunuchs, and male
and female circumcision.[15] He also reported on the observations
he had made about the size of Africans' genitalia, lending support
to the claims of sexual difference that often preoccupied racists.[16]
Other subjects deemed unsuited for mixed company intrigued

him as well. He finally found an appreciative audience for his interest in scalping and cannibalism, practices that he believed to be characteristic of societies at a particular stage of social development.[17] He reported on hermaphrodites, albinos, pygmies, and other human oddities.[18] Above all, however, he welcomed the Anthropological Society as a venue for his views on racial difference and the implications they carried for contemporary debates about slavery and the status of Africans and their brethren in the Americas.

In collaboration with Dr. James Hunt, the new society's dynamic president, Burton sought to turn ethnology into a biological science of race, signified by the term anthropology. This meant giving greater attention to the anatomical dimensions of human variation such as skull size and body shape, differences that could be measured, weighed, and otherwise quantified and classified, a key criterion of scientific status. The philological line of inquiry that the Ethnological Society favored was not amenable to quantification; furthermore, it relied on a diffusionist model of difference that presumed common origins. In rejecting that approach, Burton turned his back on a key element of his Orientalist heritage. While continuing to study the various languages he encountered in his travels, he made no attempt to apply his linguistic knowledge to a philological understanding of human difference, and he dismissed the efforts of the great late nineteenth-century Orientalist, Max Müller, who continued to pursue that line of inquiry. Instead, he turned to craniometry and other aspects of comparative anatomy. During his expedition to Lake Tanganyika, Burton had collected African skulls, donating them upon his return to the Royal College of Surgeons. He would continue to seek out specimens of human remains during his subsequent travels in West Africa, the Middle East, Iceland, and elsewhere, collaborating with Charles Carter Blake, another member of the Anthropological Society's inner circle, in a series of articles analyzing his findings.[19] Phrenological and cranio-logical terminology crept into his travel books, which increas-ingly referred to the shapes of peoples' skulls as either "doliocho-cephalic" or "brachycephalic."[20] He gave his characteristically meticulous attention to other physical markers of racial differ-ence, such as the shape, texture, and color of hair, skin, nose, eyes, hands, and other body parts. His preoccupation with these mat-ters was very much within the mainstream of physical anthropol-ogy during its early years as an academic discipline.[21]

Another dimension of the Anthropological Society's efforts to move the study of humankind in a racialist direction was its re-markably active program of translating and publishing promi-nent continental scholarship on the subject of human diversity. In 1864 alone it sponsored the English-language publication of Paul Broca's *On the Phenomena of Hybridity in the Genus Homo*, Geor-ges Pouchet's *Plurality of the Human Race*, Carl Vogt's *Lectures on Man*, and Theodor Waitz's *Anthropology of Primitive Peoples*, fol-lowed in 1865 by Johann Blumenbach's *Anthropological Treatises*.[22] Although these authors disagreed on certain key points—Broca, for example, was a polygenist, while Waitz took a monogenist stance and Pouchet straddled the two camps—all of them ap-proached the issue of race from the bracing, unblinkered "scien-tific" standpoint that the Anthropological Society admired and sought to emulate in Britain, where Christian humanitarian sen-timentalism was seen as constraining the pursuit of racial knowl-edge. Hunt was the figure mainly responsible for introducing this continental literature on race to his countrymen, but Bur-ton was deeply engaged in the issues it raised about the sources and nature of human diversity. He published a lengthy review of Theodor Waitz's book for the Society's journal and he struck up a lasting friendship with Carl Vogt.[23]

This promotion of the works of Broca and other European writers is simply one indicator of how aggressively the Anthropological Society took up the cause of the new racial science. It moved quickly to establish its reputation as a learned society, recruiting over five hundred members within its first two years of existence, sponsoring an active program of lectures and debates, and publishing its transactions in a steady stream of volumes.[24] Burton and Hunt and their colleagues saw themselves as engaged in a genuine scientific enterprise that presented a radical, free-thinking challenge to what they considered the tired dogmas of British intellectual life. But had they simply "hijacked the rhetoric of political radicalism and scientific skepticism," as one historian has charged?[25] Thomas Huxley, the great religious skeptic and apostle of Darwinism, thought so: he called Hunt a "low bred ill instructed imposter."[26] Huxley's Darwinians clashed repeatedly with Hunt's Anthropologicals, especially over the issue of monogenesis versus polygenesis. There is no evidence, however, that the Anthropologicals were motivated in this dispute by cynical or opportunistic designs. At the core of their project was a sincere if misguided effort to come to grips with the problem of how to fit humans into the biological scheme of things. What they proposed was a radical shift away from the conventional Christian view of the species as God's favored creation, existing "apart from nature," in favor of "a sense of man as primarily a biological being, embedded in nature and governed by biological laws."[27] On this essential point they were entirely in concurrence with the Darwinians, with Burton declaring the *Origin of Species* to be the "best and wisest book of this, or perhaps, of any age."[28] Where they diverged from the Darwinians was over the implications they drew from this scientific challenge to religious dogma.[29] As they saw it, the biological evidence about races refuted evangelical Christian claims of the common brotherhood of all peoples. Although the new biological science did not, of course, necessitate an emphasis on racial difference, and, indeed, would eventually discredit such views, it supplied what seemed at the time fertile ground for such inquiries. Burton and Hunt collaborated closely in advancing the view that biological laws were racial laws. Hunt dedicated his notoriously racist tract, *On the Negro's Place in Nature* (1863), to Burton, who he declared to be "one of the few men who are competent to give any decided opinion as to the value of my communication." Burton reciprocated by devoting a chapter of his next book, *A Mission to Gelele* (1864), to a defense of Hunt's views, leaving little doubt about his own: "I believe in the inferior genesis of the Negro," he bluntly declared, "and in his incapacity of improvement, individually and *en masse.*"[30]

Such provocative pronouncements had their polemical purposes as well. The Anthropological Society appeared on the scene at a time when Britain was in the throes of a heated debate about the American Civil War. The new organization immediately established itself as a vigorous advocate of the Confederate cause; one of its more active members was Henry Hotz, the Confederacy's agent in London.[31] This context gave an added edge to the Society's controversial stance on race. Any assessment of the innate abilities of peoples of African heritage was inextricably bound up with the issue of slavery, which carried a hefty political charge in British society. The evangelical campaign to abolish slavery in British territories had mobilized public opinion in the early nineteenth century on a scale never before seen, and although the passage of the Emancipation Act in 1834 quieted its concerns, the antislavery caucus remained a formidable political force, as it demonstrated through the pressure it placed on the British government to support the Union cause in America.[32] It faced strong opposition, however, from textile manufacturers and other groups with ties to the South's plantation economy. The result was a highly polarized climate of opinion that hinged on the problem of slavery.

Burton leapt into the fray, adopting the role of agent provocateur on behalf of the "peculiar institution." Slavery, he declared, was "the great civilizing agent of primitive races."[33] Since "the Negro cannot improve in his own country . . . it is a mercy to remove him from it" and place him under the supervision of a white master.[34] Indeed, the "removal of the negro from Africa is like sending a boy to school; it is his only chance of improvement."[35] Evangelicals who objected to the Negro's enslavement on religious or moral grounds were simply blind to the benefits that made it a necessary stage in the development of every civilization, according to Burton, who offered evidence from the Bible in support of his views.[36]

Burton's defense of slavery is in fact riven with contradictions. His claim that blacks could be civilized or at least regenerated through slavery contradicts his claim that their innate inferiority made them incapable of improvement. Both positions rest on notions of racial inferiority, but one presumes that this inferiority can be rectified while the other does not. It also is difficult to reconcile his argument for the civilizing effects of slavery with his concession that the slave trade was responsible at least in part for the degeneration of East African societies. These are not the only inconsistencies in Burton's racialist rationale for slavery. In the essay he wrote in defense of Hunt, he endorses the polygenist position that blacks are a "sub-species or permanent variety of the *genus homo*," a claim for their biological difference that carries with it the conviction that sexual unions with whites are either sterile or result in weak, degenerate offspring. Yet he argues in the same essay that those blacks who bred with "semitic" peoples from North African benefited from an admixture of "Asiatic blood," becoming an improved race he calls "negroids"—as opposed to putatively pure-blooded "negroes."[37] This assertion contradicts a strict polygenist interpretation of Africans as a race, as Hunt was quick to appreciate. When he pressed Burton at an Anthropological Society meeting to explain the differences between "negroids" and "negroes," Burton could not do so: he lamely replied that "they were indefinable."[38]

This remark is indicative of the strains that arose as Burton sought to harness the unruly human diversity he detailed with such meticulous care in his journeys through Africa and other parts of the world to the rigid racialist categories favored by his polygenist coterie. He was torn between a determination on the one hand to characterize Africans as a homogeneous racial group and a recognition on the other that "each tribe requires a specific study."[39] He also found it hard to reconcile his theoretical allegiance to the idea of fixed racial types with the empirical evidence of mixed ethnicities that continually confronted him. His efforts to associate the physical features of "hybrid types" with the immutable markers of race would lead him down some strange byways. He characterizes the mix of Semitic (Arab) and Hamitic (African) features in the Swahili people of the East African coast as follows: "The upper, or intellectual part, though capped by woolly hair, is distinctly Semitic. . . . The lower, or animal half, especially the nostrils, lip, jaws, and chin, is unmistakably African."[40] He makes similar remarks about some Islamicized blacks he meets in West Africa, whom he describes as having "faces like the Semiticized negroids generally, Arab in the upper and African in the lower half."[41] Burton reads the hybridity of these peoples in a phrenological fashion, ascribing the superiority of Arab over African blood to their relative rank as influences on the physical features of the face, with the former dominating the sites of intellect (the brow) and sensitivity (the eyes). Even so, such hybrid creatures pose questions about the fixity of racial types. As Burton acknowledges, "when speaking of the permanence of type, it is well to bear in mind that our poor observations hardly extend over 2500 years."[42]

When Burton turns his attention from Africans to the various other peoples he has observed in his travels, his views on race prove even more complicated and contradictory. In the American West he encounters settlers who seem to him to have been racially transformed by their environment. "The Western man," he declares, "had been worked by climate and its consequences . . . into a remarkable resemblance to the wild Indian. He hates labor."[43] This stress on the malleability of race under the influence of climate echoes his earlier claims about the degeneration of the Portuguese in India. In Brazil he again turns to climate to explain what he believes are significant changes in peoples of European stock. Brazilian Creoles, he claims, have smaller hands and feet, straighter hair, and thinner noses than their Portuguese ancestors, not to mention other "modification[s] of form and approximation to the Indian type . . . [that] I cannot explain . . . except as the effect of climate." Nor is their metamorphosis merely physical: "the Luso-Brazilian, as well as the Anglo-American, has been modified morally as well as physically by climate, and has assimilated in national character to the aborigines"—though Burton does not indicate what that national character might be.[44]

When it comes to Europeans, then, Burton is prepared to accept that racial characteristics change under the weight of environmental forces. But he resists the same logic when he turns to Brazil's African slave population. Although he believes that the African in Brazil is "an exotic . . . out of his proper ethnic center"—a claim that presumably applies to the European in Brazil as well—what that means in this particular case is not racial modification, but racial extinction. Although the system of slavery has sustained the Brazilian black so far, "emancipation will annihilate the African race," a fate he predicts for the slave population of the United States as well.[45] Strangely, Burton says almost nothing about blacks and slavery in his book on the American West, even though he had journeyed through the United States immediately before the outbreak of the Civil War. He does, however, say a great deal about the American Indian, whom he places in the same analytical category as the African. "Like the negro, the Indian belongs to a species, sub-species, or variety—whichever the reader pleases"—in short, a separate racial group, which is evidenced by the fact that the Indians' "half-breed" offspring (a group for whom Burton expresses utter contempt) exhibit all the signs of "quasi-mules," whose degeneracy and sterility ensure that they will be "short-lived." But the same fate, he suggests, awaits "pure-blooded" Indians as well: the Pawnee are "declining"; the "other Prairie tribes will degenerate, if not disappear, when the buffalo is 'rubbed out'"; the "extinction" of the Delaware "appears imminent."[46] Unlike the African in Brazil or the United States, however, the Indian is not an exotic in the American West, and although there are plenty of other reasons to anticipate the destruction of this "dying race," as it was often termed, it seems curious, to say the least, that Burton should at the same time suppose that white settlers, who are responsible for this harsh outcome, might themselves mutate into the Indians' simulacra.

It is easy sport to expose the intellectual incoherence of such racial notions, but their persistent power in our own age makes the exercise an important one nonetheless. There are some indications that Burton himself was not entirely oblivious to the flaws in his reasoning. Although he never managed to find his way out of the mental maze of race, he did make occasional comments

West Africa, etc...

that suggest some awareness of the dilemma he confronted. At one point he declares himself opposed to Prichard's monogenist belief in the brotherhood of man but also expresses unease with Robert Knox's doctrinaire insistence that "race is everything": "I venture to opine that the truth lies between the two," though exactly where he does not (cannot?) say.[47]

The key question, however, is why Burton engaged in such racial theorizing at all. What were its attractions? What purposes did it serve? The standard interpretation of racist thinking is to regard it as a strategy to enforce social distance and bolster social status, to give expression to deep-seated fears and to support assertions of power.[48] Although these motives certainly had some influence on Burton (they are, after all, broad enough to be applicable in some sense to almost everyone), they only go so far in helping us to understand the circumstances that made racist ideas appealing to Burton and the purposes to which he put them. To gain a fuller appreciation of what race meant for Burton and why he found it such a compelling if problematic concept, we need to give closer attention to the experience that gave full force to his preoccupation with race, his service as British consul in West Africa.

※※※※※※

The region to which Burton was sent on his first posting as a British consul in 1861 had a long and troubled association with Britain. For several centuries, Britain had been a major participant in the trade for slaves from West Africa, becoming its dominant player in the eighteenth century. In 1807, however, Parliament abolished the British trade in slaves and instituted a naval blockade to intercept slaving ships. This altered, but did not end, Britain's involvement in the region. It acquired peninsular Sierra Leone from its evangelical missionary founders in 1808, establishing a crown colony there for the repair and resupply of patrol vessels and the repatriation of freed slaves, known as recaptives. It also assumed a modest presence elsewhere in the region, acquiring use of a base at Fernando Po in 1827, establishing a loose protectorate over the Gold Coast in the 1840s, and annexing the port of Lagos in 1861. Beyond its continued efforts to suppress the slave trade and protect the interests of a small but growing contingent of traders and missionaries, however, there was little to keep Britain in West Africa. The high death toll from malaria, yellow fever, and other diseases gave the region a reputation as "the white man's grave," which led in turn to the recruitment of Western-educated blacks from Sierra Leone and the West Indies, who were thought to be less susceptible to the fatal fevers, for government service in the region. In 1865, a parliamentary select committee recommended that Britain reduce its commitments in West Africa, a decision that Burton heartily endorsed in his testimony before the committee.[49]

Burton's consular headquarters were located at Fernando Po, the large island in the Gulf of Guinea owned by Spain but leased to Britain as a base for its antislavery patrols. If any part of West Africa had a special claim to be the white man's grave, this was it. According to a British naval surgeon writing in 1847, there was not "any spot in the whole world more detrimental to health."[50] Burton sailed for this posting without his new bride, convinced that the fevers of West Africa would be fatal to her. His initial impression of the place was that it was "the very abomination of desolation," and he "felt uncommonly suicidal through that first night on Fernando Po."[51] Although one reason he may have received the appointment was the belief that his previous experience in East Africa had "seasoned" him to the climate, Burton was hardly immune from malaria and other fevers, and he fell ill almost immediately upon his arrival.[52] Poor health, however, did not prevent him from undertaking arduous journeys through the region. In fact, it often served as their rationale, as when he climbed the mountains of Cameroon in 1862 in search of a site for a sanitarium.[53] When he informed his superiors in 1863 that he had left his consular post and ventured up the Congo River for health reasons, an anonymous Foreign Office bureaucrat wryly remarked: "as long as there is a river unexplored or a mountain unascended within Capt. Burton's reach, his health will always be impaired until he has accomplished both the one and the other."[54]

The charge of a British consul was to assist local British subjects and oversee British trade, mainly through the regulation of shipping.[55] Burton's obligations extended across much of the Gulf of Guinea, a culturally complex and politically fragmented region where European garrisons and African kingdoms, Western traders and recaptive middlemen, Christian missionaries and native elites all jockeyed for power, wealth, and influence. Burton spent much of his time trying to settle disputes between these contending parties. He reformed the Court of Equity that served to regulate contracts and resolve grievances; he mediated British and African traders' claims of restitution for economic injury; he accompanied naval gunboats on punitive expeditions against recalcitrant tribesmen.[56] But he had little stomach for the job and even less for the parties with whom he had to deal.

As Burton saw it, the region was in the throes of social disintegration. He charged that the so-called legitimate trade that British antislavery advocates lauded as the salvation of Africa consisted mainly of arms, ammunition, and alcohol. Its effects were "perfectly demoralising, and as injurious to the interests of the people as the slave trade ever was."[57] In some coastal areas, he claimed, much of the population was perpetually drunk. The easy access to arms, in turn, fueled conflicts between neighboring peoples, making their enmities more deadly than ever before. He rested much of the blame for this deplorable state of affairs on the heads of local European traders, whom he held in contempt. "Really," he sneered, "in this part of the world climate makes the white man a more degenerate thing than the nigger."[58] What especially dismayed Burton, however, was the traders' corrosive influence on Africans. "The chiefs are thoroughly demoralised"—again that damning, crucial verb—"by contact with the worst class of European."[59] When called upon to intervene in trade disputes, he often found that "what is brought forward as a grievance against the natives is the work of Europeans."[60]

He had little regard for European missionaries either. They too were a "source of trouble," in part because of their low "mechanic origin," but above all because of their detrimental impact on Africans. He impishly offered as evidence of their influence the case of Tom Honesty IV, a chief on the Cameroon River, who "after conversion to Christianity and to the practice of monogamy died of a confirmed syphilis."[61] But he had a far more serious complaint against the missionaries: they were responsible for the region's growing contingent of Christianized, Westernized Africans, a group that Burton regarded as the most socially and morally subversive force in the region.

The main objects of Burton's disdain were the recaptives from Sierra Leone, who had undergone a religious and cultural rebirth under the care of the colony's missionaries. Their allegiance to the Christian faith and customs and their understanding of the English language and laws made them well suited for the role of intermediaries in trade and negotiations between the British and indigenous peoples. As a result, they occupied port towns all along the Guinea Coast, establishing an influential presence everywhere they went. Among their most distinguished representatives were Samuel Ajayi Crowther, bishop of the Anglican Church in Nigeria, and James Africanus Horton, an Edinburgh-trained army surgeon in the West African service. Along with other deracinated, often mixed-race West Africans (as well as some educated blacks recruited from the West Indies), they constituted a nascent professional elite, a comprador class of merchants, lawyers, publishers, educators, doctors, and government officials who embraced British bourgeois values of respectability and independence.[62]

Although Burton admired a few members of this Westernized elite—"Bishop Crowther [is] by far the best specimen of African that I have yet met"—he disdained them as a group.[63] To his eyes, they were mimic men, a hybrid breed lacking any stable identity or moral certitudes. This was evident to him from their choice of dress: they insisted on wearing "the cast-off finery of Europe," a sorry sartorial imitativeness that he contrasted to "the picturesque and beautiful costumes of Asia"—a judgment that speaks in intriguingly discrepant ways to his own fondness for cultural cross-dressing.[64] He considered the recaptives a lazy, litigious lot, addicted to various vices. *Wanderings in West Africa* was replete with defamatory remarks about their character. The typical Sierra Leonean, Burton asserted, was "an inveterate thief; he drinks, he gambles, he intrigues." He complained time and again about "their puerile inept ways, their exceedingly bad language, their constant intoxication, and their disposition to quarrel on all occasions."[65] His consular dispatches were filled with warnings against the "ever increasing evil in all these rivers [caused by] the immigration of Sierra Leone and other liberated men."[66] Much of his antagonism to them lay precisely in their sense of themselves as "liberated." They presumed to believe they were Burton's equals, behaving in a manner he interpreted as "insolence." He worried that the "white man's position is rendered far more precarious on the coast than it might be, if the black man were always kept in his proper place."[67]

No better illustration can be offered of Westernized Africans' able challenge to racist ideas about their "proper place" than their responses to Burton's own vituperative remarks. In 1865 a lawyer and newspaper editor from Sierra Leone named William Rainy privately published *The Censor Censured: or, the Calumnies of Captain Burton (Late Her Majesty's Consul at Fernando Po) on the Africans of Sierra Leone.* This pamphlet had two main aims: one was to refute Burton's "vile national slander" against the people of Sierra Leone; the other was to prove that Burton had illegally profited from the consular sale of a vessel to settle its late owner's debts.[68] The charges brought glee to enemies of Burton such as Christopher Rigby and James Grant, who hoped they would spell the end of Burton's consular career.[69] The Foreign Office did in fact launch a malfeasance investigation, which concluded that the acting consul had improperly conducted the sale during one of Burton's frequent absences. Burton, however, was considered financially accountable for his subordinate's actions, and his salary was temporarily suspended to recover the embezzled funds.[70] Railing against the decision, Burton insisted that the charges had been trumped up because "I do not hold the black to be equal to the white man and . . . prefer seeing the missionary at home in Spitalfields than abroad in West Africa!"[71] Nearly two decades later he still smarted from the incident, writing with ugly petulance that to call an African a "nigger" in Sierra Leone or to commit a "mild assault" on one of its citizens would incite litigation from "Lawyer Rainy."[72]

Burton's views were the target of a far more substantial and penetrating critique by James Africanus Horton. One of Sierra Leone's greatest sons, Horton achieved renown as a physician, scientist, banker, and army officer in West Africa. He was an ardent proponent of the Victorian Christian values nurtured in Sierra Leone's mission-centered society, embodying their premise that the benefits of British civilization were attainable by all, regardless of race.[73] He responded to Burton's attacks on his countrymen in his encyclopedic survey of the region, *West African Countries and Peoples* (1868). There he sought to expose the "false theories of modern anthropologists" (the title of chapter four) and demonstrate that Africans possessed the same capacity for improvement as any other people. Horton referred to Burton in his preface as "the *noli me tangere* of the African race" and took him to task throughout the book.[74] This rebuttal appeared after Burton had drawn back from his polemical involvement in the racist cause, and his only public reference to Horton appeared more than a decade later in his final work on West Africa, where he noted some minor inaccuracies in Horton's book. In a telling indication of how far he had retreated from his earlier bellicosity, Burton now declared: "Most Englishmen know negroes of pure blood as well as 'coloured persons' who, at Oxford and elsewhere, have shown themselves fully equal in intellect and capacity to the white races of Europe and America. These men afford incontestable proofs that the Negro can be civilized."[75]

⚜⚜⚜

Burton's disgust with conditions on the coast and antagonism toward its residents during the years he served as consul at Fernando Po reinforced his innate restlessness, causing him to venture into the interior whenever possible. Whether it was a climate suited for a sanitarium in the Cameroon Mountains or the challenge of the cataracts on the Congo River, the lure of mineral wealth in the Gold Coast or reports of gorillas and cannibals in Gabon, Burton found an excuse to escape his official responsibilities. He was in his element off the beaten track, ever eager for those unpredictable encounters with strange peoples that allowed him to exercise his wits and sate his curiosity. His accounts of those encounters possess an ethnographic amplitude that in combination with recurrent expressions of empathy and flashes of insight stand in stark contrast to his sweeping generalizations about Africans as a race. They compel a closer examination of what race meant for Burton.

Perhaps the best example of this discordance between Burton's racial doctrines and his impressions of particular peoples can be found in *A Mission to Gelele* (1864), an account of his visit to the independent African state of Dahomey. This is the book that includes his notorious chapter in defense of Hunt, with its crude claims about the innate inferiority of Africans. Both in style and in substance, this chapter stands at odds with the overall thrust of the work, which presents a rigorously empirical and surprisingly sympathetic account of a regime that was widely regarded in Britain as one of the most savage and bloodthirsty in Africa. Burton visited the court of Gelele, king of Dahomey, in 1863 on a Foreign Office mission to persuade the king to cease the practice of human sacrifices. What topic could have better served his racist agenda? Far from playing up this lurid practice, however, Burton sought to mitigate its horror. He insisted that the state's annual toll of human sacrifices was far less heavy than the popular press reported. He pointed out that the victims were mainly war captives and criminals, many of them the same class of persons who went to the gallows in Britain. He reminded his readers that until recent times executions in their own country had been far crueler than those he observed in Dahomey. He explained that the sacrifices were carried out in obeisance to royal ancestors and were intended to legitimate the established political and religious order. They were, he suggested with obvious relish, "a touching instance of the King's filial piety, deplorably mistaken, but perfectly sincere." In obvious dissent with the policy of his own government, he warned that Gelele's subjects "would deem it impious were he to curtail or to omit the performance [of human sacrifice], and suddenly to suppress it would be as if a European monarch were forcibly to abolish prayers for the dead."[76]

Much the same message appeared in the letters that Burton wrote from Dahomey to his friend Richard Monckton Milnes. Though he adopted a more intimate and insouciant tone, he again emphasized the contrast between the fearsome reputation the kingdom had acquired in England and the mundane reality he observed first hand: "At Benin . . . they crucified a fellow in honour of my coming—here nothing! And this is the blood-stained land of Dahomè!! The 'monster' as your papers call the King is a jolly looking party about 45 with a pleasant face, a frank smile and a shake of the fist like a British shopkeeper. . . . About these individuals a fearful amount of bunk has been written."[77]

Burton gave a similarly normalizing account of Dahomey's famed regiments of women warriors, supposed Amazons who attracted a good deal of erotically charged interest in the British press. He observed that most of them were old and physically unattractive, suggesting that the "toil, hardships, and privations" they endured had masculinized them.[78] (He hammered his point home with an oft-reproduced illustration of a rather repellent figure armed with a musket.) He also presented a brief but learned discourse about the use of women warriors in societies through history, making the point that the practice was less distinctive to Dahomey than his readers might suppose.

Not only did Burton dampen the sensationalist reports of women warriors and human sacrifices, but he devoted most of his attention to the everyday aspects of Dahomean life. *Mission to Gelele* recounted his journey to and from the kingdom, his observations of court rituals and ceremonies, and his impressions of Dahomean religious beliefs, social practices, and political institutions. Because it took him weeks to gain an audience with Gelele,

Burton sketched this member of Dahomey's regiment of female warriors during his diplomatic mission to the African kingdom in 1863. By accentuating her unattractive features, he sought to counter romanticized descriptions of these "Amazons" while giving visual expression to his own racist sentiments. From Richard F. Burton, *A Mission to Gelele, King of Dahome* (London: Tinsley Brothers, 1864).

he had plenty of time to observe his hosts, study their language, and acquire an understanding of their culture. A political reactionary himself, he praised the regime's social order: "Except in the case of serfs, slaves, and captives, there is throughout Dahome, and I may say Africa, more of real liberty and equality— I will not add fraternity—than in any other quarter of the globe, and the presence of the servile renders the freemen only freer and more equal." He defended Dahomean religion against the charge that it was mere fetish worship, arguing that it possessed a conception of a "Deity as the Cause of Causes and the Source of Law." By the time he left the kingdom, he claimed to be capable of "understanding most conversations in Ffon, and of being able to join in a simple dialogue." As a result, according to several modern authorities, his is the most informed account of Dahomey written in the nineteenth century.[79]

This same determination to understand traditional African customs and beliefs is evident in Burton's accounts of the Mpongwe and Fan of Gabon, the Ibo of Abeokuta, and various other West African peoples. He was highly sympathetic to the Asante state in its series of wars with the British and their Fanti allies. "Those who talk of the benighted African," he declared during the first of these clashes in 1863, "should have seen the envoy who conveyed to the Governor the ultimatum of the Ashani King. There was not a European on the coast to compare with him in dignity, self-possession and perfect savior-faire touching the object of his mission." When war broke out again in 1873, Burton declared the Asante to be "thoroughly in the right whilst we are utterly in the wrong."[80] It is hardly surprising that his offer to act as a mediator in this war was ignored by the British government.

Time and again in his writings about West Africa Burton makes similar comments about the indigenous peoples he comes into contact with, exhibiting a curiosity about their lives and an empathy for their perspectives that stand in disconcerting contrast to his racist pronouncements. This, then, is the curious thing about his attitudes toward Africans: his racism does not close him off from an appreciation of their world.

Perhaps the most interesting and revealing of Burton's West African works in this respect is the only one that does not recount his own experiences in the region. *Wit and Wisdom from West Africa* is a compilation of proverbs drawn from the oral traditions of the Wolof, the Asante, the Yoruba, and four other ethnic/linguistic groups. Burton offers several motives for the volume: "It seems to me that the readiest, indeed the only, way of understanding the Negro is to let him speak for himself in his own words." That is exactly what his collection proceeds to do. Moreover, he notes that such proverbs offer access not only to African languages, but to African literatures as well. "For Africa *has* an embryo literature," he declares, "and hardly requires that one should be begotten by strangers." Proverbs constitute an "oral literature, if the phrase be allowed." Praising the moral messages that African proverbs communicate (the book's subtitle refers to "Proverbial Philosophy"), Burton adds an utterly unexpected comment in a footnote: "There is more of equality between the savage and the civilizee—the difference being one of quantity, not of quality—than the latter will admit. For man is everywhere commensurate with man."[81]

How can these remarks be reconciled with Burton's insistence on the innate inferiority of the African? How, for that matter, can he immerse himself with such evident enthusiasm in the intimate world of Africans while professing his disgust with their physical features, bodily odors, behavioral characteristics, and the like? It is tempting to chalk up these apparent contradictions to the workings of an undisciplined and volatile mind, but this conclusion would miss what may have been Burton's most intriguing contribution to Victorian conceptions of race. His understanding of race as a closed space defined by difference serves a double purpose: it supports the standard racists' contention that biology is destiny, but it also ventures the view that races have their own systems of beliefs and behavior, each incommensurate with the other and implicitly standing against any universalist standard of values. To put it another way, it opens the door to a relativist conception of culture.

This places the animus that Burton harbored toward Christian missionaries and their African converts in a new light. Although he certainly took their efforts to breach the boundaries of race as a threat to his own authority and prestige, he also opposed them because of their corrosive effects on indigenous African societies, whose institutions and traditions he felt deserved more respect than the Christian Westernizers granted them. Hence his appreciation of African proverbs and his curiosity about the religious beliefs, social practices, and other characteristics that distinguished these peoples. Burton was prepared to push his own position to its logical extreme. He noted that the missionaries in West Africa "must in duty oppose the customs of the people, their sacrifices, their wars, their polygamy, and their system of slavery."[82] From his perspective, however, such efforts were not so self-evidently beneficial to Africans as they seemed. He insisted that human sacrifice could not be abolished without eroding the entire ethico-political system it served, the consequences of which were potentially destructive. He was even more explicit in his defense of polygamy and slavery, arguing that both practices served important social purposes. And, as a military man, he certainly had no ethical objections to war, which he felt weeded out the weak. His broader point, however, was this: "All races now known to the world have a something which they call right, and a something which they term wrong; the underlying instinctive idea being evidently that something which benefits me is good, and all which harms me is evil. Their good and their evil are not those of more advanced nations; still the idea is there, and progress or tradition works it out in a thousand different ways."[83]

No declaration of beliefs could have been more profoundly at odds with the aims of the Christian missionary enterprise in Africa. Although Burton admired individual missionaries for their knowledge of local languages and customs and relied on them for information and assistance during his travels, he considered their project to be misconceived at its core. By professing to represent the one and true faith, they asserted the universalism of a religion that actually arose out of a particular historical context on behalf of a particular cultural tradition. The proof was to be found in the changes missionaries required of converts: the promise that they would become part of an egalitarian community unconstrained by racial inequalities was contingent on their adoption of a culturally specific set of practices, such as the English language, Western dress, and monogamous marriage. It was this determination to bring about the erasure of cultural difference that Burton found so objectionable.[84]

When it came to the influence of Islam on Africans, however, Burton harbored no such concerns. On the contrary, he believed that "El Islam has wrought immense good in Africa . . . it has taught the African to make that first step in moral progress."[85] Far more than Christianity, he insisted, Islam instilled habits of honesty, sobriety, and industry. As evidence of its positive influence, he had to look no further than his own factotum, an African Muslim named Selim Aga, whom he eulogized in his last book about West Africa.[86] He praised Islam's tolerance of other faiths and its treatment of women. He admired the value it placed on learning.[87] He considered it "the Perfect Cure for the disorders which rule the [African] land."[88]

The apparent contradiction between his views on Africans' conversion to Christianity and their conversion to Islam was not lost on his critics. They saw it as confirmation that he was a not-so-secret convert to Islam who could not conceal his hatred of Christianity. Yet his contrasting assessments of the two faiths were not as inconsistent as they seemed. He never claimed that Islam's doctrines were inherently superior to those of Christianity, offering advantages to everyone, Europeans included. If Islam offered more benefits to Africans than Christianity, that was merely because it spoke more directly to their particular needs. It prohibited the consumption of alcohol and other vices that undermined African communities. It reinforced traditional practices such as polygamy and domestic slavery that contributed to their social stability. Its advantage, then, was situational. Unlike Christianity, which left its converts socially deracinated and morally unmoored, it supplied them with a syncretist faith that accommodated itself to ancestral traditions while contributing a new social and ethical framework for meeting the wider world.

As an enemy of the missionary assault on indigenous cultures, Burton was determined to confront the central conviction that underwrote the Christian position, the monogenist belief in the common ancestry of all human beings. If monogenism made it possible to argue for the erasure of cultural difference and the imposition of a Euro-Christian universalist standard of conduct, then it is hardly surprising that the determination to preserve difference and insist on its importance as a source of knowledge led some of its proponents to the polygenist position that racial differences were innate and immutable. Burton's embrace of a polygenist understanding of race was motivated not just by his belief in the separate genesis of Africans, but by his desire to defend their distinctive social practices and sense of cultural identity against extinction. He was most fervently outspoken in his advocacy of the polygenist position during his years in West Africa because it was there that the missionaries had made their most significant inroads against indigenous systems of behavior and belief. His experiences in the Near East had convinced him of Islam's importance in sustaining local cultures against Euro-Christian subversion; hence his hopes for the spread of Islam in West Africa.

Racism freed Burton from the obligation of evaluating Africans by the standards of his own society. Ironically, then, it made it possible for him to move in the direction of cultural relativism.[89] What appears to us a paradox—the convergence of curiosity about other cultures as autonomous systems operating outside any absolute standards *with* the view of race as a biological fact whose various groupings are distinct, fixed, and hierarchically ordered—was entirely consistent and logical to Burton. Thus his chapter endorsing the racist views of Hunt includes the following statement: "Nations are poor judges of one another; each looks upon itself as an exemplar to the world, and vents its philanthropy by forcing its infallible system or systems upon its neighbour. How long is it since popular literature has begun to confess that the British Constitution is not quite fit for the whole human race, and that the Anglo-Saxon has much to do at home, before he sets out a-colonelling to regenerate mankind?" Similarly, Burton remarks in his book on Abeokuta: "'What a wretched existence!' the European reader will exclaim [about the lives of Africans]. I vehemently doubt this. The so-called reflecting part of Creation will measure every other individual's happiness or misery by its own; consequently it is hoodwinked in its judgment. Considering the wisdom displayed in the distribution and adaptation of mankind, I venture to opine that all are equally blessed and cursed."[90]

Such comments alert us to the complex and unexpected ways in which notions of race and culture played out for Burton. His claims of racial difference need to be seen as much in terms of the importance he placed on the autonomy of indigenous cultures as in terms of the notion that Europeans possessed innate biological advantages over other peoples.

Because Burton's pronouncements on Africans are so repugnant to modern sensibilities, they have caused some to regard him as a crank, advancing opinions too intellectually purblind and morally bankrupt to bear serious attention.[91] Yet Burton was engaged in a serious if flawed endeavor to come to terms with the world of difference that confronted the Victorians across the globe. He sought to respond to that difference without resorting to the shackling assumptions of a Euro-Christian universalism. The influence of his endeavor extended far beyond the confines of the small coterie of midcentury racists let by Hunt. It in fact contributed to an intellectual genealogy of a surprisingly different sort. A brief review of three individuals whose West African careers either paralleled or followed Burton's gives some indication of the remarkable trajectory of his efforts to define and defend difference.

The person whose views on Africa and Africans most closely corresponded to those of Burton is a now largely forgotten figure, Winwood Reade.[92] A novelist and journalist who wrote several books about his travels through West Africa, Reade admired Burton both for his achievements as an explorer and for his advocacy of controversial opinions. Reade orbited in the same intellectual circles as Burton, joining the Anthropological Society and presenting himself as a scientific freethinker who was not afraid to speak his mind on matters of race and religion. Like Burton, he stirred controversy with his criticism of the Christian missionary impact on "savage" Africans and his conviction that Islam was far better suited to their needs.[93] He had his greatest impact, however, with his book *The Martyrdom of Man* (1872), a self-described "Universal History" that sought to subvert a Christocentric view of the past. This ambitious work, which told the story of the human experience from a Darwinian-inspired perspective, came to be regarded as "a kind of substitute Bible for many Secularists."[94] Burton praised its "heroic honesty."[95] What deserves particular note is that the book had its origins in Reade's desire "to prove that Negroland or Inner Africa is not cut off from the mainstream of [historical] events."[96] It went through dozens of editions and influenced a surprisingly diverse array of readers, among them Sidney Webb, H. G. Wells, and W. E. B. Du Bois, who admired it for insisting that Africa and Africans have their own history. Whether Reade's book was responsible for Burton's own thoughts on Africa's contribution to history is difficult to say, but by the early 1880s he had embraced what a century later would be referred to as an Afrocentric view of the past, proclaiming that "Egypt is the source of all civilization (except China?)" and that the Egyptians were black Africans who had migrated from Ethiopia.[97]

Another figure whose views bore considerable resemblance to those of Burton was the West African explorer Mary Kingsley. Burton was "one of Mary's great heroes."[98] She had read his books about West Africa as a youth and she followed in his footsteps on her own trips through the region, giving similar study to local languages in order to gain greater understanding of African societies. No less a controversialist than Burton, Kingsley shared his conviction that Africans derived from different evolutionary origins and she too defended African practices such as polygamy and slavery. She believed that missionary Christianity was engaged in the "murder" of indigenous cultures.[99] Though she would have wished her Africans to remain untouched by any outside cultural influences, she considered Islam a better alternative than Christianity because it accommodated itself to African customs. Her position on West Africa was seemingly paradoxical: she made a forceful case for African cultural preservation on the one hand and British economic imperialism on the other, though her imperialism slipped at times into a nascent support of African nationalism. She is often credited with making the first sustained case for viewing African culture from a relativist perspective.[100]

Finally, it is possible to find common threads between the views of Burton and those of the great pan-African nationalist Edward Blyden. Born on the Caribbean island of St. Thomas, Blyden immigrated to Liberia under the auspices of the New York Colonization Society in 1851. In a series of books and articles published over the next half century, he established himself as the most prominent and articulate advocate of the view that blacks possessed their own distinctive racial talent and personality, which could only achieve its full realization in their African homeland under their own rule. Blyden's biographer notes that his "concept of race was strongly influenced by . . . the English school of anthropology led by James Hunt and Richard Burton."[101] Blyden fiercely opposed racial intermixture, insisting that mulattoes were weak and degenerate.[102] He was scathing in his denunciation of Christianity's impact on Africans, claiming that it trained them to "servility." He gave high praise to Islam for its receptivity to African institutions and practices, arguing that it "was a healthy amalgamation, and not an absorption or an undue repression."[103] He claimed that Africans had made great contributions to past civilizations and that they would do so again once they recovered their self-respect and their racial-cum-cultural heritage. As V. Y. Mudimbe has observed, he insisted that Europeans and Africans had different talents and destinies, stressing the "relativity of social cultures and progress."[104] When Burton returned to West Africa in 1881, he stopped off in Liberia in order to meet the man he admiringly referred to as the "Honorable Professor E. W. Blyden," though the encounter, regrettably, never took place.[105]

The views articulated by Reade, Kingsley, and Blyden may not have been directly inspired by Burton, but he clearly had more in common with these figures than is generally recognized. Burton, Reade, Kingsley, and Blyden shared some intriguing and important lines of thought. Each of them criticized Christianity for its assault on Africa's indigenous cultures; each of them applauded Islam for its accommodation to those cultures; each of them credited African cultures with moral and functional values that deserved respect, insisting that they had made distinctive and important contributions in the past. Each of them placed a high premium on cultural difference and objected to efforts by the West to erase it. And each of them associated culture with race. Though their views on race varied in some respects, they agreed that Africans constituted a distinct race that possessed its own array of characteristics and capacities, which manifested themselves in culture. Needless to say, they shared a rigid and reductionist notion of race, and it would be foolish to deny that their views were susceptible to dangerous and destructive uses. But their claims regarding race served in some sense to free them from the confines of their own ethnic habitus and to think of difference on its own terms. Race, in short, was how Burton and those who followed in his footsteps gained purchase on cultural relativism.

VI

The Relativist

The decade and a half between 1865 and 1880 was a troubled time for Burton, both personally and professionally. At its start he gloried in his public reputation as a fierce controversialist who exhibited bohemian proclivities. But his transfer in 1865 from West Africa to Brazil reduced his participation in London scientific and literary circles, in part because his new post carried fewer health risks, thereby scotching his main excuse for home leaves. Though he initially responded to the change of scene with renewed enthusiasm for his consular career, his mood soon deteriorated. He lapsed into an alcoholic depression that made his South American years one of the darkest and least productive periods of his life. His appointment to the Damascus consulship in 1869 temporarily boosted his spirits, but the disgrace of his recall several years later devastated him emotionally and withered his professional ambitions. From 1873 onward he languished in Trieste, a quiet port city where his sinecure as consul provided him with plenty of time to contemplate what had gone wrong. His resentment found its most troubling expression in a bitter burst of anti-Semitism. But he also used his enforced leisure in more productive pursuits, drawing on his immense experience and knowledge of the world to lay the groundwork for the great burst of creativity and controversy that marked the final decade of his life.

These troubled years are bordered at each end by an important work that reveals the varied ways relativism continued to shape

Burton's thinking. At the height of his involvement in the heated debate about the racial character of Africans, Burton put his nascent relativism to use in *Stone Talk* (1865), a bitter, free-wheeling satire in verse that was directed at Britain itself, and in particular at its arrogance, dogmas, and hypocrisy, which he argued were responsible for warping the lives of the nation's inhabitants and wreaking havoc on other peoples around the globe. Fifteen years later he published *The Kasîdah* (1880), another work of poetry that adopted a relativist stance, this time in order to show how spurious were all religions' exclusive claims to truth and how feeble their dependence on faith in the face of reason. In both works he assumed a fictive identity to advance his relativist views, in the first case channeling what he wanted to say through the voice of an ancient Indian Brahmin, in the second through a medieval Persian Sufi. This ventriloquism served as the imaginative equivalent of impersonation, and it provided Burton with the emotional and intellectual distance he evidently needed to edge toward a fully articulated relativism.

⁂

For someone who spent most of his career abroad, Burton managed to acquire an exceptional array of friends and acquaintances in Britain. His celebrity made him a person of interest to the elite that counted itself as "society," an interest that his wife, with her connections to aristocratic circles, did much to cultivate. They socialized with various lords and ladies and enjoyed weekends at the country estates of politically influential benefactors like Richard Monckton Milnes (Lord Houghton), Lord Salisbury, and Lord Stanley. Burton's wide-ranging interests also brought him into association with persons from various other walks of life, especially those who contributed in important ways to Victorian culture and letters. He was an active member of various clubs and learned societies and an avid reader of—and frequent correspondent to—the nation's leading newspapers and periodicals. With no residence to call his own, when alone in London he usually stayed at one of the several clubs of which he was a member and when accompanied by Isabel at her father's townhouse or a hotel, an unfettered existence that allowed him to dine with friends, attend the theater, and otherwise do as he pleased.

Burton seemed especially at home in the company of urban artists and writers. Over the years he counted among his confreres the painters Frederick Leighton, George Frederick Watts, and Val Prinsep, the caricaturist Carlo Pellegrini (*Vanity Fair*'s "Ape"), the actors Henry Irving, Ellen Terry, and Henry Murray, the journalists A. B. Richards, Andrew Wilson, and Frank Harris, and the novelists Bram Stoker, Wilkie Collins, and Ouida. These associations placed Burton in the midst of an emerging bohemian culture in London. The idea of the bohemian had originated in France in the second quarter of the nineteenth century, when a term originally employed as a synonym for gypsies (a telling association) came to refer to the Parisian artists who led independent lives unconstrained by the strictures of bourgeois society. By the mid-nineteenth century this new usage had entered the English lexicon, giving a label to what had become an increasingly self-conscious coterie in London who relied on their intellectual and creative talents for a livelihood.[1] The journalist Justin McCarthy, who was part of what he called "London Bohemia" in the 1850s and 1860s, recalls that it was "made up of young newspaper writers, young painters, young actors, and meant, for the most part, late hours of conviviality, much brandy and soda, many cigars, unlimited tobacco, a good deal of temporary poverty, a common faculty for running into debt, and that common tie . . . the bond of 'poor devilship.'"[2] Often disaffected from the mainstream values of Victorian society, these bohemian types sustained a subterranean current of iconoclastic thought and behavior that Burton found refreshing and consonant with his own outlook.

McCarthy identifies Burton as a leading member of this bohemian set, "a man of domineering presence and almost overbearing manners." He was "loud-voiced, self-asserting, bearing down all argument and all contradiction with a vehement self-reliance which had something almost fierce in it." McCarthy admired him, but did not like him, finding him too eager "to startle and shock."[3] Francis Galton also noted that he was much "disposed to shock," and added: "What a 'Bohemian' is to ordinary persons that Burton was to a Bohemian."[4] This outré quality is precisely what attracted others to him. Two of his closest friends were Monckton Milnes, the politician, poet, and collector of pornography, and Algernon Swinburne, the *enfant terrible* of mid-Victorian letters. What drew these men together were their transgressive interests, convictions, and personal proclivities, all of which fueled a deep disdain for the sexual prudery and religious piety that pervaded polite society.

Milnes was one of Burton's closest confidants, sharing an interest in literature and pornography, supplying advice on the advancement of his career, and introducing him to intellectual luminaries such as Thomas Carlyle, James Anthony Froude, and Charles Kingsley. Burton's frank and irreverent letters to his well-connected friend and mentor detailed his curiosity about African sexual practices, his sympathy for the Islamic faith, and his annoyance at Christian cant and British bluster.[5] A similar irreverence characterized his correspondence with Swinburne.[6] The two men met at a party hosted by Milnes in May 1861 and soon became close friends, going on great drinking bouts together. When Swinburne succeeded in publishing his *Poems and Ballads: First Series* (1865) after its original publisher stopped its sale for fear of prosecution, Burton congratulated him for "bruising the head of British virtue."[7] Swinburne pronounced Richard "my tempter and favourite audience,"[8] and expressed his admiration by dedicating his *Poems and Ballads: Second Series* (1878) to Burton, who reciprocated by dedicating the first volume of his translation of Camoes's *Os Lusiadas (The Lusiads;* 1880) to Swinburne.

Burton, Swinburne, and Milnes were among the members of a curious dining club that appeared on the London scene in 1863. Called the Cannibal Club, it arose out of the intellectual ferment surrounding the newly founded Anthropological Society, whose president, James Hunt, also was the leader of this gustatory gathering. The very name of the new club signaled the determination of its organizers to create an atmosphere where subjects deemed deviant by society could receive an open airing. The club's official symbol was a mace carved to look like an African head gnawing on a thighbone. These iconographic and rhetorical references to cannibalism had Burton's fingerprints all over them. They also hinted at the tone of the table talk, which must have given far freer reign to participants than the sober, "scientific" etiquette that governed the proceedings of the Anthropological Society.

Although most commentators have dismissed the activities of the Cannibal Club as "frivolous" and "an excuse for the stag revelries which Burton called 'orgies,'"[9] these assessments fail to appreciate the iconoclastic spirit that underlay its boisterous bouts of heavy drinking and smoking. Dining clubs were often identified with bohemian activity in mid-Victorian London.[10] McCarthy recalls meeting Burton at a dining club of this sort, and though he does not identify it by name, he indicates that it convened at a hotel near Fleet Street, which accurately describes the venue of the Cannibal Club.[11] The club figures prominently in a recent history of pornography in England, described as an institution that was emblematic of "the emergence of a new relationship between sexuality and society" in the mid-nineteenth century. Members included a number of active collectors of pornography, among them Sir James Plaisted Wilde, General Studholme John Hodgson, and Charles Duncan Cameron, as well as Burton, Milnes, and Swinburne, most of them drawn together by the shared conviction that their interest in sexuality constituted a kind of scientific study that was "a radical act in and of itself."[12] We also know that Burton and other club members asserted what they considered radical racial views, evoked in the club's infamous mace. But perhaps the most telling evidence that those who attended the club dinners had more on their minds than merely boisterous behavior comes from the *Cannibal Catechism,* which Swinburne wrote as a kind of club anthem. Although intended for the members' amusement, the poem carried a profoundly subversive message, one that would have seemed sacrilegious to most Victorians. It mocked the Christian faith with a faux-catechism for cannibals, equating the eucharist to a cannibal feast. The opening stanza gives the flavor of the piece:

> Preserve us from our enemies
> Thou who art Lord of suns and skies
> Whose meat and drink is flesh in pies
>   And blood in bowls!
> Of thy sweet mercy, damn their eyes
>   And damn their souls![13]

The *Cannibal Catechism* certainly reflected Swinburne's personal and highly polemical antagonism to Christianity and turn to agnosticism,[14] but its place in the club's rituals suggests that it reflected the views of other members as well. Burton, for one, shared Swinburne's intense skepticism about the claims of Christianity. So did several other men known to have been members of the club. One was Charles Bradlaugh, the well-known atheist

who established the National Secular Society in 1866 and later refused to take the religious oath when elected to Parliament, pre-
cipitating a five-year legal battle to gain admission to the legisla-
tive body. Another was the freethinker Thomas Bendyshe, who,
in addition to translating Johann Blumenbach's *Anthropological
Treatises* for the Anthropological Society, owned and edited *The
Reader*, a periodical known at the time as "the recognized organ
of the Scientific Societies."[15] There can be little question, then,
that the Cannibal Club was much more than a meeting place for
homosocial merriment; it was in fact a venue for venting what
were considered at the time subversive opinions about religion,
race, sex, and much more.

⚜ ⚜ ⚜

This context is essential to an appreciation of *Stone Talk*, a 121-
page satirical poem that Burton published under the pseudonym
Frank Baker in 1865, when the Cannibal Club and the Anthropological Society were at their height.[16] Although this "Squib," as
Burton called it in a letter to Swinburne,[17] is arguably the most
original and provocative thing he ever wrote, copies of it are so
rare that its significance has been largely overlooked. Isabel Burton reveals one reason for its scarcity in her biography of her husband. She explains that she first learned of *Stone Talk* when Richard gave her a freshly printed copy of the book during a railway
journey, recommending that she read it, but not revealing that he
was its author. She immediately recognized that the irreverent
views it expressed bore a striking resemblance to those of Richard, and she told him that she suspected its author "has been associating with you at the club, picked up your ideas and written
this book." Although Isabel does not specify what club she has
in mind, the obvious candidate is the Cannibal Club. When it
dawned on her that her husband had in fact written the book, she

became alarmed at the impact it might have on his consular career if his identity as author were publicly exposed. On the advice of Monckton Milnes, who shared her concerns, she states that she bought up and destroyed as many copies of the book as she could find, thereby making the publication the rarity it is today.[18] Isabel never mentions how her husband responded to her action, which foreshadows her notorious burning of "The Scented Garden" manuscript after his death.

Stone Talk gives us unmatched insight into Burton the bohemian, a man disaffected by British society and determined to challenge its values, mock its pieties, and expose its hypocrisies. Although the work is marred by erratic shifts in topic and tone, a plethora of obscure references, and various other flaws, it remains in many respects a striking achievement. The farcical premise of the work is that a drunken Dr. Polyglott, staggering home from a night of carousing with a friend, collapses in a stupor on Fleet Street (the bohemian set's home turf), where he finds himself face to face with a talking paving stone, the reincarnated spirit of a Hindu Brahmin. The stone launches into a lengthy, learned discourse on a wide range of topics, with the drunken man occasionally interjecting ineffectual objections. Hence the book's subtitle, *Marvellous Sayings of a Petral Portion of Fleet Street, London, to one Doctor Polyglott, Ph.D.* Burton scatters a number of clues that allude to the resemblance between Dr. Polyglott and himself. These include the character's fondness for drink, the time he spent in India, and, of course, his name, which alludes to Burton's own multilingual talents. Why he grants Polyglott a Ph.D. is more difficult to determine. Perhaps it is an expression of regret over the youthful indiscretions that prevented Burton from completing his university education and realizing his intellectual ambitions in a conventional fashion. Perhaps it is a sly way of suggesting that he regarded the knowledge he had acquired through less formal means as the equivalent to a doctorate. Or perhaps his intent is to mock academic distinctions altogether, exposing them as poor indicators of real knowledge and insight. Dr. Polyglott, after all, is continually bested in his debate with the inert stone, and his character seems modeled in certain respects after Voltaire's naively optimistic and ineffectual Dr. Pangloss.

What makes *Stone Talk* such an intriguing and destabilizing work is the intellectual dominance that the stone holds over the proceedings. Though Dr. Polyglott exhibits some of Burton's superficial attributes, it is the Brahmin-possessed stone that actually expresses his opinions. Blunt, commanding, worldly, angry, and full to bursting with an eclectic array of knowledge, the stone is the true voice of Burton in 1865, his self-portrait as a bohemian intellectual. (At one point in the poem, the stone urges "Bohemians of the scribbling sort / To call the critic rabble out," a stanza that is revealing both for its use of the word "bohemian" and its identification with the interests of the writers whose bohemianism has made them the enemies of high culture's literary critics.)[19] A psychoanalytic interpretation of *Stone Talk* would no doubt detect some sort of emotional trauma lurking behind Burton's choice of a paving stone for his mouthpiece. Burton himself attributes the entrapment of the Brahmin's spirit in a stone to a traumatic event. The stone explains that its unfortunate reversion from the twice-born status of the Brahmin came about when it fell in love with the widow of a pariah, but failed to muster the courage to save her from a funeral pyre. This story closely resembles another that Burton related some fifteen years earlier in *Goa, and the Blue Mountains,* suggesting that this rather tired romantic trope of love lost to the constraints of social convention struck a deep emotional cord with Burton, perhaps because it spoke in some way to his own experience in India. But the animated stone also is a literary device for Burton: it is the *deus ex machina* that establishes the virtually limitless historical perspective from which the spirit of the Brahmin draws his knowledge and authority.

What seems most striking about Burton's choice of interlocutor, however, is not the fact that it is a stone, but that it is inhabited by an Indian Brahmin's spirit. It could, of course, be argued that transmigration as a plot device demands a Hindu (or a Buddhist) interlocutor, but when Dr. Polyglott becomes aware that the stone is speaking to him, he also notices that the street's other paving stones are human heads, "whites, blacks, browns, and reds," which implies that reincarnation extends to all peoples. Later in the poem Burton embellishes this point by declaring: "All are but One—One Universe." The use of the Brahmin as the voice for Burton's views, then, is less transparent and more intriguing than it might at first appear. By investing this spectral representative of a colonial society and a polytheistic religion with a body of knowledge and depth of insight that far surpasses anything exhibited by its degree-enhanced English disputant, Burton hits upon a provocative and powerful way to speak the unpleasant truths he believed his own society was reluctant to hear. His exercise in ventriloquism provides him with the distance and disguise he requires to give free expression to his unorthodox, freethinking, relativist views.

So what does the stone say? A great deal, ranging in subject matter from the evolution of the human species to the failures of British foreign policy. It begins with an account of the origins of the solar system. "'Tis true," the stone acknowledges, "e'en I can't recollect / When atomies did first collect," but it goes on to assure Dr. Polyglott that the universe came into existence millions of years ago through the centripetal convergence of physical matter, not a deliberate act of God.[20] This refutation of the biblical account of creation is followed by the stone's endorsement of the

Darwinian theory of evolution: "By freak of matter Adam burst / Through Simian womb!"[21] Even though the Bible supplies "tales enough to hide / Your origin and salve your pride," the fact remains that man is nothing more than a "reformed orang-utang . . . King of the genus Chimpanzee!" Other articles of Christian faith are dismissed as nonsense as well, culminating with the rejection of the belief that man is the special creation of God. In a ferociously antihumanist peroration, the stone proclaims that the world would be far better off without the human race, a sentiment it suggests is shared by all other living things. It hopes for a future cataclysm that would be "Enough to exterminate the pest / Of nature and to spare the rest."

The stone then turns to the philosophical insight that has to be seen as the lynchpin of Burton's position—his relativism. He advances the argument that there are no universal truths, that all efforts to extract them from the facts of experience are fated to fail because they are channeled through the perceptual filters of the human mind, which invariably modifies and distorts them. This point is made metaphorically in the following stanzas:

> Facts are chameleons whose tint
> Varies with every accident:
> Each, prism-like, hath three obvious sides,
> And facets ten or more besides.
> Events are like the sunny light
> On mirrors falling clear and bright
> Through windows of a varied hue,
> Now yellow seen, now red, now blue.

The impossibility of escaping the subjectivity of personal place and perspective is the theme advanced over three pages of verse, with the stone concluding, "Why need I prove that each man's thought / Is each man's fact, to others nought?" Burton returns to the point still later in the poem, when he connects a relativist understanding of moral truth to the varieties of religious traditions: "Chance birth, chance teaching—these decide / The faiths wherewith men feed their pride."

What follows from this relativist stance is an excoriating assault on British policies, practices, and beliefs. The stone sets on this course with a reminder to Dr. Polyglott that the British once were the colonial subjects of the Romans, whose "skins are dark, while yours are fair." It recites what it claims was the speech Queen Boadicea gave to stir her people to patriotic resistance against their conquerors, contrasting it to the ruthless power their descendents now wield round the world. Burton himself was, of course, an agent of British imperialism, advancing its interests in India, Africa, and elsewhere. Yet the remarkable screed that follows indicates that he was never naive about the impact that British colonial expansion had on conquered peoples or unmoved by the suffering it produced. Indeed, these stanzas pulse with genuine anger at the swathe of destruction his country's imperial ambitions have left behind.

> Look at th' unfortunate Chinese,
> Who lost their Sycee[22] and their teas
> Because they showed some odium
> To Fanqui's[23] filthy opium;
> See India, once so happy, now
> In scale of nations sunk so low—
> That lovely land to which was given
> The choicest blessings under heaven,
> Till ravening Saxon, like simoom,[24]
> With fire and sword brought death and doom,

And, lo! a wretched starv'ling brood
From horse-dung picks disgusting food;
Whilst, in the Commons, India's name
Clears every bench to England's shame.
Of old, the Red Man in the West,
How different his lot, how blest,
How happy in his wigwam home!
By Saxon's poisonous pox and rum
Now what a vile and ruined race!
A few years more its every trace
Will vanish clear from Earth's fair face, . . .
Witness th' old Turk, Mahomet Ali,
Whom Malcolm stuffed with many a lie, . . .
Yet scarce ten years had 'lapsed before
You tried to seize his little store
Of piastres, that the East might 'count
You plunderers Lord Paramount, . . .
Had the Hawaiian known his fate,
A hundred Cooks had slaked his hate,
Each child had murd'rous hand imbrued
In circumnavigating blood.
O'er far Tasmania's sounding shore
Of aborigines a score
Now wanders (where, some years ago,
A hundred thousand souls could show),
Australia-like, exterminate
By your corrosive sublimate.
And now again your tricks you try
On Japanese and Maori:
Because they choose to live in peace,
Nor lend a ready back to fleece,
You arm yourselves with fire and steel
Their towns to burn, their lands to steal,

High raising the ennobling cry
Of Cotton and Christianity;
And, armed with these, each man of sense
Ascribes his course to Providence,
Favouring your pre-eminence,
And purposing to occupy
The globe with Anglo-Saxon fry—
One marvels how! One wonders why!
Man, Rome might come to Britain's school
And own herself a bungling fool!

The global sweep of Burton's critique is remarkable, and lines elsewhere in the poem expand its range even further. The stone, for example, points out how little interest the British public showed in the slaughter committed by its forces during the Sikh wars: "who cares for distant blacks, / Die they by ones, die they by lacs?"[25] Where was Britain's vaunted sense of philanthropy on this occasion, the stone asks? When Dr. Polyglott responds by praising the evangelical humanitarian campaign that brought slavery to an end, the stone launches into an irate assault on Christian hypocrisy, which condemns a custom that the biblical prophets and patriarchs found acceptable while turning a blind eye to a far more pernicious form of slavery thriving in Britain itself—the industrial wage slavery to be found in the "dread dens of Manchester" and the "ravening maw of Birmingham."

One of the most fierce and uncompromising passages in the poem comes when it turns to the poor young women who take up domestic service for employment and thereby become susceptible to sexual abuse. Humanitarian sympathy, the stone suggests, is in scarce supply when such a woman ends up pregnant and is "shown the gate." Bereft, she is driven by hunger to infanticide, and "when all foul resources fail, / She dies in Magdalen[26] or jail."

Nor do her indignities end there. Her body is sold to a medical school to train its students in dissection:

> And, when he's learned to cut and maim,
> The pauper-corpse no friends will claim.
> The scalpel's work when past and done,
> They shove pieces, not of one,
> But half-a-dozen subjects dead—
> One arm, three legs, and dubious head—
> That, ere the mass begin to fester,
> The priest may pray for "this our sister."

These stanzas tap into the Victorians' outrage at the dissection of human bodies, an outrage that derived from ignorance of the intentions of medical researchers, fear of the incentives their practices gave to grave robbers, and resentment at the degrading treatment meted out to the bodies of the poor even after their deaths.[27] None of these considerations, however, are as important to Burton himself as the message communicated in his final line, which charges that Christian institutions sanction these obscene practices with their complacent rituals.

The stone's criticisms of contemporary British society extend to a number of other topics as well. It objects to the sartorial fashions that harness the waists of women in corsets and cover the faces of men in whiskers. It laments the marital requirements that prepare young women for no other purpose than to catch a husband, then condemn them to a kind of slavery once they have succeeded. It decries the familial expectations that oblige young men to seek their fortunes in the far-flung corners of the empire, where loneliness and danger is their lot. It condemns the prevalence of prostitution, alcoholism, and petty crime on the streets of London, pointing out the contradictions their existence presents to British claims of moral superiority.

Unfortunately, *Stone Talk* loses much of its focus and fire in its latter pages. Burton seems unsure—or uneasy—about the end-game of his satire, and he drifts into a directionless rant on an assortment of unrelated topics. He vents his opinions on the various international issues of the day, ranging from Russian oppression of the Poles to the American Civil War. He worries that Britain may have grown too "old" and "stupid" and "cold" to defend its national interests—contradicting, it would seem, his earlier complaint that Britain was too aggressive and ruthless in its use of power. At one point in the poem, he recites a series of irreverent limericks of the sort that must have been popular with members of the Cannibal Club. This increasingly helter-skelter set of concerns and enthusiasms undermines whatever thematic consistency the work may have had in its early going, and it ends on a flat note. Dr. Polyglott, restored to sobriety as the day dawns, concludes that the stone must be the Devil and flees from the scene.

Burton probably composed *Stone Talk* in bits and pieces, dashing off stanzas amid the various other activities and interests that occupied his time in the mid-1860s—the meetings of the Anthropological Society, the debates about the racial character of the African, the controversy over the source of the Nile, his responsibilities as British consul in West Africa, and the publication of a half-dozen other books (four of them two-volume tomes) in the five years leading up to the appearance of *Stone Talk*.[28] Yet it gave fuller expression to Burton's bohemian spirit than anything else he ever wrote, giving us a glimpse of that proclivity to "shock" that so unsettled Justin McCarthy and Francis Galton. At the same time, Burton took care to insulate himself from the outrage he hoped the work would stir by publishing it under a pseudonym. But how much risk of controversy did he really run? There is some evidence that the book would have fallen on deaf ears even if Burton's wife had not preempted his purposes by removing it from circulation. Even though the publisher managed to send out thirty-five review copies of *Stone Talk* to the press before Isabel got wind of what had happened, we know of no published reviews.[29] The poem's premise and plot may have been too outlandish to attract the interest of Victorian critics and readers, its sins against literary conventions too egregious to warrant notice.

Stone Talk is of interest to us, however, because of what it reveals about the author, his opinions, and his epistemological orientation. It supports the contention that Burton was consciously engaged in the construction of a relativist conception of difference. Here he took his familiarity with other cultures and societies as the point of departure for a critical assessment of British views and values. And even though the book sunk without a trace, Burton never forgot it. His own copy is filled with additional verses and other annotations in his spidery, all-but-unreadable handwriting, which suggests he had hopes of issuing a revised edition some day. Although that never happened, the spirit that inspired *Stone Talk* would again find expression a decade and a half later when Burton published his far more accomplished volume of verse, *The Kasîdah*.

❧❧❧❧

Soon after the publication of *Stone Talk* in 1865 Burton sailed for Brazil to assume the British consulship at Santos, a port town near São Paulo. Socially and professionally, this posting was an improvement over Fernando Po. Isabel was able to accompany her husband without inordinate fear of contracting a fatal fever. Burton found the country's Latin culture congenial and socialized with members of the Brazilian elite, including the royal family. He immersed himself in Brazil's history, culture, and geography with characteristic gusto, reading everything he could lay his hands on and traveling to distant territories at every opportunity.[30] On one occasion he made a lengthy journey by horseback into the highlands of Brazil, then returned via the San Francisco River, following its rapids-strewn course fifteen hundred miles to the sea.[31] Later he ventured to Paraguay to get a first-hand look at that country's war with Argentina, Brazil, and Uruguay, a ferocious conflict that left more than half of the Paraguayan population dead.[32]

Underlying this restlessness, however, was his growing boredom and dissatisfaction with a career that seemed to condemn him to one obscure posting after another. "I am still a Pariah," he wrote to Swinburne with more than a touch of self-pity.[33] He neglected his consular duties and drank too much. It is telling that he left no written trace of his final South American journey, which took him across the Andes into Chile. Wilfred Scawen Blunt, who encountered him in the closing stage of his Brazilian consulship, judged him to be "a broken man."[34]

Burton had in fact decided to resign from the Foreign Service when in 1869 he got word that his old friend and admirer, Lord Stanley, had appointed him to the Damascus consulship as one of his final acts as foreign secretary. Burton had long sought an appointment in the Near East, arguing that his familiarity with Arabic and Islam made him well suited for such a post. Stanley's decision came over the objections of Sir Henry Elliot, the British ambassador at Constantinople, who feared that Burton's presence in Damascus would antagonize the local population. Projecting long-standing British suspicions about Burton's religious loyalties onto an Ottoman public, Elliot suggested that Muslims would regard him "either as having insulted their religion by taking part as an unbeliever in their most sacred rites, or else as having been a Mahomedan and having since become a Renegade."[35] Stanley's successor, Lord Clarendon, felt obliged to send Burton an official letter of warning that he would be recalled if his presence provoked complaints.[36]

Burton was in fact supremely unsuited to the demands of his new post, though not for the reasons cited by Elliot. Damascus was a stew of sectarianism, populated by Muslim, Christian, and Jewish communities whose relations with one another were uneasy and occasionally violent. Each of these religious groups was in turn divided into distinct and often antagonistic sects. The Muslim population consisted of various Sunni and Shiite orders, several different Sufi brotherhoods, and pockets of Kurds and Druzes. The minority Christian community was fragmented even further, with Maronite, Greek Orthodox, Roman Catholic, Protestant, and other denominations jockeying for position. Even the relatively small Jewish population was divided between the Sephardim and the Ashkenazim. In 1840 a number of the city's Jews lost their lives in a pogrom precipitated by charges that they had carried out the ritual murder of Padre Tomaso, a Capuchin friar. Another spasm of communal violence broke out in 1860, resulting in the massacre of some three thousand Christians by a Muslim mob. The city remained a tinderbox when Burton arrived a decade later.[37] Moreover, much of the surrounding territory was only nominally under the control of the Ottoman state, which struggled to pacify Druze and Bedouin tribesmen. These circumstances demanded a consul who had patience and political savvy, qualities that Burton sorely lacked.[38] His authoritarian personality soon antagonized a number of the region's religious communities, as well as the local Ottoman authorities.[39]

Burton arrived in Damascus in late 1869, determined to demonstrate his expertise in the affairs of the region and make a name for himself as an active consul. It was not long before he was embroiled in controversy. The first crisis occurred when he learned in June 1870 that an evangelical preacher named Mentor Mott was distributing Christian tracts to Muslims in prison and on the street. Burton put a stop to Mott's proselytizing activities, arguing with good reason that they were "highly dangerous" to the peace of Damascus. This action, however, did not sit well with a Protestant missionary lobby that was already antagonistic to Burton because of his antimissionary reputation.[40]

Soon thereafter he clashed with several members of the local Jewish community, who had come under British legal protection in the aftermath of the Padre Tomaso pogrom. In August or September 1870 he arrested two Jewish boys, apprentices to a local tailor, charging them with stirring up communal tensions by drawing crosses on the walls of a Muslim school. He also accused several Jewish merchants of making usurious loans to Muslim peasants, then using their protected legal status to coerce repayment from the debtors. Not only did Burton refuse to lend support to their activities, but he recommended that they be stripped of their rights as protected subjects. The merchants responded by charging that Burton was anti-Semitic and they garnered the assistance of Sir Moses Montefiore, president of the Board of Deputies of British Jews, and other prominent British Jews to lobby for his recall.[41]

Burton's problems quickly multiplied. When he caught wind of rumors in early 1871 that Christians were targeted for another round of communal violence, Burton took preemptive action, believing he had nipped a genuine conspiracy in the bud. Ambassador Elliot was unconvinced, complaining that his consul had a "habit of spreading alarming news of impending massacres" that "unsettle the public mind at Damascus."[42] A month later the Foreign Office received a report that Burton had been involved in a fray in the town of Nazareth, where he fired his pistol over the heads of a Greek Orthodox mob when it began pelting members of his party with rocks. Burton may have precipitated this dispute by objecting to a land transaction in Nazareth that he believed unfairly benefited the Greek Orthodox Church.[43] Soon thereafter the governor-general of Syria, Mehmet Rasid Pasha, who had endured repeated interference by this troublesome consul in the internal affairs of his province, issued a formal complaint to British authorities when he learned that Burton had met with Druze chiefs in the Lebanese hills without his knowledge.[44] This "determination to meddle with the internal administration of the district," Elliot observed, was "liable to be taken by the restless population of those countries as an encouragement to resist" Ottoman authorities. What Elliot aptly described as Burton's efforts to "assume the virtual position of Governor" could be tolerated no longer.[45] In August of 1871 he was recalled.

Burton was nearly expelled from the consular service: only vigorous lobbying by Isabel managed to save his career. Left to cool his heels for over a year on half-pay, he was finally offered the consular post at Trieste, an Adriatic port city tucked in the southwestern corner of the Austro-Hungarian empire, where it was assumed he could do little harm. He would spend the last seventeen years of his career there.

The Damascus debacle affected Burton deeply. It put an end to his ambitions to be a player in British policy toward the Muslim world, and even though he continued to voice strong opinions about the region, he lost all influence in official circles. His recall convinced him that mediocrity and timidity reigned supreme in Britain, providing no place for a man of his talents and ambitions. Henceforth an acute sense of aggrieved self-pity colored his alienation from British society. This experience reaffirmed his view that all established religions were entrapped in their own subjectivity, making a mockery of their exclusivist claims to universal truths. Nowhere was the fraudulent nature of those claims more readily exposed to view than in Damascus, where the weight of the past and the mix of faiths left little doubt in his mind that religious identity and belief were the arbitrary outcome of time and place. Finally, Burton's bitter interlude in Damascus served as the springboard for his troubling foray into the swamp of anti-Semitism.

⚜︎⚜︎⚜︎

Burton's late-blooming antagonism toward Jews is a subject that requires serious attention in any consideration of his life and thought.[46] Anti-Semitism is a kind of racism, so it is hardly surprising that someone who objectified and essentialized Africans would do the same to Jews. What is perhaps more surprising is that Burton's anti-Semitism should come so late in life. This is not to suggest that Burton was untouched by the anti-Semitic sentiments that suffused European Christian society during his youth and early manhood. Its rhetorical echoes could be heard, for example, in his accusation that Hindu "Shylocks" in Sindh exploited the local peasantry. Yet there is no evidence that Burton was an overt anti-Semite before his Damascus debacle. On the contrary, we have good reason to believe that he shared his wife's romantic philo-Semitism, which Disraeli's novel *Tancred* did so much to inspire. One of the few explicit remarks Burton made about Jews before the 1870s appears in his book on Brazil, where he notes the pervasive anti-Semitism in that country, then adds a surprising personal comment: "Had I a choice of race, there is none to which I would belong more willingly than the Jewish—of course the white family."[47] Though the qualifying clause in this favorable comment alerts us to the racialist assumptions that allowed him at a later date to adopt an anti-Semitic posture, there was nothing in his reference to Jews as a "race"—a common characterization by Victorians of various persuasions, not least Jews themselves—that required such a move. Furthermore, for much of his career he showed less interest in Jews as a people than he did in Judaism as a religion.

Only after Damascus did Burton turn his attention from Judaism to Jews, a shift in focus that signaled his active engagement in anti-Semitic thought. It is clear that the resentment he felt toward the Jews of Damascus and their allies in England for seeking his recall gave him a motive for this turn, but we should resist the conclusion that it was the sole cause of his anti-Semitism.[48] Jews, after all, were not the only peoples with whom he clashed in Damascus, yet they were the only ones toward whom he acquired an animus *as a people.* Moreover, his anti-Semitism seems to have reached its peak only after he had assumed his consular duties at Trieste. This suggests that his attitudes toward Jews also need to be framed in the context of the rise of political anti-Semitism in central and eastern Europe in the late nineteenth century. As it happens, Trieste at this time offered its own special inducements to those susceptible to anti-Semitic appeals.

When Burton arrived there in 1872, Trieste was a bustling port city, providing the largely landlocked Hapsburg empire with its main outlet to the sea. Most of its population was Italian, but it had significant numbers of Albanians, Greeks, Turks, and others as well. Most notably, Jews were a highly visible presence in the city. Indeed, "people in Vienna considered Trieste a Jewish city."[49] Jews dominated the shipping insurance industry and constituted a large portion of the city's social and intellectual elite. Many poorer Jews from eastern European origins also found refuge there. For Burton, already smarting from what he saw as his humiliation at the hands of Jews, these circumstances must have inflamed his sense of resentment and suspicion. Moreover, Burton made frequent visits to Vienna, Munich, and other central European cities during his years in Trieste and kept apprised of political events and intellectual trends there by reading Austrian and German periodicals. He could hardly have been unaware of the rise of political anti-Semitism in the region.

Trieste's location also placed Burton on the doorstep of the most serious European international crisis of the late nineteenth century, the conflict over the fate of the Balkans. Here the long-smoldering mixture of regional nationalist aspirations and great power rivalries burst into flames when Serbia went to war against the Ottoman empire in 1876. This precipitated the notorious massacre of Bulgarian Christians by Turkish authorities, which led in turn to Russia's entry into the war in 1877. The Tory government took the position that British strategic interests necessitated the guarantee of the Ottomans' territorial integrity, even if this meant that Britain had to fight the Russians. Although Burton was a long-standing Tory, an admirer of Benjamin Disraeli, and a veteran of the Crimean War, having assisted the Turks against the Russians, he adamantly objected to the government's decision to lend its support to a regime he had come to view as corrupt and decadent.[50] In a professionally risky move, he wrote a series of pseudonymous letters to the *Daily News,* the *Daily Telegraph,* and other newspapers, criticizing official policy and advocating the breakup of the Ottoman empire. Like some prominent Liberal critics with whom he corresponded, he believed that international Jewry had swayed the British government to lend its support to the Ottoman empire, which was far more tolerant toward Jews than its Russian antagonist, by appealing to Disraeli's Jewish heritage. These anti-Semitic suspicions were voiced most explicitly in his private correspondence with Grattan Geary, the managing editor of *The Times of India,* but they appeared in some of his opinion pieces as well.[51] Burton claimed that Jews were "a power in every European capital, conduct the financial operations of nations and governments, and are to be found wherever civilization has extended and commerce has penetrated."[52]

Burton's anti-Semitic fulminations found their most sustained and disturbing expression in a manuscript titled "Human Sacrifice among the Sephardine or Eastern Jews, or the Murder of Padre Tomaso," which he signed with the pseudonym Hans Barker. Although the work was never published during Burton's lifetime and most of it has remained unpublished and inaccessible to this day, its title leaves little doubt about its content.[53] Most of the unpublished portion of the manuscript evidently takes the form of an inquest into the death of Padre Tomaso, seeking to prove that the friar was in fact the victim of ritual murder by the Sephardic Jews of Damascus.[54] It frames this charge in the context of a broader claim that Ashkenazi Jews had engaged in ritual murders in medieval times and that Sephardic Jews continued to do so. The "blood libel" was the most explosive accusation that could be made against Jews. It had sparked terrible pogroms in Russia and elsewhere in Eastern Europe in the late nineteenth century. Though Burton may have rationalized his interest in the purported practice of ritual murder by Jews in much the same ethnographic terms as he had justified his curiosity about the human sacrifices carried out by the Dahomean state—as another of the many strange customs that human beings devised to give expression to their spiritual feelings and fears—there is little doubt that it was motivated at its core by an animus toward Jews.

As is often the case with anti-Semites, that animus was not unmixed with admiration. The portion of the essay that posthumously appeared in print expresses the view that Jews possess "a prodigious superiority of vital power." Burton attributes this power to "the purity of their blood," a consequence of their endogamous marriage practices, which have made them "physically and mentally . . . equal in all respects to their Gentile neighbours, and in some particulars . . . superior to them." He places emphasis on what he claims to be the ability of the Jews to acclimatize to almost "any part of the habitable globe," unlike "Europeans," who "degenerate" in inhospitable climes. He believes that they show less susceptibility than other "races" to most illnesses, including cholera, plague, leprosy, and venereal disease, and insists that their women are more fecund than other women. This is an argument—or perhaps more accurately a phantasm—that racializes Jews. By the same token, Burton attributes the variations among Jews to "almost a series of sub-races"—a claim that closely resembles the one he made when obliged to account for the evident diversity among black Africans. He gives particular attention to the differences between Sephardic and Ashkenazi Jews, which he identifies as a distinction between "Eastern" and European Jews. By attributing "horrible and disgusting superstitions" to the former group while crediting the latter with more advanced or rational views, he draws on Orientalist stereotypes. These distinctions, however, disappear in the face of his insistence that Jews in general pose a threat to the rest of humankind. Even his acknowledgment that Jews have endured repeated persecution by Christians over the centuries is turned against them by suggesting that their victimization has fomented a desire for vengeance. The Jew's "fierce passions and fiendish cunning, combined with abnormal powers of intellect, with intense vitality, and with a persistency of purpose which the world has rarely seen, and whetted moreover by a keen thirst for blood engendered by defeat and subjection combined to make him the deadly enemy of all mankind."[55]

The only possible mitigation that might be granted to Burton regarding this venomous essay is that he did not publish it. Why he failed to do so is not entirely clear, though the fact that his career remained beholden to a Disraeli-led Tory government until

1880 may have been one consideration. Still, the manuscript remained on the shelf even after the Tories fell from power, and when Burton did express himself in print on the subject of Jews, his remarks took a rather different turn.

In 1881 he published a commentary on the passion play at Oberammergau, Bavaria, which he had seen with his wife in 1879. A popular attraction among Catholics, this theatrical descendant of the medieval German "mystery" play dramatized the persecution, crucifixion, and resurrection of Christ in a narrative that tended to blame Jews for his death.[56] Few circumstances would seem better suited to inspire an outburst of anti-Semitism from Burton, but he turned his invective instead toward Christianity. He attended the passion play, he explains, because of his "Orientalistic and anthropological" interest in the possible parallels between this annual attraction for Catholics and the pilgrimage to Mecca for Muslims—a motive that itself is likely to have offended devout Catholic readers, particularly since Oberammergau gets the worst of the comparison: it comes across in his account as a place where tourism has trumped spirituality. Commenting on the biblical events the play represents, he sympathetically compares the problems confronted by Pontius Pilot with those of British colonial officials attempting to mediate between rival religious groups in India. When he turns to the issue of the Jews' role in Christ's crucifixion, he asks whether "there is nothing to be said on their side?" and then offers this answer: "They held the grand vivifying principle of antiquity—Do right because it is right. . . . But then came another doctrine: Do right in order to save your souls, in order to win a reward in heaven. . . . Surely these Stoics of Judaism, whatever they may have practiced, held in theory the true principle, the Higher Law." For this reason, he suggests, Judaism may in the end outlast Christianity, an outcome that he appears to regard with favor. Here, as earlier in his career, his focus on Judaism as a faith lends itself to a more sympathetic stance.[57]

The last significant commentary by Burton about Jews as a people appears in an essay he wrote on the occasion of Disraeli's death in 1881. Disraeli, he declares, was "in nature as in name a very Hebrew of the Hebrews," an identity he could not escape because it was encoded in his racial being. He exemplified the "peculiar racial vitality" of the Jews, "the energy, the foresight, and the marvelous tenacity" they had exhibited throughout history. The Jews, thus, are represented as a distinct and immutable race. Although Burton avoids the more egregious anti-Semitic slanders that had characterized his earlier essay on the Jews, he does condemn Jewish involvement in usury and other "immoral" practices and objects to the Rothschilds' influence on European affairs. Moreover, he remains as critical of Disraeli's policy toward the "Eastern Question" as ever. And yet, for all its anti-Semitic references to Disraeli's Jewish heritage, the essay is an appreciation of the great Tory prime minister, a eulogy to his talent and determination. Burton clearly admires the man, and one of the sources of that admiration is evident in a remark that appears at the beginning of his essay. The "English public, the middle-class mass," he declares, "never understood him [Disraeli]." Burton recognizes in Disraeli something of himself—an outsider who had to struggle against the insular snobbery of a philistine public. This flash of empathy is perhaps as close as Burton ever came to an appreciation of the challenges that confronted the Jew in European society.[58]

Burton never succeeded in reconciling the contending categories of difference that informed his attitudes toward Jews. When he framed the issue of Jewish difference in religious terms, he was able to maintain some degree of impartiality, in part because he was not invested in the adversarial claims of Christianity. But when his understanding of Jews took a racial turn, his position became fraught with confusion and contradiction. At first, he seemed well disposed to Jews—at least those of European heritage, as his admiring reference to "white" Jews suggests. But the racial distinction implicit in that characterization never made much sense as a framework for differentiating between Ashkenazim and Sephardim or any other category of difference among Jews. Rather than abandon the idea of race, however, Burton simply reclassified these internal distinctions as "sub"-racial, placing stress instead on those supposed racial characteristics that he convinced himself Jews of all sorts shared. His unhappy experience in Damascus, which brought prominent British Jews in alliance with the local "Eastern" Jews he despised, provided the emotional impetus for this shift in orientation, while the political and intellectual influences he absorbed in Trieste gave it credence. It hinged on his claim that Jews possessed a unique capacity to adapt to diverse environments and hence to assume different characteristics while retaining a common racial essence.[59] In advancing this argument to explain the ubiquity and diversity of the Jews, Burton complicated any possibility of making a move similar to the sort that turned his racism toward Africans in a relativist direction. Such a move necessitated the association of a people with a place, a natal location that could explain and sustain their separate and incommensurate being, as Africa did for Africans. It is perhaps for this reason that in the midst of the "Eastern Question" crisis, which critics like Burton hoped would bring about the breakup of the Ottoman empire, he proposed the establishment of a homeland for the Jewish peoples in their biblical birthplace of Palestine.[60] This was only a fleeting thought, however. With the resolution of that crisis and the death of Disraeli, Burton's interest in Jews seems to have waned.[61] Even so, his troubling excursion into anti-Semitism served as an eerie augur of the ideas and events that would do so much to rend the world apart in the twentieth century.

꿏꿏꿏꿏꿏

The consular post at Trieste supplied Burton with a modest sinecure without imposing many administrative demands to tie him down. He was often on the road—to Iceland to investigate sulfur deposits for an investor in 1875; to India on a nostalgic tour of his old haunts in 1876; to the Midian precincts of Arabia in a preliminary reconnaissance of ancient gold workings in 1877; back again to Midian at the head of a full-fledged expedition in search of gold in 1878; and to West Africa to report on the region's gold mines for a London entrepreneur in 1881. In addition, he made countless trips to Britain and various continental European destinations. He also continued his torrid pace of writing, publishing accounts of his travels in Iceland (*Ultima Thule,* 1875), India (*Sind Revisited,* 1877), Midian (*The Gold-Mines of Midian,* 1878, and *The Land of Midian [Revisited],* 1879), and West Africa (*Two Trips to Gorilla Land,* 1876—which recounted a journey he had made a decade earlier—and *To the Gold Coast for Gold,* 1883), as well as translations of several historically significant travelers' tales (*The Lands of Cazembe,* 1873, and *The Captivity of Hans Stade of Hesse,* 1874), an archeological study of the Etruscans (*Etruscan Bologna,* 1876), and even a proposal regarding the military use of swords (*A New System of Sword Exercise for Infantry,* 1876). In addition, Burton found time to pursue his interest in Luis Vaz de Camoes, whose epic poem about Portuguese exploration in Asia and Africa, *The Lusiads,* had fascinated him since his days in India, when he had published a translation of several stanzas from the poem in a Bombay newspaper in 1847. In 1880 he published his two-volume translation of *Os Lusiadas (The Lusiads),* followed a year later by a biography of the author and critical analysis of his work,

Camoens: His Life and His Lusiads (1881), and, last, a translation of Camoes's other poems under the title *Camoens: The Lyricks* (1884).

Burton saw little return from the physical and intellectual investment he made in these varied enterprises. His prospecting expeditions never brought the financial windfall he hoped for, while his books generated mixed reviews and weak sales. Meanwhile, his health began to deteriorate. Trapped in Trieste, he grew increasingly embittered by what he regarded as his country's lack of appreciation for his achievements. He gave expression to these grievances in his biography of Camoes, which included some self-serving allusions to himself. Burton felt a deep affinity for Camoes, who exemplified that rare combination of qualities—grand adventurer and great writer—that he had sought to cultivate. It is apparent from the opening passage of his portrait of the Portuguese poet that he was writing about himself as well. Camoes, he declares, was "one of the most romantic and adventurous [figures] of an age of adventure and romance," but his life was blighted by unrealized hopes: "Opening with the fairest and brightest promise; exposed in manhood to the extremes of vicissitude, to intense enjoyment and 'terrible abysses'; lapsing about middle age into the weariness of baffled hope; and, ending, comparatively early, in the deepest glooms of disappointment, distress, and destitution, the Student, the Soldier, the Traveller, the Patriot, and mighty Man of Genius, thus crowded into a single career the effort, the purposes, the events of half-a-dozen."[62]

Burton goes on to describe Camoes as "Captain Sword as well as Captain Pen," an "aristocrat to the backbone" who "had the courage of his opinions" and who stood in contrast to "the weakly, sickly Humanitarianism of our modern day." Unhappily, he also "never had a talent for success," and, in the end, "his spirit was broken."[63] The allusions to his own character and career are unmistakable, but lest the reader miss the point, Burton has his wife drive it home. "Captain Burton," she declares in an essay attacking her husband's critics at the close of volume 2, "by virtue of sympathy and perhaps similarity of career, seems to have raised the spirit of Camoens himself."[64] There was, of course, more than a touch of self-promotion to these remarks, a conscious effort to remind British readers that their own "mighty Man of Genius" remained neglected, but the overall intent is valedictory, offering an oblique reflection on a life of oversized ambitions and accomplishments that is coming to its close without the public recognition Burton feels he deserves.

A similar spirit pervades *The Kasîdah* (1880), though here it is transformed into a detached and reflective meditation on life. This work, the second and most accomplished of Burton's book-length ventures into verse, is shot through with an acute awareness of the fleeting nature of existence. It ventures into the ethical and philosophical thicket that preoccupied many Victorians, addressing questions of faith, truth, and morality. Though far more skillfully wrought than the eccentric, uneven *Stone Talk*, it shares with the earlier work a similar intent: it too is determined to counter religious and other orthodoxies with freethinking views framed within a relativist context. British public opinion was arguably more receptive to such views in the 1880s than it had been in the 1860s, but Burton still preferred to cloak his authorship in a pseudonym, identifying the work's supposed translator and editor as F.B., the initials of the same fictive author—Frank Baker—he had introduced in *Stone Talk*. More tellingly, he once again adopts the voice of an "Oriental," inventing for the purpose a Sufi poet named Hâjî Abdû. Burton's long-standing appreciation for Sufi poetry and sympathy for the culture that inspired it make Hâjî Abdû a character well suited to his ventriloquist purposes.

Numerous critics and biographers have rightly noted that *The Kasîdah* bears a close resemblance to *The Rubaiyat of Omar Khay-*

yam. In 1859 Edward Fitzgerald, a little-known English country gentleman with an interest in Persian language and literature, published a very loose translation of selected *rubaiya,t* or quatrains, written by the medieval Persian poet Omar Khayyam, whose manuscripts a friend and fellow Orientalist had discovered in the Bodleian Library and the Bengal Asiatic Society Library in Calcutta. Bernard Quaritch, the specialty bookseller and publisher who later issued Burton's works on Camoes, offered the slim volume for sale in his shop, eventually consigning it to his bargain box when it found few buyers. There is disagreement about who actually "discovered" the book, but we know that Burton shared with Swinburne, Milnes, and the pre-Raphaelite artist Dante Gabriel Rossetti an early appreciation for its importance.[65] Its popularity spread by word of mouth, necessitating a second edition in 1868. By the late nineteenth century, *The Rubaiyat of Omar Khayyam* had become a literary sensation, stirring widespread interest and generating new editions and translations, including one by Burton's friend Justin Huntly McCarthy (son of the journalist who had met Burton in London's bohemian circles in the 1860s).[66] Much of this interest in the poem derived from its exotic atmosphere and epicurean themes, which praised the life lived in the here-and-now. Many readers also understood the work to be "a repudiation of traditional religious morality" in favor of a tacit agnosticism.[67] It elicited strong objections from some, who condemned it for advocating what they regarded as "speculative Nihilism and cynical sensualism."[68] Others, however, found comfort in its religious ambivalence, which gave eloquent voice to their own growing doubts about Christianity.[69]

The *Rubaiyat* was in turn reflective of a broader surge of interest on the part of the late Victorians in Oriental themes, which increasingly made their mark on art and literature, architecture and design, and various other elements of British culture.[70] Burton was naturally sympathetic to these trends and contributed to their promotion. When his friend Lord Leighton, the wealthy academy painter, added the magnificent Arab Hall to his Holland Park mansion in 1877–1879, Burton supplied him with Islamic tiles he had acquired during a visit to Sindh a few years earlier.[71] During an extended stay in London in 1875, he organized a weekly "smoking party called Haji Abdullah's Divan," a late-night homosocial gathering organized around an Oriental motif.[72] His home in Trieste had a "Moroccan" room and he took to wearing a fez and pointed-toed slippers.[73] On a less frivolous note, he also began at this time to give careful thought to the project that would become his magnum opus, a new translation of the tales of the Arabian Nights. His more immediate literary preoccupation, however, was "a lovely poem on a *future life*" that Isabel informed Monckton Milnes he was immersed in writing in 1876.[74] This must have been *The Kasîdah*.

Burton clearly sought to feed off the success of *The Rubaiyat* by crafting a work that imitated its poetic tone, not to mention its Orientalist trappings. As a result, critics have tended to dismiss *The Kasîdah* as a poor imitation of *The Rubaiyat*, a knock-off with little literary merit of its own.[75] This view is understandable, but unfair. It fails to consider the differences of intent between a genuine, though free, translation of medieval Persian poetry and a work that imitates the tone of such poetry in pursuit of its own objectives. The irony is that Burton's literary impersonation proves to be too effective, preventing many of his readers from recognizing the modern, independent voice that speaks through the guise of Hâjî Abdû. *The Kasîdah* is in fact a serious and accomplished poem that pursues a highly provocative theme, centered on the inadequacy of all religions' appeals to faith. Contrary to Isabel's claim, it is a poem not about "a future life," but about how to live this life with the realization that it will end in utter

The "Moroccan" room in Burton's Trieste villa was one manifestation of the late Victorian turn to Orientalist themes and motifs. Burton's involvement in this endeavor would culminate in his famous translation of the tales of the Arabian Nights. Photograph by Dr. Grenfell Baker. Courtesy of the Orleans House Gallery, Twickenham.

extinction.[76] *The Kasîdah*, in short, is the testament of a man who knows there is no God.

The poem begins with a pensive meditation on mortality. "All wearies, changes, passes, ends; alas! the Birthday's injury," laments Burton. He rehearses the standard expressions of consolation, ranging from calls to live for the moment to admonitions to prepare for the afterlife. But he will have none of them, particularly the assurances of those who claim to know that eternal existence awaits us after death. Their faith is nothing more than the absence of knowledge, the inability to apprehend the material forces that generate and extinguish life. "There is no God," Burton bluntly declares, and what goes by that name is nothing more than an idealized representation of man himself. "Man worships self: his God is Man; the struggling / of the mortal mind / To form its model as 'twould be, the perfect of itself / to find." Burton draws on his knowledge of comparative religions to support this assertion, observing that the different images of God offered by the Hebrews, Greeks, Arabs, and others reflect their distinctive images of themselves.

This leads to the philosophical keystone of Burton's position, his relativism. He rejects all moral absolutes: "There is no Good, there is no Bad; . . . They change with place, they shift with race; and, in / the veriest span of Time, / Each Vice has worn a Virtue's crown; all Good was / banned as Sin or Crime." The absence of any universal standard of morals makes any assertion of one true faith equally empty. No religion possesses the key to truth. "All Faith is false, all Faith is true: Truth is the shat / tered mirror strown / In myriad bits; while each believes his little bit the / whole to own." Above all, the faith in an afterlife is a futile fantasy. Burton categorically declares that "Man hath no Soul," that what religions refer to as the soul is nothing more than consciousness, "the work of Brain and nerve," which ends with life itself. Hence, "There is no Heav'en, there is no Hell; these be the / dreams of baby minds" whose prayers are pointless.

"How then," Burton asks, "shall man so order life . . . when his tale / of years is told"? He rejects the pleasure-seeking choice that Omar Khayyam advocates, mischievously dismissing as "fools" those "who believe a word he said." Instead, he advocates a life of relentless struggle against ignorance and superstition, insisting that "Reason is Life's sole arbiter, the magic Laby'rinth's / single clue." The path he proposes is one that demands a skeptical stance toward all systems of belief: "Spurn ev'ry idol others raise." All we can rely on is our own critical reason, our ability to "See clear, hear clear." The logic of this argument draws him in the end to a position that echoes that of Friedrich Nietzsche: "He noblest lives and noblest dies who makes and keeps / his self-made laws"; and, more daringly, "Be thine own Deus: Make self free, liberal as the cir / cling air: / Thy Thought to thee an Empire be; break every pris- / on'ing lock and bar."

The Kasîdah is a fully sustained, powerful performance, and one that draws on Burton's wide-ranging experience and knowledge to fine effect. Following the poem are two extended "notes" (more accurately, essays) that summarize and comment on its themes. Though useful for the insight they give into Burton's state of mind and the intellectual debts he acknowledges, they are for the most part redundant and pretentious, the labored performance of an author who is determined to leave his reader in no doubt about the breadth of his learning and the depth of his understanding. The first note purports to be the editor's account of what he knows about Hâjî Abdû and his beliefs, though it is evident from the start that Burton is describing himself, much as he did in his biography of Camoes. The author "had traveled far and wide with his eyes open. . . . To a natural facility, a knack of language-learning, he added a store of desultory various reading. . . .

Nor was he ignorant of 'the -ologies' and the triumphs of modern scientific discovery. Briefly, his memory was well-stored; and he had every talent save that of using his talents."[77]

What follows is a straightforward prose restatement of the views expressed in the poem—straightforward, that is, insofar as a text that creates for its author not just one, but two false fronts can be so regarded. Assuming the identity of the "editor" Frank Baker commenting on the "author" Hâjî Abdû, Burton declares himself to be an "Agnostic" who "looks with impartial eye upon the endless variety of systems." He is "weary" of "finding every petty race . . . claiming the monopoly of Truth." He condemns both Christianity and Islam for "their demoralizing effects," which "become clearer every progressive age." He denounces the notion of original sin, dismisses the belief in an afterlife as "a day dream," describes the soul as simply "a convenient word denoting a sense of personality," and rejects the idea of "a beneficent or maleficent deity [as] a purely sentimental fancy, contradicted by human reason." He asserts the view that the mind is merely a manifestation of matter and describes the human species as "a Tailless catarrhine anthropoid ape, descended from a monad or a primal ascidian." This defense of evolutionary science is not meant, however, to deny all spiritual feeling. Burton declares his philosophical allegiance to the views of "the Sufi, with the usual dash of Buddhistic pessimism."[78]

The second "note" takes the form of an exegesis that traces the intellectual influences on the author. Here is Burton at his most unreadable, dragging his reader into a welter of esoteric terms, references, and quotations, some of them in French, Latin, Greek, Arabic, and even a snatch of Sanskrit. There is something poignant about his effort to validate the views expressed in *The Kasîdah* by associating them with some of the most illustrious names in European philosophy and literature. He manages in the course of a few pages to cite Euripides, Aristotle, Plato, Luther, Bacon, Milton, Shakespeare, Pope, Johnson, Diderot, Rousseau, Kant, Schiller, Schopenhauer, Comte, and Huxley—a virtual "great books" of Western literature. He also puts his formidable knowledge of the world's religions on display with references to Buddhism, Zoroastrianism, Jainism, Hinduism, Confucianism, and the Egyptian Book of the Dead, not to mention, of course, Judaism, Christianity, and Islam. Again, however, he gives "the last word" to Sufism, which he distinguishes from Islam as a philosophical doctrine that is "neither spiritualist nor idealist."[79]

Burton was hardly alone in rejecting the religious dogmas that had done so much to shape Victorian society: it is in fact hard to find a prominent intellectual in the latter part of the century who was not plagued with spiritual doubts.[80] Several things make Burton's views on religion worthy of attention, however. The frank and uncompromising nature of his rejection of the core elements of religious belief—the existence of God, the promise of an afterlife, a universal moral code—is striking. So, too, is the use he makes of various religious and ethical traditions in order to undermine the exclusivist claims of any single system of belief. This breadth of knowledge provides him with the resources not only to challenge the claims of Christianity, but indeed to reject any system of belief that exceeds the bounds of human reason and denies its ultimate authority. Burton comes to this position through the exercise of relativist reasoning, an approach that provides him with the theoretical means, if not always the practical consistency of purpose, to break free from a hierarchical, culturally inscribed perspective on difference.

⁓✿⁓✿⁓✿⁓

Burton's venture into the realm of relativism was not wholly without parallel among his contemporaries. Although the rise of a relativist frame of reference is usually associated with modernism in the arts and humanities around the turn of the century (along with related developments in theoretical physics), its roots ran deep in Victorian thought. It emerged, according to a recent study, out of the radical struggle against religious dogmatism and political authoritarianism, contributing to the critiques of those reactionary forces by John Stuart Mill, Herbert Spencer, James Frazer, Karl Pearson, and other prominent intellectuals in the mid- to late nineteenth century.[81] Relativism served as a key philosophic foundation for their objections to institutionalized religion, their support for evolutionary theory, and their restiveness with regard to the social constraints imposed by the bourgeois regime of respectability. Burton shared those attitudes and convictions. Unlike most of the Victorians who have been identified with relativism, however, he felt no sympathy for the radical struggle to extend political rights to greater segments of the population. He retained an abiding distrust of representative institutions, believing that most societies required the disciplined grip of authoritarian rule.[82] As the journalist Frank Harris recalled, Burton "preferred the tyranny of one to the anarchical misrule of the many. 'Eastern despotisms,' [Burton] asserts, 'have arrived nearer the ideal of equality and fraternity than any republic yet invented.'"[83] For Burton, then, the relativist perspective turned him against political liberty and in favor of "Eastern despotisms." Although this Orientalist rhetoric referred in part to his respect for indigenous political institutions in Asia and Africa, the model he most likely had in mind was the British colonial regime he had served in Sindh.

The imperial project that Burton contributed to in Sindh was significant not only as an inspiration for his own reactionary political convictions, but also as a constraint on his radical counterparts' advocacy of representative politics. It stood there like a great barrier reef, a submerged but formidable boundary beyond which the relativism of Victorian liberals was unable to pass. John Stuart Mill and his counterparts simply could not conceive of applying their critique of political oppression to the various peoples across the globe who lived under Britain's authoritarian colonial rule.[84] Victorian social theorists, it has been suggested, embraced an evolutionary schema in order to place constraints on their relativism, to ensure that it did not erode the boundaries between themselves and those they regarded as less civilized.[85] In effect, they contained its subversive implications by insisting that most other peoples had not yet reached that stage of evolutionary progress that justified self-government. It was not until this intellectual defense mechanism began to break down in the twentieth century that substantial numbers of Britons were prepared to accept the premise that colonial peoples were capable of exercising the same political rights that Victorian liberals had struggled to win for their own society. Yet, as heirs to this ideological tradition, we often overlook the opposite premise:that Britons were no more capable of governing themselves than were other, non-white peoples. Although Burton never articulated an explicit argument for such a view—in part, perhaps, because he too was enmeshed in an evolutionary frame of reference—his frequent expressions of admiration for the authoritarian regimes he encountered abroad and his undisguised disdain for democracy in Britain demonstrate that his relativist instincts drew him in that direction.

Finally, it should be noted that Burton brought to the discussion of difference—a concept that lies at the philosophical heart of relativism—a richer and more intimate appreciation of its range of registers among individuals and cultures than can be claimed for the Victorian worthies who have been credited with advancing the relativist cause. The efforts made by Burton to draw meaning from his own observations and experiences serve as a reminder that we cannot divorce the philosophical consideration of relativism from the practical matters of travel and trade and colonialism that brought Victorians face to face with the quotidian world of difference.

VII

The Sexologist

As Richard Burton's physical powers waned in the final decade of his life, he turned his still formidable intellectual energies to the study of sexual desire and its varied expressions and means of gratification. He took up the translation and publication of a genre of literature that many of his countrymen considered obscene. The first and most famous of these works was the *Kama Sutra,* the ancient Sanskrit guide to lovemaking that Burton and his collaborators were responsible for introducing to Western readers in 1883. It was followed by the *Ananga-Ranga* (1885), another Sanskrit sex manual, and *The Perfumed Garden* (1886), an Arabic text of similar intent. All were issued anonymously under the imprint of the Kama Shastra Society, a fictive organization that served in combination with other publishing stratagems and subterfuges to protect its producers from legal prosecution. In one instance, however, Burton proudly proclaimed his responsibility for a work suffused with explicit sexuality; by so doing, he deliberately provoked a confrontation with those forces in British society he associated with moral intolerance and intellectual pedantry. Unlikely though it might seem, the instrument of this provocation was a work widely regarded as children's literature—the tales of the Arabian Nights. In 1885–86 Burton published a ten-volume translation of the tales, *The Book of the Thousand Nights and a Night,* followed in 1886–1888 by an additional six-volume *Supplemental Nights.* The mammoth scale of the project was matched by its audacity. Burton not only offered an English-language reading public the first frank and unexpurgated translation of the tales themselves, but also peppered the text with footnotes about esoteric aspects of Islamic culture, especially sexual customs, and closed the tenth volume with a "Terminal Essay" that included a lengthy discourse on homosexuality across time and cultures. This quixotic enterprise thrust Burton into the middle of an intersecting network of debates about sexuality and purity, state regulation and personal freedom, the Occident and the Orient.

The late Victorian crisis of identity serves as a crucial backdrop for Burton's enterprise, informing his motives for undertaking these erotic translations and shaping the controversial reception they received. This crisis was characterized by the disintegration of the high Victorian moral and cultural consensus, and it occurred in conjunction with a growing public consciousness of the non-Western world.[1] The so-called new imperialism of the late nineteenth century, which fueled an unprecedented expansion in the reach of the British empire, brought that empire to the attention of the British public as never before.[2] The Muslim lands of North Africa became a special focus of parliamentary debates and press headlines as the British occupied Egypt in 1882 and the messianic General Charles "Chinese" Gordon died in the Sudan in 1885, "martyred" at the hands of Islamic fundamentalists in the opinion of his mourners. Orientalism acquired a new life in this context, reasserting its long-lasting associations with imperial power, but also serving as a source of inspiration for English men and women who sought an outlet for dissatisfaction with their own society.[3]

For Burton, this renewed interest in Orientalist concerns brought him full circle, returning him to his intellectual roots while allowing him to recast them for new purposes.[4] These purposes were related only secondarily to the "Oriental" world. Burton was above all intent on deploying his Orientalist knowledge and the perspective it provided to resist and subvert what he regarded as one of the central tenets of Victorianism, its repression of sexual knowledge. In so doing, he helped to give rise to two related strands of British modernism, one traceable in the transition from a moral to a psychological view of sexuality, the other marked by the embrace of instinct and emotion as a means of liberation.

༺ ❧ ༻

From his earliest years in India, Burton exhibited an abiding and unabashed interest in the manifold expressions of human sexuality. His ethnographic study *Sindh and the Races That Inhabit the Valley of the Indus* (1851) included discussions of aphrodisiacs, courtesans, and Sindhi matrimonial guides such as the *Lawful Enjoyment of Women,* a work that included a chapter he described as "quite unfit for the perusal of the fair sex."[5] Wherever he traveled thereafter, he studied the sexual practices of the local peoples, particularly when they contrasted with Western norms. Among the various customs connected to sexuality that attracted his attention were polygamy, male and female circumcision, prostitution, abortion, eunuchism, and phallic worship. British obscenity laws prevented him from discussing most of these matters in anything other than the most vague and euphemistic terms; when he tried to speak openly about them, he was censored.[6] Hence his interest in the Anthropological Society and the Cannibal Club derived in large measure from the opportunity they presented to engage in a frank and free discussion of sexuality.

Burton also had a personal appreciation for those publications that British law deemed pornographic. His close friend Monckton Milnes had collected what was reputed to be the largest library of pornography in Britain at his country estate, Fryston, and Burton perused its shelves during his frequent visits.[7] He was familiar as well with the formidable collection amassed by Henry Spencer Ashbee, author of the *Index Librorum Prohibitorum* (1877) and several other Latin-titled volumes that gave summary accounts of this subterranean world of erotic literature.[8] What forced this literature into subterranean channels was the Obscene Publications Act of 1857, which permitted authorities to issue warrants in search of pornographic publications and imposed harsh penalties on those found guilty of purveying them.[9] A few British publishers and booksellers continued to skirt the law, most notably John Camden Hotten, who, in addition to conducting an underground trade in pornography, issued Swinburne's *Poems and Ballads: First Series* (1865) after its original publisher withdrew the work for fear of prosecution. For the most part, however, the production of pornographic literature and images was driven abroad, mainly to Paris and Rotterdam, where dealers continued to cater to British customers through the postal system and private channels. Parliament responded with the Customs Consolidation Act of 1876, which prohibited the importation of obscene materials, but smugglers managed to find ways to circumvent its restrictions. Milnes's main supplier was a British expatriate in Paris named Frederick Hankey, a strange figure whose erotic tastes ran along de Sadean lines. Burton met Hankey through Milnes. When Burton was sent as a British emissary in 1863 to the West African kingdom of Dahomey, where the rivers were reputed to flow with the blood of human sacrifices, Hankey evidently asked him to acquire the skin of an African woman. This says all that needs to be said about Hankey's disturbed psyche, and although we do not have Burton's response to Hankey himself, the jocular remarks he made to Milnes show that he was prepared to play to, if not act on, the sadistic fantasies of his friend. "Poor Hankey must still wait for his peau de femme," he reported to Milnes, explaining that Dahomey did not quite live up to its fearsome reputation.[10]

This incident has been offered into evidence as proof that a "combination of imperialism, sadism, and sexism" suffused the erotic interests of pornography's British patrons after mid-century.[11] By this reckoning, Burton and his circle of friends were the poster boys for a new kind of pornography that sought intercourse with power and prejudice. Although they created a scientific veneer for their prurient interests, providing a scholarly apparatus of references, footnotes, and Latin terminology for the pornographic material they collected, catalogued, and printed, the purpose of their scrutiny, it has been argued, was to objectify women and nonwhite peoples, to naturalize them as intrinsically inferior. They sought to legitimate their colonizing desires through the language of science, using it to advance a pornographic agenda that was underwritten by the erotic appeal of power.

If we grant that individual tastes and interests are informed by larger social and ideological forces, then it is reasonable to assume that widely held Victorian attitudes regarding race, gender, and other categories of difference would leave their mark on the pornographic preoccupations of Burton and his circle. Sexual desire is no less shaped by the values of the society within which it finds expression than are other forms of human behavior, as Burton himself readily acknowledged. The argument advanced in the preceding paragraph, however, runs the risk of projecting contemporary preoccupations onto the past, giving anachronistic emphasis to impulses and intentions that may have been peripheral to pornography's appeal to Burton. It also imposes an overly determined reading onto some ambiguous and rather circumstantial evidence. Burton's association with Hankey, for example, does not prove that he shared the latter's sadistic proclivities: we know, in fact, that he regarded the works of de Sade as "monstrous" and was appalled by the sadistic cruelties he observed in Dahomey.[12] Nor did his actions conform to the conventional patterns of allegiance to an imperial racism: most of his British contemporaries, for example, would have been shocked to learn that his gifts to the king of Dahomey had included "three very degagé coloured prints of white women in a state of eve-ical toilette," which reversed the regular flow of traffic in cross-racial pornography and subverted the standard conviction that imperial authority rested on the symbolic importance of the white woman's sexual inaccessibility to black men.[13] The larger problem that these facts pose for the charge that Burton's interest in pornography was infused with "imperialism, sadism, and sexism" is its presumption that these categories are unproblematic and transparent. To attach such tags to the erotic interests of Burton and his coterie does little to explain how these men in their desire for sexual titillation deployed notions of race and gender and power differently from their antagonists, whose efforts to suppress pornography were in fact overlaid with much the same panoply of prejudices. We need a more nuanced reading of the various ways these ideas and practices intersected with one another, making it possible for shared discourses regarding race and the like to appear in markedly different registers. An examination of the varied uses made of Orientalism by Burton and his critics will help to substantiate this point.

Furthermore, we need to distinguish more carefully between the public production and private consumption of pornography. The powers of the law were directed against the former, not the latter. Men like Milnes and Ashbee could acquire large collections of pornography with little or no risk of prosecution by authorities because their activities occurred within their own homes, private domains that were outside the purview of the limited Victorian state. Similarly, so long as Burton's interest in pornography was purely personal, the only constraints it confronted were those that derived from governmental efforts to squeeze supply. But once Burton turned from a consumer to a producer of work that collided with the obscenity standards of the day, he placed himself knowingly in legal harm's way. Why he chose to do so requires explanation if we are to fully understand what purposes such literature served for him. The publication in the 1880s of the *Kama Sutra* and his other openly erotic projects presents us with abundant evidence of the aims, attitudes, and assumptions that underwrote his engagement with pornography.[14] By giving careful scrutiny to the contents of these works, the considerations that motivated their production, and the environment within which they were issued, we can gain greater insight into the social and political issues that Burton believed to be at stake in the late Victorian debate about sexuality and obscenity. His willingness to launch such a legally risky undertaking as the Kama Shastra Society's series of publications reflected his determination to challenge prevailing social norms regarding sexuality, rejecting the prudery and silence that characterized the public stance toward the subject. He presented the *Kama Sutra,* the *Ananga-Ranga,* the *Perfumed Garden,* and the *Thousand Nights* as evidence of the superior sexual knowledge of other cultures, which recognized that women had sexual needs, men had sexual responsibilities, and sexuality itself had varied avenues of expression, including same-sex love; and he portrayed his translations of these works as means to the emotional liberation of his countrymen—and women.

No examination of Burton's cross-cultural inquiries into sexuality can proceed, of course, without some consideration of his personal sexual proclivities. This issue has preoccupied biographers ever since Fawn Brodie advanced the view in *The Devil Drives* (1967) that Burton had bisexual or homosexual proclivities, a claim given even greater emphasis in Frank McLynn's *Burton: Snow on the Desert* (1990). Mary Lovell has taken the contrary position in her recent *Rage to Live* (1998), insisting that Burton was a confirmed heterosexual and loving husband who simply showed a "scientific" interest in homosexuality. In contrast to the problem that confronts the biographers of most Victorians, it is not the dearth of evidence about Burton's private life that has fueled this debate, but rather its diverse and contradictory character. Burton is remarkably frank in his published writings about his sexual adventures. His first book, *Goa, and the Blue Mountains,* includes a picaresque account of his visit to the village of Seroda, famed for its *bayaderes,* dancing girls who often served as prostitutes.[15] The profusion of appreciative references to women he encountered in his subsequent travels leaves little doubt that he enjoyed their favors wherever he could. One example will suffice: tucked into his report to the Royal Geographical Society on the East African expedition is the comment that the Wagogo "women are well disposed towards strangers of fair complexion, apparently with the permission of their husbands."[16] Some biographers have doubted whether Richard and Isabel Burton enjoyed a healthy physical relationship, but they have found little to support such doubts beyond a report or two of quarrels between the couple and the absence of any children or indications of pregnancy during their marriage. Yet one telling and poignant page in a scrapbook that Isabel filled with her personal medical prescriptions is headed, "Pills supposed to make people have children."[17]

There also are indications, however, that Richard was attracted to men and may have had sexual relations with them. Much of the evidence is admittedly ambiguous and open to the danger of misreading homosociality for homosexuality. Victorian culture tended to segregate men and women into separate social spheres, encouraging a level of intimacy among members of the same sex that would be interpreted in our society as evidence of homosexual feelings, but that rarely carried such connotations in the nineteenth century. It was natural for men to socialize in the exclusive company of other men. Still, it is striking how frequently Burton established close and lasting relationships with single younger men, among them Algernon Swinburne, Charles Tyrwhitt-Drake, Verney Lovett Cameron, and Foster Fitzgerald Arbuthnot (though the latter two married late in life). Moreover, Burton's testimony in the *Nights* about his investigation of the boy brothels of Karachi in the 1840s hints at his involvement in same-sex intercourse. Finally, we have a remarkable letter written in 1875 by Swinburne, who refers to "that lost love of Burton's, the beloved and blue object of his Central African affections, whose caudal charms and simious seductions were too strong for the narrow laws of Levitical or Mosaic prudery which would confine the jewel of a man to the lotus of a merely human female by the most odious and unnatural of priestly restrictions."[18] Given how close Swinburne was to Burton and what we know about Swinburne's own homosexuality, it is difficult to deny that this letter, however ambiguous in its particulars, suggests that Burton had engaged in sexual activities his society would have deemed deviant.

So where does this evidence leave us? Perhaps it suggests that the efforts to determine whether Burton's inclinations were heterosexual or homosexual are framed around a false dichotomy. We might make better sense of our man if we acknowledge that Burton's curiosity about sexual matters, like his curiosity about so many other aspects of human experience, simply could not be contained within a single channel of expression.

꙳ꙮ꙳ꙮ꙳ꙮ꙳

Burton's involvement in the publication of the *Kama Sutra* and other erotic works had its origins in his friendship with Foster Fitzgerald Arbuthnot, a member of the Bombay Civil Service and a student of Indian and Persian literature. The two men most likely met in 1854, when Burton returned to Bombay after his pilgrimage to Mecca. They soon discovered that they shared a common interest in the subcontinent's classical treatises on lovemaking, and they began to make plans to translate and publish some of them. The initiative in launching these projects came from Arbuthnot, with Burton content to play a more modest advisory and editorial role—until, that is, their decision to found the Kama Shastra Society in the early 1880s provided the impetus for what became his personal campaign against the forces of moral purity.

The two collaborators faced several problems in producing English editions of India's erotic literature. The first was that neither of them knew classical Sanskrit. This problem was more easily surmounted in the case of the *Ananga-Ranga,* a fifteenth- or sixteenth-century work written in fairly simple Sanskrit and available in several modern Indian-language translations, than it would become when they later confronted the *Kama Sutra.* Arbuthnot either obtained a preexisting Hindustani translation of the *Ananga-Ranga* or hired a local Indian pundit to translate a Sanskrit copy into Hindustani or English. He also may have drawn on the assistance of Edward Rehatsek, an eccentric Hungarian living in Bombay who had devoted decades to the study of Indian languages and literatures.[19] In 1873, while on furlough in England, Arbuthnot delivered the manuscript to Burton, who polished the prose.[20] Three years later, when Burton made his valedictory visit to India, the two men turned their attention to the *Kama Sutra*, a third-century Sanskrit text that had served as the model for the *Ananga-Ranga* and several similar works. Arbuthnot hired Bhugwuntlal Indraji, an authority on classical Sanskrit who had assisted in the translation of the *Laws of Manu* and various other texts for European Orientalists, to collect and compare various copies of the Sanskrit manuscript and prepare a composite translation. With the assistance of Shivaram Parshuram Bhide, a student at the University of Bombay who was well versed in Sanskrit and English, Indraji produced the text that Arbuthnot supplied to Burton.[21] Rehatsek again may have played an unacknowledged role in the enterprise. Although Burton is identified in modern reprints of the *Kama Sutra* as its translator, his contribution was limited to polishing the English text, adding some annotations, and perhaps authoring or coauthoring the preface.

The second problem confronting Burton and Arbuthnot was how to bring the translated works into print in the face of the Obscene Publications Act. Burton must have been contemplating a solution to this problem when in 1872 he broached the idea of a "General Translation Fund" that would be financed by a thousand men, each contributing an annual subscription of a guinea. It is not known how this proposal, which appeared in the *Athenaeum*'s letter column, was received, though those who responded were very likely added to a list of potential subscribers to Burton and Arbuthnot's project.[22] The following year the two men tried to publish the *Ananga-Ranga* (under the title *Kama Shastra*), only to have the printer get cold feet and suspend production after a few proof copies had come off the press.[23] A decade later Burton approached John Payne, a noted Arabist who was preparing to publish his translation of the Arabian Nights through private subscription, to ask "advice about publishing" on behalf of "my friend F. F. Arbuthnot," who "has undertaken a peculiar branch of Literature—the Hindu Erotic which promises well."[24] Burton represents himself in this letter as an intermediary for a friend, perhaps in part to minimize his own involvement, though his remarks also confirm that Arbuthnot was still the leader in their enterprise.[25] Nearly six months later, Burton informed Payne that Arbuthnot "has founded a Society consisting of himself and myself. The idea is Rabelaesian." Soon thereafter he revealed the name of their new society—the "Hindu Kama Shastra (Aro Amoris) Society."[26] These revelations were the first clues as to how they intended to evade obscenity charges—in effect, through a corporate variation of the personal alias or disguise that Burton had so often adopted over the course of his career.

Isabel Burton revealed after Richard's death that the Kama Shastra Society of London and Benares, as the sponsoring entity was identified on the title pages of the *Kama Sutra* and other works, was "a bogie name . . . invented by my husband in my presence with 2 other men [Arbuthnot and Milnes] and many a laugh they had over it for the purpose of puzzling people when they wished to bring out any book that was not for the drawing room table."[27] Whatever amusement this deception may have given them, its main purpose was deeply serious. Their fictive society, along with its equally fictive place of publication (Cosmopoli), served to mask their identity, protecting themselves and their printer from prosecution. They also followed the lead of Payne in marketing their publications through the mail by private subscription, thereby bypassing the legally vulnerable retail book trade. The first of their translations to appear under the imprint of the Kama Shastra Society was the *Kama Sutra* in 1883; the *Ananga-Ranga* followed in 1885. A year later saw the publication of *The Perfumed Garden*.[28] Unlike its Indian counterparts, this work derived from a sixteenth-century Arabic manuscript of Tunisian origin that a French officer had discovered and translated in the mid-nineteenth century. Also unlike the prior publications of the Kama Shastra Society, this one was translated by Burton alone, though in the absence of access to the Arabic manuscript he relied on the French-language edition.[29] In conjunction with his translation of the tales of the Arabian Nights, which was published between 1885 and 1888, *The Perfumed Garden* marked a turning point, as the enterprise he had hitherto served in a secondary role now became his governing obsession. He came to see these publications not merely as contributions to an erotic literary genre that offered titillation to men like himself, but as evidence of a superior sexual knowledge that offered freedom to a society afflicted by emotional repression. What had been the source of private amusement became the basis for a public crusade.

Burton's change of heart came at a critical moment in the cultural crisis of Victorianism. British society in the mid-1880s was in the throes of a "moral panic," generated in large part by the appearance of a series of public "narratives of sexual danger."[30] The most sensational of these were the lurid press coverage of Jack the Ripper's mutilation-murders of women in London's East End and W. T. Stead's dramatic exposé of child prostitution, "The Maiden Tribute of Modern Babylon," published in the *Pall Mall Gazette* in 1885.[31] Other indicators of the heightened attention paid to sexuality as a source of peril included the divorce scandal in 1886 that scuttled the political career of Sir Charles Dilke, a potential successor to Gladstone as leader of the Liberal Party, and in the same year the triumphant conclusion to the long campaign by Josephine Butler to repeal the Contagious Diseases (CD) Acts, which both critics and supporters interpreted in terms of sexual danger, though they differed over whether the acts heightened or reduced that danger.[32]

Even as the repeal of the CD Acts reduced the state's powers of intervention in one realm of sexuality, the passage of the Criminal Law Amendment Act in 1885 expanded its powers in others. Drafted in response to the public outcry caused by Stead's revelations about child prostitution, the new legislation raised the age of sexual consent for females and outlawed the procurement of women for prostitution, while the attached Labouchére Amendment imposed criminal penalties for sex between males. The Society for the Suppression of Vice and the National Vigilance Association (the former founded in 1802, the latter in 1884) became important agents in the enforcement of the act, launching their own private investigations and prosecutions while pressing authorities to suppress brothels, shut down ribald shows, and target the purveyors of erotic literature. In one of the most notorious cases to arise out of this prosecutorial climate, the British publisher Henry Vizetelly was sentenced to three months in prison in 1889 for translating and publishing several of Emile Zola's novels.[33]

Burton's actions were inextricably entwined with these events. He had long expressed dismay at the straitened moral climate in Britain, often making mocking reference to Mrs. Grundy, the fictitious symbol of British propriety and priggishness.[34] Two years after his initial attempt to publish the *Ananga-Ranga (Kama Shastra)* had fallen victim to the printer's fear of prosecution, a blistering attack on the forces represented by Mrs. Grundy appeared in Isabel Burton's *Inner Life of Syria* (1875). "Mrs. Grundy," a key passage proclaimed, was "a creature of Lucifer's. . . . She perverts England. . . . She is a cloak to cover vice; she is servile, vicious, venomous, and hypocritical. . . . To please her so-called delicate sensibilities, everybody must write as if they were ten years old."[35] Burton often colluded with his wife to present his words and opinions under her name—effectively another form of ventriloquism—and this outburst bears all the hallmarks of such a stratagem, giving a female voice to his frustration with the legal and social intimidation that had prevented the publication of the *Ananga-Ranga*.

By the early 1880s Burton had become even more dismayed by the purity forces' influence on British society. In 1882 he wrote to Payne: "Mrs Grundy is beginning to roar: already I hear the fire of her. And I know her to be an arrant whore and tell her so and don't care a damn for her." This bellicose tone reflected his growing determination to take a stand against censorship. Burton declared at one point that "if they [the purity forces] want a fight they can have it" and on another occasion announced that he aimed to tread on Mrs. Grundy's corn and cause her to "howl on her big bum to her heart's content."[36] There is more than a touch of misogyny in these remarks, which represent the purity movement as a fat female scold. They also indicate, however, that Burton knew his enemy. Despite the visibility of male spokesmen like W. T. Stead, middle-class women provided most of the organizational muscle for the purity campaign, which was an important aspect of the late Victorian feminist movement. Moreover, whatever derogatory gender stereotypes Burton may have played upon, these should be measured against the purity campaigners' own melodramatic rhetoric, which portrayed their purpose as the protection of defenseless women from the lascivious designs of ruthless men.[37] Both sides, then, framed the debate around stereotypical images of women, who assumed whatever characteristics served to advance the objectives of the contending parties.

Burton was itching for a fight with the moral purity campaign. He also realized, however, that the obscenity laws would ensure his defeat if he tried to use sex manuals like the *Kama Sutra* and *The Perfumed Garden* as his cause célèbre. He had to find another way to bring his concerns and convictions to public attention; he found what he was seeking in the tales of the Arabian Nights.

⁘⁘⁘⁘⁘

In his foreword to the *Thousand Nights,* Burton alludes to the circumstances that led him to undertake a new translation of the tales. He originally turned to the *Nights,* he states, as "a talisman against ennui and despondency" during his "long years of official banishment" from England. Translating the tales, he explained, provided a sense of release from his "dull and commonplace" consular duties, an imaginative outlet that made the "most fantastic flights of fancy, the wildest improbabilities, the most impossible of impossibilities, appear . . . utterly natural, mere matters of every-day occurrence." These remarks seem to characterize the tales in stereotypical Orientalist terms, representing them as escapist fantasies standing in opposition to the Western realm of reason and respectability, offering emotional respite from its exactions. But Burton gives his interest in the *Nights* an unexpected twist. Their appeal to him derives not merely from their exotic qualities, but from their access to truths that his own society does not wish to acknowledge. Burton concedes that, "professionally speaking, I was not a success." Yet he attributes his blighted consular career not to any failings of his own, but to "a despotism of the lower 'middle-class' Philister who can pardon anything but superiority." By drawing this connection between his own career and the *Nights,* Burton makes it clear that he regards his translation as an oblique commentary on his own society, a critique of the reign of mediocrity that prevents the advance of anyone "who knows more or who does more than the mob of gentlemen-employés who know very little and who do even less." His prodi-

His health deteriorating and his career stalled, Burton threw himself into a series of literary projects in the 1880s. This painting by Albert Letchford, copied from a photograph by Burton's doctor, shows him at work in his Trieste study. Courtesy of the Orleans House Gallery, Twickenham.

gious literary endeavor is intended to show that he does in fact know more and do more than his countrymen.[38]

This determination, as he sees it, to tell truth to power, is the impetus behind the most important and controversial aspect of Burton's translation, its treatment of the tales in an "unconventionally free and naked manner" that will stand against the morally straitened, intellectually timid climate of opinion that the middle-class mob has imposed on British society. Anticipating charges of "grossness and indecency, in fact *les turpitudes*," Burton establishes his defense on the philosophical grounds he had been preparing for several decades: cultural and historical relativism. Accusations of obscenity, he insisted, are "matters of time and place." Hence "what is offensive in England is not so in Egypt" and what is coarse in the *Nights* "will not be found in this matter coarser than many passages of Shakspeare [*sic*], Sterne, and Swift." Burton does not limit the use of relativism to the defense of his translation; he turns it into a weapon against the West itself. What the contrast to the culture of the *Nights* reveals about the West is its "innocence of the word not of the thought; morality of the tongue not of the heart." Burton's intent was not merely to defend the basic "purity" of the *Nights,* but to expose the "perfect hypocrisy" of his own society.[39]

Burton's *Nights* made its debut with a reading public that for the most part was familiar with the tales of the Arabian Nights as children's literature. Antoine Galland's famous early eighteenth-century French translation, which brought the tales to the notice of European audiences, had been the basis for the many English-language editions that generations of British readers had grown up with.[40] Geared for a general audience, these variations of Galland left out many of the bawdier tales and toned down the language and subject matter of the remaining ones. Nevertheless, the work had made its mark on the imagination of the Romantic poets, as well as Tennyson, Dickens, and many other mid-Victorian writers. The tales also attracted the interest of the British East India Company, which in 1814–1818 issued the first printed edition of an Arabic text source (known as the Shirwanee or Calcutta I text) as a study tool for officials learning Arabic, followed by a second version drawn from a much larger set of source texts (Macnaghten or Calcutta II) in 1839–1842. These years also saw the publication of the first important English translation from the original Arabic by Edward Lane, who relied mainly on another version of the text (Bulaq) that the Egyptian government had printed in 1835. His three-volume edition won praise for its extensive annotations about Egyptian life and culture, but, like Galland, he left out various tales and bowdlerized others, which drew the ire of Burton. When John Payne turned his attention to the *Nights* in the early 1880s, many of the tales known to Arabic scholars still had not appeared in English. Payne's ten-volume translation, published in 1882–1884, went some distance toward rectifying that neglect, and its lyrical use of language was much admired.[41] Burton, however, complained that Payne too was "'drawing it very mild,'" tempering those coarser passages that he viewed as essential elements of the tales.[42] Once Payne's limited edition of a thousand per volume had appeared in print and proven a financial success, Burton publicly announced that he intended to produce a new translation of the *Nights* for sale by subscription.

When Burton actually started his translation is unclear, though there is little doubt that he first became acquainted with the tales in their unexpurgated form while he was serving as an officer in India. Mary Lovell suspects that he and Dr. John Steinhaueser, a friend from the Indian army, talked about collaborating on a translation as early as 1854.[43] In *First Footsteps in East Africa* (1856), Burton observed that even though the Arabian Nights was one of the "most familiar of books in England, next to the Bible, it is one of the least known, the reason being that about one-fifth is utterly unfit for translation; and the most sanguine Orientalist would not dare to render literally more than three-quarters of the remainder."[44] Already he was aware of the gulf in moral standards that separated the original tales from the sanitized version known to the West. By the mid-1860s his interest in and qualifications for translating the tales was well known to colleagues in the Anthropological Society: several of them publicly urged him to undertake the project in order to restore the "interesting anthropological information, which was omitted from the English editions, as not being considered proper for general reading," assuring him that such an endeavor "would be conferring a great boon on science."[45] By 1871 he had already translated at least a few of the tales, which he showed to a visitor in Damascus.[46]

It is clear, then, that this project had been germinating for years before Burton's public announcement in the early 1880s that he intended to publish a translation of the *Nights*. By the same token, this long-standing ambition came to fruition at a moment in the cultural history of Britain that ensured the work an attentive reception, appearing as it did when interest in Orientalist subjects and anxiety about sexual matters had reached new heights. The translation Burton brought into print in the mid-1880s stood apart from its predecessors not merely because of its massive scale (it included seventy-eight more tales than Payne's version, the next-longest translation), but because of its determination to include material that other translators had considered too offensive to expose to Western readers and to explicate its ethnographic meaning in an encyclopedic array of annotations, many of them concerned with sexual practices.[47] Burton was well aware that his endeavor would stir controversy; his contrarian spirit welcomed it. Just as he had applauded Swinburne for "bruising the head of British virtue" some years earlier, so now he intended to do some bruising of his own.[48]

Still, Burton took care to protect himself from legal jeopardy. He retained the services of Sir George Lewis, a prominent solicitor familiar with obscenity law. He sold the *Nights* through private subscription, relying largely on the lists of potential customers gathered through marketing the *Kama Sutra*. His prospectus warned that the work was "emphatically a book for men and students [of Muslim society]; and nothing could be more repugnant to the translator's feelings than the idea of these pages being placed in any other hands than the class for whose especial use it has been prepared."[49] The unmistakable message was *buyer beware*. When the volumes appeared, they carried the fictive imprint of the Kama Shastra Society (though Waterlow and Sons was the actual publisher), and the place of publication was identified as Benares (though printing occurred in Stoke Newington.) The principal difference between the *Nights* and Burton's other excursions into the subterranean world in erotic literature was that this publication was not issued anonymously—Burton placed his name proudly and prominently on the title page.

If Burton's abandonment of anonymity was in one respect a well-merited expression of pride in his accomplishment, it also was a declaration of war against the proponents of purity. He understood that his action exposed him to genuine risks, which he dramatized with a warning to his sister and niece that the book might be burned.[50] Even before the *Nights* had been sent to subscribers, the *Printing Times and Lithographer* declared that "the work, although published by subscription, is likely enough to be pronounced 'an injury to public morals,' to the danger of [Burton] himself."[51] A member of Parliament was quoted in a National Vigilance Association publication as expressing concern about the morality of the work.[52] No sooner had the first volume made its appearance than it sparked intense reaction in the press. The public debate that ensued reveals a great deal about the uses of Orientalism in late Victorian Britain.

Criticism of the *Nights* came from various quarters. *The Echo* declared that Burton "has produced a morally filthy book. What might have been acceptable to Asiatic populations ages ago is absolutely unfit for Christian populations of the nineteenth century."[53] The *Edinburgh Review* described the notes that accompanied the work as "an appalling collection of degrading customs and statistics of vice." Comparing Burton's translation to previous versions, it recommended "Galland for the nursery, Lane for the library, Payne for the study, and Burton for the sewers."[54] Foremost among Burton's antagonists, however, was W. T. Stead's *Pall Mall Gazette,* the leading organ of the purity campaign. Fresh from its "Maiden Tribute" triumph, it first alerted readers to the dangers of the *Nights* in a notice that appeared under the leader "Pantagruelism or Pornography?" Written under the pseudonym of Sigma by John Morley, Stead's predecessor as editor of the *Gazette* and a leading Liberal member of Parliament, the piece condemning Burton's translation as "one of the grossest . . . books in the English language" and warned that it would find its way into the hands of "unripe youth, unsuspecting maidens" and other innocents ignorant of its contents. As if to confirm this warning, the *Gazette* reported that copies of the book could be found for sale in certain London bookshops, where market considerations could be presumed to predominate over moral ones when customers called. In the editorial opinion of the *Gazette,* the *Nights* was a "revolting obscenity" that "formed part of the garbage of the brothel." Sigma seconded this verdict, referring in a follow-up piece to "Captain Burton's Oriental muck heap."[55]

This jeer is indicative of the way Burton's critics drew on Orientalist discourses to articulate their objections to the work.

They did not challenge Burton's claims of expertise about his subject; rather, they charged that the subject itself was unworthy of study because it reflected the debased morality of an inferior, decadent civilization. Like all variants of Orientalism, theirs derived from the delineation of difference, the difference that religion and custom and historical experience imposed on the other. They expressed this difference in various ways: that Oriental societies lacked the sensitivities regarding women that obtained in European society; that the Oriental present stood at an evolutionary stage comparable to a European past. But the defining point of these differences for Burton's critics was reducible to the moral dimension. What they saw as the licentiousness of Islamic society lay at the core of their complaints about Burton's literary and ethnographic endeavor.

Burton, however, was not without his supporters. Some of the *Gazette*'s competitors had been dismayed by the sensationalism—and the success—of its purity campaign, and they came to the defense of the *Nights* for reasons that had as much to do with concerns about the threat of censorship as they did with the intellectual or artistic merits of the translation itself. One of the *Gazette*'s foremost critics, *The Standard*, professed the *Nights* to be "exceptionally high and pure" by comparison with the "vicious suggestion and false sentiment that pervade . . . the modern romantic school."[56] Like Burton, it claimed that the Arabian tales were no cruder than Rabelais, Boccaccio, Shakespeare, Swift, and other giants of European literature. *The Morning Advertiser,* whose editors were friends of Burton, applauded his effort to retrieve the tales from the "namby-pambyism" of children's literature, insisting that "what we would call [the *Nights*'] impropriety is only a reflection of the *naive* freedom with which talk is to this day carried on in the family circles of the East."[57] Expressions of support also appeared in the correspondence columns of various periodicals. Sigma's diatribe provoked responses from an "Anglo-Egyptian" who defended the *Nights* as a repository of Orientalist knowledge "to be conscientiously sought by all who are either administrators or philanthropists in Egypt," and from a "Public School Master" who took the position that the "licentiousness of language and life . . . [was] inseparable from Orientals."[58] The *Academy*, the high-brow weekly with which Burton was closely associated, published several letters in defense of the *Nights*, notably one by the poet and critic John Addington Symonds, who was not yet personally acquainted with Burton. Though commenting that Burton's translation "sometimes . . . transgresses the unwritten laws of artistic harmony," Symonds praised the work for its "peculiar literary vigour, exact scholarship, and rare insight into Oriental modes of thoughts and feeling" and objected to the hypocrisy of "our middle-class *censores morum* [who] strain at the gnat of a privately circulated translation of an Arabic classic, while they daily swallow the camel of higher education based upon minute study of Greek and Latin literature."[59]

Burton's champions made their own uses of Orientalism in their defense of the *Nights*, uses that were varied in intent. One was the functionalist claim that the *Nights* offered insights into Islamic society that the British would find beneficial in their role as imperial overlords of Egypt, India, and other Muslim lands. Burton himself had justified his efforts in terms of the West's need for knowledge of the Orient in order to rule it effectively. Observing that Britain "is at present the greatest Mohammedan empire in the world," he insisted that his explanatory notes were intended to "teach us to deal successfully" with those Muslim subjects.[60]

A second and related argument defended the coarseness of

Burton's translation as a reflection of the coarseness of Islamic life, giving an unblinkered glimpse into the secret world of a less civilized culture. There was not much difference between this stance and the one advanced by critics regarding the inferiority of the civilization represented in the *Nights*. Where it diverged was its insistence that important insights could be gained from greater knowledge of this unfamiliar world. These insights were not limited to the Orient: they could be turned against the West, providing a vantage point from which the over-refined, hypocritical character of English society could be scrutinized and criticized.

What linked these arguments with one another was their emphasis on the essential otherness of the society portrayed in the *Nights*. This appeared inconsistent with another line of defense, one framed around the universalist claim that the objections raised against the *Nights* also could be raised against some of the greatest works of Western literature. This argument implicitly challenged the distinctions between Western and Oriental sensibilities. It relied instead on a distinction between the lusty frankness of classic Western literature and its insipid modern counterparts. Once again, however, a major aim was to criticize the moral standards of modern English society by juxtaposing them with the standards of another time or place.

The final word on the controversy over the *Nights* came from Burton himself. "The Biography of the Book and Its Reviewers Reviewed," a lengthy essay appended to the concluding volume of the *Supplemental Nights*, was the sort of rebuttal that every author dreams of writing in response to his or her critics.[61] The *Pall Mall Gazette*, Burton declared, "works more active and permanent damage to public morals than books and papers which are frankly gross and indecent," while its editor, W. T. Stead, "has apparently still to learn that lying and slandering are neither Christian nor chivalrous." The author of the *Edinburgh Review*'s critique of the *Nights* "must be prurient and lecherous as a dog-faced baboon in rut to have aught of passion excited by" the translation. The National Vigilance Association was "a troop of busybodies captained by licenced blackmailers."[62]

For all its gibes, however, Burton's essay is much more than a diatribe against his critics. It is also a perceptive and pungently expressed critique of the consequences of prudery in British life. Burton's argument is a profoundly modern one: it charges that civilization breeds repression and repression breeds perversion. "Respectability unmakes what Nature made," he asserts aphoristically. His analysis is framed around an Orientalist juxtaposition of civilization and savagery. "Among savages and barbarians," he claims, "the comparatively unrestrained intercourse between men and women relieves the brain through the body; the mind and memory have scant reason . . . to dwell fondly on visions amatory and venereal, to live in a 'rustle of (imaginary) copulation.'" By contrast, "the utterly artificial life of civilisation . . . leaves the many, whose lot is celibacy, no bodily want save one and that in a host of cases either unattainable or procurable only by difficulty and danger. Hence the prodigious amount of mental excitement and material impurity which is found wherever civilisation extends." What raises his ire against the *Pall Mall Gazette* is that it "deliberately pimps and panders to this latent sense and state of aphrodisiac excitement." The *Gazette* and its allies actually "advertise what they condemn," thereby enhancing its market value. This ironic state of affairs is ultimately traceable to the determination in modern England to "bring up both sexes and keep all ages in profound ignorance of sexual and inter-sexual relations." Burton notes, for example, the Victorian use of euphemisms to refer to parts of the female body, which creates "a figure fit only to frighten crows." "Shall we ever understand," he sighs, "that ignorance is not innocence?"[63]

Burton saw himself as an agent of enlightenment. His Kama Shastra Society publications, from the *Kama Sutra* through the *Nights*, were intended to undermine what he regarded as the repressive moral regime that controlled public life in England. Though it would be anachronistic to attach the term Victorian to his representation of that regime, he was an early advocate of the modernist view that the forces of middle-class respectability had imposed their morally straitened, sexually shackling values on nineteenth-century British society. If the sexual attitudes of the British public were in fact a good deal more complex and varied than Burton acknowledged or appreciated, it is true that an anti-sensualism derived from evangelical Christianity held a prominent place in the ethos of the Victorians, and its influence seemed to critics like Burton to be on the rise in the highly charged social climate of the 1880s.[64] Burton saw himself as a missionary of sorts, preaching his gospel of sexual knowledge to the unenlightened, opening their eyes to the essential truths of the Orient. "On no wise ashamed am I of lecturing upon these esoteric matters, the most important to humanity," he proclaimed: "I venture to hold myself in the light of a public benefactor. In fact, I consider my labours as a legacy bequeathed to my countrymen."[65]

When Burton spoke of his *countrymen,* he probably meant the term to be understood in its gender-specific sense. Where women figured into his efforts at enlightenment was never entirely clear. On the one hand, he took an impish delight in suggesting that the women of England were eager to learn the "esoteric lore" revealed in the *Nights.*[66] On the other hand, he harbored real reservations about whether they should be permitted to peruse this sort of information. He did not want his niece to view the work, for example.[67] Even if he was pandering to authorities—and to prospective subscribers—with his claim that his version of the *Nights* was intended exclusively for male readers, he was sufficiently enmeshed in the Victorian doctrine of separate spheres to feel some unease about how much sexual knowledge was suitable for women.

Burton, then, was hardly immune to the hypocrisy he condemned in others. He kept aspects of his correspondence and writings on erotic subjects secret from his wife, yet she played a central role in the business side of his enterprise, soliciting subscribers, responding to queries, dealing with printers, mailing volumes.[68] She also knew a good deal more about the contents of his erotic publications than either of them was willing to acknowledge openly. "Richard wished that his men friends sh[oul]d think I did not know what he was engaged upon," Isabel later revealed, but "I cannot afford to be particular what words I *see*, nor do they do me any harm."[69] She shared his outrage at the influence of the purity campaigners, referring on one occasion to "that hideous humbug the Society for the Suppression of Vice."[70] And despite their public protestations that she never set eyes on the objectionable passages in the *Nights*, there is irrefutable proof that she played an active role in the expurgation of the text for *Lady Burton's Edition of Her Husband's Arabian Nights* (1886).[71] They marketed this six-volume bowdlerized version of Burton's *Nights* as one that would be suitable for female and juvenile readers, itself a claim that indicated ambivalence, if not outright hypocrisy, regarding what women should know about sexuality. In this respect, Burton's challenge to contemporary sexual mores was as indicative of Victorian values as any of his critics' efforts to defend those mores. "I never pretended to understand women," an unusually disarming Burton confessed in response to complaints about his representation of women in the *Nights*.[72] This belief that the sensibilities of women were beyond the ken of men set him in the mainstream of Victorian notions of gender difference.

Where Burton diverged from this mainstream was with regard to his views on the relative distribution of desire between men and women. In contrast to the dominant Victorian view of the male as the sexual predator and the female as the passive and often passionless partner, he believed that the "passions and the sexual powers of the females greatly exceed those of their males."[73] Although this perception of female sexuality had been widespread in British culture through the Georgian era, it became suppressed as the bourgeois ideal of female respectability—the angel in the home—assumed predominance among the Victorians: insofar as the earlier view survived, it was largely displaced onto the lower classes and foreign peoples as another marker of difference.[74] Burton most likely became aware of this alternative tradition by reading the folklore, poetry, and prescriptive literature of Sindh, which became his gateway to the larger world of Islamic social practices and beliefs. His translation of the *Nights* is replete with references to the sexual voracity of women. "Egyptians hold, and justly enough, that their women are more amorous than men," Burton declares in one of his provocative footnotes. In another he claims that "the venereal requirements and reproductive powers of the female greatly exceed those of the male," especially in "hot-damp climates" such as Egypt, Persia, Malabar, and, curiously enough, California.[75]

This nod toward climatic determinism has been taken as evidence that Burton constructed an Orientalist interpretation of desire, equating the Muslim world in particular with a realm of unrestrained sexuality. One critic, Rana Kabbani, has charged that the "Orient for Burton was chiefly an illicit space and its women convenient chattels who offered sexual gratification denied in the Victorian home for its unseemliness." This "myth of the erotic East," she argues, expressed the patriarchal urge to free itself from the constraints of female will and social propriety.[76] Though Burton does indeed draw on Orientalist stereotypes in his representation of the women of the Islamic world, his purpose is entirely at odds with Kabbani's interpretation. He vigorously objects to the view that such women are chattel intended to gratify the desires of men, condemning it as a Western misconception about relations between the sexes in Eastern societies. He believes Muslim women enjoy freedoms all but unknown to their Christian British counterparts, especially regarding property and inheritance rights. One of the most noteworthy features of the Arabian Nights is the independence and influence of its female characters,[77] a quality that is particularly apparent in Burton's translation. He observes that "readers of these volumes have remarked to me with much astonishment that they find the female characters more remarkable for decision, action and manliness than the male; and are wonderstruck by their masterful attitude and by the supreme influence they exercise upon public and private life." This "manliness" is apparent in sexual matters. Far from the female serving the sexual needs of the male, it is instead the male who is obliged to serve the sexual needs of the female. What sets the Orient apart from the Occident for Burton is not so much the disproportionate desire of the female, but the superior ability of the male to gratify that desire. This ability is due above all to the fact that "Moslems and Easterns in general study . . . the art and mystery of satisfying the physical woman." The evidence of this study is to be found in love manuals like the *Kama Sutra,* and it is because of his efforts to make such knowledge available to the West through his translations that he proclaims himself a public benefactor.[78]

Burton's critique of the West centers on its failure to satisfy the physical woman. English men, as he sees it, "have the finest women in Europe and least know how to use them."[79] In footnotes to the *Kama Sutra*, he observes that "many men utterly ignore the feelings of the women, and never pay the slightest attention to the passion of the latter," which "is not complete" until they attain orgasm. In his preface to the *Ananga-Ranga*, he insists that the work is intended to "prevent the separation of husband and wife . . . by varying their pleasures in every conceivable way," placing particular emphasis on the importance of mutual gratification.[80] Similarly, *The Perfumed Garden* stresses, as its most recent translator puts it, the "husband's responsibility to ensure that his wife is sexually content."[81] Burton believes that British ignorance of these sexual skills has produced a climate of prudery and psychological repression. Its effects, he argues, are most pronounced with women, since they are the ones left sexually starved: "How many an old maid held to be cold as virgin snow, how many a matron upon whose fairest fame not a breath of scandal has blown, how many a widow who proudly claims the title *univira*, must relieve their pent-up feelings by what may be called mental prostitution." Among the most visible manifestations of this "mental prostitution" is the purity movement itself, with its perverse interest in the erotic matters it professes to condemn. The prominent role that women play in this movement is itself a measure of the failure of men to satisfy their sexual needs.[82]

Burton saw female sexuality as a source of disorder if left unsatisfied. It was the obligation of men to keep it in its appropriate channels, something he felt his countrymen had failed to do. His translation of the *Nights* was intended to provide male readers with the insights of the Orient into the physical woman, to inform them of the erotic responsibilities they were obliged to shoulder in their relations with the opposite sex, responsibilities that an overrefined civilization had sought to repress. It was not intended for female readers: Burton feared that it would further arouse sexual appetites that were already unsatisfied. The anxieties that he expressed would reverberate through the fin de siècle, with its tropes of sexually aggressive vamps and social degeneration.[83]

The Orient opened another area of sexuality to inquiry—male homosexuality, or, as that term had not yet made its way into the English lexicon, what Burton referred to as pederasty. Although lesbianism also had Orientalist associations in the Western imagination, which often attributed it to the harem, it interested Burton far less than male-on-male sex. In 1883 Burton informed Payne that he had written a paper "showing the geo[graphical] limits of sodomy" that "I shall publish . . . some day and surprise the world."[84] And so he did. The occasional references to homosexual practices in the Arabian Nights tales provided Burton with the pretext he had been seeking to publish the paper. Its appearance in the "Terminal Essay" was the chief reason this lengthy endpiece to the *Nights* generated such controversy.[85] Burton's daring enterprise, unprecedented in its frank and detailed discussion of practices long suppressed in Britain by social opprobrium, demonstrated both the subversive power and the limitations of his use of Orientalism.[86]

Burton led his readers on a densely documented, fifty-page tour of "what our neighbours call *Le vice contre nature*—as if anything can be contrary to nature which includes all things."[87]

237

Starting with the classical Greeks, he followed the trail of pederastic practices across time and place, ranging from the Mediterranean and North Africa through the Middle East and Persia,
across Afghanistan and the Punjab to China and Japan, and then
into the Americas via the South Pacific, concluding with references to the presence of pederasty in contemporary Europe. He
approached the subject from a historical and anthropological perspective, drawing on examples and anecdotes from a formidable
array of sources—classical Greek and Latin literature, biblical and
Qur'anic references, ethnographic and travel writings, medical
treatises, and so on. Burton made few concessions to public sensibilities. Although some of the more explicit anecdotes were veiled
in Latin and French, others appeared in unvarnished English.
And taken together they provided an unprecedented account of
the historical, geographical, and sociological dimensions of homosexual love.[88]

The essay's tone is set in its opening pages, where Burton reveals that as a young officer in India he had investigated the male
brothels of Karachi at the behest of General Napier. This audacious announcement is followed by a brutally candid account of
what he found there, including details about the range of services
offered and their costs. In words that retain their power to shock,
he remarks that boys brought higher prices than eunuchs because
"the scrotum of the unmutilated boy could be used as a kind of
bridle for directing the movements of the animal."[89] The studied
ambiguity that Burton creates regarding his own involvement in
these activities gives a daringly intimate, even confessional, quality to the essay.

Burton frames his study of pederasty around the proposition
that its practice was most prevalent in what he termed the
Sotadic Zone (named after the classical Greek poet Sotades,
whose verse dealt with homosexual themes). Describing this zone

as "geographical and climatic, not racial" in nature, he claims that it ran along the latitude roughly parallel to the Mediterranean through some of the warmer regions of the globe. His explanation for what made peoples in this zone susceptible to same-sex liaisons is perfunctory at best. He argues that the climate produced "a blending of the masculine and feminine temperaments" through some obscure alchemy. Furthermore, his examples often are at odds with his argument for a climatic cause: he concedes that pederasty is uncommon among the Hindus of the Indian subcontinent, in contrast to their Muslim neighbors; he claims that it is pervasive both in China and the Americas, lands that encompass widely varied climates; and he acknowledges that it has "gained considerable development" in England, even though his homeland is incontrovertibly outside the Sotadic Zone as defined in the essay.[90]

Why does Burton bother to make claims for a Sotadic Zone when his own examples of pederastic practices so manifestly contradict its existence? These claims seem to have served several purposes. First, by pointing to the climate as the cause of pederasty, Burton seeks to naturalize the phenomenon, removing it from the realm of religious and moral strictures. He is well aware that homosexuals are "utterly repugnant to English readers," but insists that they "deserve, not prosecution but the pitiful care of the physician and the study of the psychologist."[91] This statement presages efforts by Havelock Ellis and other pioneers of sexology to represent homosexuality in medical rather than moral terms. To open the subject to scientific scrutiny, however, demands the ability to overcome moral taboos. Hence the second purpose of Burton's claim for a Sotadic Zone: it allows his readers to maintain some psychic distance from pederasty by presenting it as an Oriental phenomenon. To be sure, this Orient is an exceptionally expansive one, including the greater part of the inhabited globe within its parameters, but it does possess geographical limits circumscribed by climate, and England and northern Europe as a whole—the Occidental heartland—stand outside those boundaries. The association in the English mind of hot climates with the absence of sexual restraint and its suspicion that the Islamic world is a sink of erotic iniquity, especially with respect to homosexual practices, are some of the conceits that sustain the claims for a Sotadic Zone.[92]

How fully persuasive Burton found his own interpretation remains an open question. His determination to document examples of the practice of pederasty among Europeans certainly stands at odds with a strictly Orientalist posture. Moreover, John Addington Symonds reports that Burton had told him three months before his death that "he had begun a general history of 'le Vice,'" which suggests that he may have been reconsidering the conceptual framework that placed pederasty in the category of the Other. Symonds himself was critical of the thesis that same-sex love was "specifically geographical and climatic" in its origins, and he undoubtedly voiced those objections to Burton.[93]

What is clear is that the "Terminal Essay" did not conclude Burton's inquiries into homosexuality. It had become his "special subject."[94] Though we cannot be sure what happened to the study that Symonds referred to, its traces probably exist in a heavily annotated copy of the "Terminal Essay" from Burton's personal library. These annotations, which are unmistakably in Burton's hand, give far greater attention to homosexuality in Europe than did the original essay.[95] They probably were intended for a revised edition of the essay on pederasty: Burton prepared a prospectus for such an edition in 1890, announcing that it was to be "read in conjunction" with Symonds's privately printed essay on homosexuality in classical Greece, *A Problem in Greek Ethics*.[96]

Homosexuality also figured prominently in Burton's final, ill-fated literary endeavor, a new translation of Muhammed al-Nafzawi's manual on lovemaking, which he had already issued under the title *The Perfumed Garden.* In the late 1880s he began to seek copies of the original Arabic manuscript. His "chief want," he told a friend at the British Library, was a chapter on homosexual love that the original French translation had excised.[97] He scoured North Africa in search of the elusive chapter in late 1889, but never found it.[98] Nevertheless, he is reported to have used the text as a point of departure for a lengthy series of annotations on the subject of homosexuality.[99] He showed a copy of the unfinished manuscript to Lord Redesdale, who states that he declared "with conscious pride, 'I think I have shocked Mrs. Grundy this time.'"[100] Isabel, however, ensured that this did not happen: her own apparent shock at the attention the manuscript gave to homosexual love appears to have been the principal motivation behind her decision to burn the work after her husband's death, leaving the public to speculate about its contents and posterity to condemn her action.

If, as some historians have suggested, homosexuality as a distinct type of sexual identity began to take shape in the late nineteenth century,[101] Burton made a more significant contribution to that development than most scholars have appreciated. His "Terminal Essay" was the first serious inquiry into same-sex liaisons published for a public audience in Britain. Symonds's *A Problem in Greek Ethics* appeared somewhat earlier, but only in a privately printed edition of a hundred copies, distributed entirely among personal acquaintances. It did not reach a general readership until Havelock Ellis reprinted it as an appendix to his *Sexual Inversion* (1897), the work that is commonly regarded as the pioneering English-language study of homosexuality.[102] Ellis's book does mark a significant step in the cultural formulation of homosexuality as a separate category of sexual identity, but its understanding of the subject was not as remote from Burton's earlier inquiry as the absence of commentary might lead one to assume. A crucial personal link between the two men was, of course, Symonds, who sought, on the one hand, to wean Burton from his climatic interpretation of pederasty and, on the other, to dissuade Ellis from portraying sexual inversion as a morbid abnormality.[103] Moreover, it is possible to detect traces of Burton's views in certain passages of *Sexual Inversion*. Although Ellis stresses that homosexuality exists "among all the great divisions of the human race," he notes a "special proclivity to homosexuality . . . among certain races and in certain regions," notably "the hotter regions of the globe." He also claims that the European lower classes, and especially criminals, exhibited little of the repugnance toward homosexual practices that preoccupied the middle classes: "In this matter," he observes, "the uncultured man of civilization is linked to the savage."[104] Thus his interpretation of homosexuality is hardly untouched by Orientalist influences.

Still, Ellis does distance himself from Burton in important ways. Although his introduction sketches the historical, geographical, and social range of homosexual practices in a manner resembling that of the "Terminal Essay," his study is otherwise almost entirely concerned with the phenomenon among the British middle classes. His approach is self-consciously scientific in its language and intent. He makes extensive use of a standard trope of medical literature, the case history, and he refers frequently to the work of Karl Heinrich Ulrichs, Richard von Krafft-Ebing, and other continental sexologists who presented homosexuality as a pathological condition. In his only direct reference to Burton, Ellis charges that he is "wholly unacquainted with the recent psychological investigations into sexual inversion."[105] The unmistakable intent is to draw a clear distinction between Ellis's own inquiries, which are legitimated by their scientific method, and those of Burton, which are not.

With its internally unstable argument for the climatic otherness of homosexuality and its humanist use of classical and ethnographic anecdotes as evidence, Burton's Orientalist approach appeared archaic when set against the sexologists' claims that homosexuality should be studied in terms of the value-neutral methods of modern science. But the sexologists' own assertions of scientific objectivity have since lost much of their credibility, and the distinctions between Ellis and Burton look rather less significant than they once did. Although his discourse was in some respects more idiosyncratic, Burton too was appreciative of the psychological costs of sexual repression, and his assessment of its impact was not much different from that of Ellis, who argued that "the evil of ignorance is magnified by our efforts to suppress that which never can be suppressed, though in the effort of suppression it may become perverted."[106] Burton, like Ellis, sought to free the homosexual self from the constraints of contemporary moral censure, and he did so at the very moment that male homosexuality had begun to enter the public consciousness as a source of danger and a cause for hysteria, with the Labouchère amendment, the Cleveland Street male prostitution scandal (1889–90), and the Oscar Wilde trial (1895).[107] If it appears in retrospect that Burton took a wrong turn with his Orientalist retreat into the Sotadic Zone, it must be recognized that this dubious thesis gave him the critical distance to conduct his inquiry in the first place

❧❧❧

For all the controversy it provoked, the *Nights* proved to be an unexpected commercial and critical triumph for Burton. Its limited edition of a thousand copies was snapped up by private sub-scribers, bringing Burton a handsome profit of £10,000. The demand proved so much greater than the supply that Burton followed up the ten-volume *Nights* with his six-volume *Supplemental Nights,* which also sold out. Burton received critical acclaim as well. Even his fiercest antagonists acknowledged his formidable learning, and the completion of his herculean literary endeavor confirmed his reputation as one of the greatest Orientalists of his age. The objections that the purity forces raised against the *Nights* did not prevent him from receiving a knighthood in 1886 in public recognition of his lifetime accomplishments.

Nor did it prevent him from undertaking further projects that skirted the laws against obscenity. In addition to devoting further attention to the issue of homosexuality with his preparations for a revised edition of the "Terminal Essay" and a new translation of *The Perfumed Garden,* Burton began to collaborate on the translation of several volumes of erotic Latin poetry with Leonard Smithers, then an obscure Sheffield solicitor who shared Burton's enthusiasm for this literature.[108] The two men issued a volume of sexually explicit poetry concerning Priapus, the Greek god of male virility, and were preparing a translation of the work of the Roman poet Catullus when Burton died.[109] Their efforts placed them at serious risk of prosecution. In May 1890 Scotland Yard launched an investigation of their activities, forcing Smithers to suspend production of the Priapus volume, destroy the title page that identified Burton as one of its translators, and hide all correspondence, page proofs, and other culpable evidence. Upon learning that Smithers had been served with a search warrant, Isabel became distraught, fearing that public exposure of her husband's involvement in these illicit publications would jeopardize his pension.[110] Burton, however, did not live long enough to retire; he died five months after the Smithers crisis. But he remained actively engaged in his erotic projects to the end.

The story of Burton's valedictory campaign to promote the study of sexuality can be seen both as an expression of and a contribution to the crumbling of a high Victorian moral consensus. His frank inquiries into the varieties of sexual desire challenged the socio-religious convictions and conventions that regulated sexuality among the British bourgeoisie in the nineteenth century. He was an early exponent of the view that prudery and sexual ignorance imposed a heavy psychological burden on individuals. He can be considered an important precursor to certain strands of modernist thought that appeared at the fin de siècle.

One of these strands sought to subvert the normative claims that came to be characterized as Victorianism through a candid scrutiny of the varieties of human sexual behavior. Burton can be linked by intellectual and personal lineage to this endeavor. Whatever the eccentricities of its analytical framework, his essay on pederasty in the *Nights* cleared the way for the public examination of homosexuality that Symonds and Ellis conducted more than a decade later in *Sexual Inversion.* When Edward Carpenter gave the subject further scrutiny in the years immediately before World War I, he made more direct use of Burton's work in his *Intermediate Types among Primitive Folk.*[111] If the *Nights* is considered in conjunction with Burton's translations of the *Kama Sutra,* the *Ananga-Ranga,* and *The Perfumed Garden,* a serious case can be made for him as a harbinger of the modern sexologists. The fact that this case has not been made can be explained in part as a result of Burton's use of Orientalist and classicist sources as the main inspiration and evidence for his advocacy of sexual enlightenment. This set him at odds with the Western medico-scientific ethos and discourse adopted by Ellis and his successors and obscured the contribution he made to the modernist effort to give sexuality the same scrutiny that other aspects of human behavior received.

Burton's approach to the issue of sexuality fed much more directly into another stream of modernism, one that embraced as a source of liberation those instinctive, emotional, even irrational forces that were associated in the West with the Orient. Perhaps the strangest exemplar of this tradition was the writer Aleistar Crowley, who much admired Burton and sought to emulate him in seeking "knowledge and powers beyond the accepted and acceptable."[112] This effort led him to the Algerian desert, where he engaged in occult practices and sexual role playing with a male lover. More influential were the poets and artists associated with the Decadent movement. They are well known to have drawn on Orientalist themes and images in their explorations of otherwise forbidden topics. As was the case with Symonds and the sexologists, this movement can be traced by direct line of descent to Burton. Leonard Smithers, his collaborator on those late erotic Latin translations, would soon become a key figure in the Decadent movement, publishing the *Savoy* magazine and other outlets for the work of Oscar Wilde, Aubrey Beardsley, Arthur Symons, Ernest Dowson, and others.[113] Like these figures of the fin de siècle, Burton found that an Orientalist stance gave him the emotional and intellectual distance he needed to carry out his critique of the repressive moral regime that ruled British society.

Among the many marginal notes that Burton scrawled in his printed copy of the "Terminal Essay" is the following: "Nothing could be more grotesque [than] Orientalism drawn from the depths of European self-consciousness."[114] However much he may have wished otherwise, his use of Orientalism in that final decade was in fact drawn from "the depths of European self-consciousness." Its preoccupations were primarily European ones.

What Burton sought to do was to turn European claims of difference against themselves, to expose those claims to a mirror and subject them to scrutiny, the self-same scrutiny that Europeans had so often directed against others in their Orientalist inquiries.[115]

VIII

The Afterlife

Richard Burton died of heart failure at his Trieste residence on the morning of October 19, 1890. His rational materialism made him skeptical of an afterlife, at least as Christianity interpreted that notion. Whether this accounted for his "horror of a corpse, deathbed scenes, and graveyards" is unclear,[1] but it is evident that he faced death without the faith that sustained his wife. He did, however, believe that human consciousness extended into realms that science had scarcely begun to detect, much less comprehend. This conviction left open the possibility that the spirit did not die with the flesh, that some manner of sentience survived the clinical cessation of life. Burton also appreciated the fact that an afterlife of a very different sort awaited him, this one manifested in his posthumous reputation. Even though he was enough of an egotist to have sought to influence its character by sanctioning the two biographies that appeared in the last few years of his life,[2] he could scarcely have imagined that his reputation would become the source of so much controversy immediately after his death or that his life would remain the subject of so much attention so far into the future.

~⚘~⚘~⚘~

Throughout his eventful life, Burton had shown an intense interest in the ethical doctrines and spiritual beliefs of the peoples he came across in his travels. This inquiry had entailed the study of most of the world's major religions—Christianity, Islam, Judaism, Hinduism, even Buddhism—as well as a good many others, ranging from animism to Jainism.[3] He was particularly attracted to forms of spiritual heterodoxy. This was the source of his sympathy for Mormonism, with its Occidentalizing of polygamy, and especially for Sufism, which diverged from the mainstream doctrines of Islam in many ways, not least in the space it opened up for a personalized mysticism. He also was drawn to magic and the occult—charms, divination, clairvoyance, and so on—ever curious to learn all he could about the role they played in various cultures.[4] Although most Britons spoke dismissively of the "superstitions" of primitive peoples, Burton rejected this smug assessment and the assumption of superiority on which it was based, noting that strikingly similar ideas and practices persisted in Europe as well.[5]

Another manifestation of Burton's interest in the paranormal was Mesmerism, also termed animal magnetism and later known as hypnotism, which became the rage in mid-Victorian Britain.[6] Mesmerism lay in that twilight zone between science and religion, exposing those recesses of the mind that some commentators claimed gave access to the soul. It produced a trancelike state that resembled the condition attained by certain Hindu and Buddhist holy men, an otherworldly realm insensible to pain and other external stimuli, a kind of death-in-life. Burton was "a great mesmerizer" who often practiced on his wife, using the technique to ease her discomfort during illness, but also to read her private thoughts, much to her dismay.[7] He viewed Mesmerism as a mechanism for investigating subjects such as "introvision, thought-reading, and medical clairvoyance," all of which he regarded as evidence that the human mind possessed powers that science had yet to understand and explain.[8]

From the late 1870s onward Burton acquired an interest in

Spiritualism, which shared with Mesmerism several distinguishing characteristics. It too sought to draw connections between
reason and instinct, between the material and the metaphysical
worlds, between the past, the present, and the future. It promoted
activities or "experiments," as it preferred to call them, that were
intended to permeate the boundaries between science and religion: séances with the dead, mind-readings, astrological predic-
tions, investigations into the presence of poltergeists, and much
more. One of its most striking features was the role played by
mediums, individuals who claimed to channel the voices of the
dead, thereby engaging in what was termed spirit possession in
so-called primitive societies.[9] Spiritualism tapped far more explicitly than Mesmerism into the Orientalist notion that the superior spirituality of Indian and other Eastern cultures gave them
privileged access to esoteric knowledge. This strand of Spiritualism found its fullest expression in Theosophy, an influential
movement framed around the pseudo-Indian occultism of Madame Blavatsky.[10]

Spiritualism's efforts to forge a syncretic system of knowledge
that integrated materialism with metaphysics and Western rationalism with Eastern mysticism appealed to Burton, though he
was no more willing to swallow its doctrines whole than he was
those of any other faith. He described himself as "a Spiritualist
without the Spirits." He believed that those inexplicable events
advertised as evidence of the "Supernatural [are] the Natural mis-
understood or imperfectly understood." The problem, as he saw
it, was that we still did not have the scientific means to determine
"where Nature either begins or ends."[11] An enthusiastic participant in séances, he was persuaded that they evidenced some
sort of sixth sense, but not communication with the dead.[12] He
adopted a materialist perspective toward paranormal phenomena,
attributing their cause to the mind's magnetic or electrical forces,

often termed electric telepathy.[13] "Spirit," he declared, "is essentially material, i.e., subject to the five (or six) senses."[14]

Burton also realized, however, that Spiritualism "satisfies a real want" in those who had rejected traditional religious beliefs; indeed, it spoke to his own metaphysical longings as well. In 1881 he drafted a "creed for the Spiritualist," an intriguing document that offers insight into his efforts as a freethinker who rejects religious dogmas to find some other avenue of spiritual solace. It begins with a declaration enunciating his position on the relationship between reason and relativism: "Intellectual truth is eternally one: moral or sentimental truth is a geographical or chronological accident, that varies even with the individual." His spiritualist creed rejects belief in original sin, redemption, heaven, hell, purgatory, and a personal deity. Yet it leaves open the possibility that death does not extinguish the spirit: "Death, physically considered, dissolves a certain organic unity; it is not, however, annihilation, but change." He does not say what kind of change this might be, but he comes closer here than anywhere else in his writings to embracing the notion of an afterlife. "Man's individuality," he declares, "survives the death of his body." Though this is a seemingly unambiguous assertion that the spirit endures, he quickly qualifies himself by observing that the spiritualist must make this claim because "the idea of utter annihilation is painful . . . , a burden too heavy to be borne."[15] Thus even in his most transcendental mood, Burton could not entirely escape a rational materialism that insisted he was merely rationalizing his dread of extinction.

It is perhaps fitting in light of these ambiguous reflections that a degree of uncertainty and controversy surrounds Burton's own death. On his final day, he awoke in discomfort around 4:00 A.M., and within half an hour it was apparent that he was having a heart attack. Anticipating that the end was near, Isabel sent for a parish priest to administer the last rites to her husband, hoping thereby to pave the way for their reunion in heaven, even though that required her to bear false witness to his conversion to the Roman Catholic faith. When the priest arrived at 6:00 A.M., Burton seemed to him already to be dead, but Isabel insisted that he was simply unconscious. She persuaded the priest to carry out his prayers while demanding that the doctor in attendance continue to administer electric shocks in an effort to revive her husband. Although the doctor declared Burton dead at 7:00 A.M., Isabel continued to maintain until that evening that he was simply in a coma.[16]

Isabel's conduct has been interpreted as the hysterical reaction of a grief-stricken wife, but it was motivated at least in part by the same uncertainties about the nature of death that informed the views of her husband. Mesmerism, Spiritualism, and Eastern forms of meditation and magic had persuaded both of them that it was possible for life to mimic death, for people to enter trance-like states of suspended animation that doctors could not distinguish from the expiration of life. So many late Victorians shared these anxieties, worrying about what would happen if they were mistakenly taken to be dead, that they founded the London Association for the Prevention of Premature Burial in 1892.[17] Isabel herself was terrified of being buried alive, once having explained to her sister that "it is my nature to lie in a trance" when given opiates—and, though this was left unstated, when mesmerized as well.[18] Her will instructed doctors to pierce her heart with a needle before preparing her for burial so as to leave no doubt that she was dead.[19] The larger issue looming over this requirement was that "no doctor knows when the Soul leaves the body. . . . Death is only apparent to the scientific eye, not *real* in a spiritual sense. The risk is too great, and there is no after remedy."[20] This statement expressed the mixture of hope and dread that Richard Burton almost certainly shared as his body drew its final breath and his mind lost contact with the material world.

Beginning with her insistence that last rites be administered to a man who most likely was already dead and most certainly was not a Roman Catholic, Isabel made a number of decisions that ensured her husband's posthumous career would be no less controversial than the one he had pursued in life. In the days after his death she requested that a series of masses be held on his behalf in Trieste's Catholic churches, and these were followed on the fourth day by a large public funeral conducted in accordance with Catholic rites. Burton's coffin was then shipped to England, where another funeral service was held in June 1891 at St. Mary Magdalene's Catholic Church in Mortlake, a suburb west of London. Here in the church cemetery his body was laid to rest in the tentlike tomb designed by Isabel. Many of Burton's friends and family were outraged by what they saw as a betrayal of his lifelong stance as a freethinker and critic of the rituals and dogmas of Christianity.

Isabel also opened herself to attack as a result of her decision in the weeks following her husband's death to cull the mass of unpublished manuscripts, journals, letters, and notes that her husband had accumulated over the course of his prolific literary and public career, burning those papers she judged unimportant or harmful to his reputation. Her own reputation would suffer disastrously from this decision. She would come to be portrayed as a religious prude who was driven to obliterate a lifetime's worth of priceless observations and insights into other lands and cultures by the discovery that her husband harbored deviant sexual interests and tastes. Documents only recently opened to the public demonstrate that the scale of the destruction carried out by Isabel was not nearly as sweeping as critics have charged.[21] What most certainly did go up in flames, however, was "The Scented Garden" manuscript, the heavily annotated retranslation of the Arabic sex manual that was either near completion or had just been completed when Richard died.

The destruction of "The Scented Garden" manuscript would have remained unknown to all but a few of Burton's most intimate acquaintances if Isabel had not advertised what she had done in a letter that appeared in the *Morning Post* only a few days after the Mortlake funeral. Isabel stated in her letter to the *Post* that the manuscript was her husband's *"magnum opus,"* but it "treated of a certain passion" so deviant that it could only be mentioned in this vague and euphemistic way. She insisted that her husband's interest in the subject was purely scientific—he "dissected a passion from every point of view, as a doctor may dissect a body"—but she feared that others would "read it for filth's sake," and insofar as it stirred their immoral desires, it jeopardized Richard's immortal soul. Therefore, to protect both public morals and her husband's prospects for a place in heaven, she committed the manuscript to the flames.[22]

We will never know, of course, whether this was the real reason Isabel burned "The Scented Garden" or whether it was merely a post hoc rationalization. It is worth asking, however, why she felt compelled more than eight months after committing the deed to publicly proclaim what she had done. Although she does not explain her motives in the revelatory letter itself, a year and a half later she wrote a defense of her action in which she claimed that her intent was to notify the many men who had written to ask about the status of the manuscript that it no longer existed.[23] Given the fact that no prospectus had been sent out announcing the work, it seems highly unlikely that such a flood of inquiries had actually occurred. And if it had, she could hardly have chosen a more provocative manner and means of responding to this interest. Her comments taunted potential purchasers with the suggestion that the now-destroyed work had been Burton's greatest achievement while it simultaneously accused them of depravity for expressing interest in it. Moreover, she made her announcement in an open letter to the press rather than the discreet private correspondence that had characterized all of her previous dealings with subscribers to Burton's erotic publications. All of these considerations tell against Isabel's professed motive in writing the *Post* letter.

A more likely explanation for the letter hinges on how Isabel sought to improve her dismal financial fortunes in the face of a morally straitened public climate that worked against the few assets she possessed. Isabel was nearly destitute when she returned to England from Trieste in early 1891, possessing just £59.[24] Her only real legacy consisted of her late husband's unpublished manuscripts. The problem she faced was that the manuscripts most likely to bring a profit by their publication were those most likely to raise the ire of the moral purity forces. By publicly announcing that she had destroyed "The Scented Garden" in order to protect public morals, Isabel probably hoped to assure the National Vigilance Association and its ilk that she could be counted on to shoulder her task as executor of her husband's literary estate in a responsible manner.[25] Once Isabel had established her *bona fides* with the purity forces, she could set about the task of getting Richard's manuscripts into print with much less risk of legal harassment.

A strategic motive for the *Post* announcement is supported by the actions Isabel took soon afterward. Within a month of the notorious letter's publication, she had established a business relationship with Leonard Smithers, the furtive figure in the underground book trade whose collaboration with Burton in the translation and publication of the *Priapeia* had been the target of an obscenity investigation in 1890. "I must warn you," Isabel informed Smithers when they reached their confidential agreement, "that if anything went wrong I should be annoyed."[26] What did she mean? Given the fact that the purpose of their partnership was to bring into print several works that the purity movement would regard as coarse if not obscene, she was most likely worried that any exposure of her activities would undermine the public image she had so carefully crafted with her revelation in the *Post.* Isabel worked with Smithers to bring into print *The Carmina of Caius Valerius Catullus* (1894), a sexually explicit classical Latin text that her husband had been translating in collaboration with Smithers when he died. She also relied on Smithers to issue Burton's manuscript translation of Giovanni Batiste Basile's *Il Pentamerone* (1893). Both works were privately printed and marketed through the mail to the same list of subscribers who had purchased Burton's earlier erotic translations.[27] The *Pall Mall Gazette,* ever alert to threats against public decency, complained in its review of the *Pentamerone* that it contained stories on "forbidden topics" and phrases of "astonishing coarseness."[28] Isabel also sold to Smithers the rights to reissue in a new "Memorial Edition" various other books by Burton that were then out of print. The prospectus for this venture stressed that "in no case will any expurgation or omission be made either in the text or notes."[29] In addition, Isabel sanctioned a new "Library Edition" of Burton's *Nights,* with Smithers serving as its editor. Apart from the excision of the essay on pederasty, which was deleted at her insistence, the new edition left the bawdy original essentially intact.[30] These publishing ventures went a long way to improving Isabel's finances, if not her reputation for moral probity.[31] She left an estate valued at £11,766 when she died in 1896.[32]

What Isabel failed to anticipate was that her announcement of the destruction of "The Scented Garden" manuscript, coming as it did directly on the heels of the Catholic burial of her husband, would provoke a firestorm of criticism from family and friends. Her appropriation of Burton to the Catholic fold had already antagonized a number of people, including his sister and niece, Maria and Georgiana Stisted, who pointedly refused to attend the Mortlake funeral. Now she found herself surrounded by a wider and more articulate circle of critics, many of them people with whom she had enjoyed a long-standing association. Algernon Swinburne, who had once referred to Isabel as the "best of all wives," now charged that she had "befouled Richard Burton's name like a harpy."[33] His "Elegy" to Burton, published in the *Fortnightly Review,* included a scorching stanza condemning her and the Catholic Church:

> Priests and the soulless serfs of priest may swarm
> > With vulturous acclamation, loud in lies,
> About his dust while yet his dust is warm
> > Who mocked as sunlight mocks their base blind eyes[34]

The writer Eliza Lynn Linton, whose assistance in procuring legal counsel for the Burtons when they issued the *Nights* had led Isabel to effuse over her as a "dear kind and deliciously shocking woman,"[35] penned an equally ferocious attack on her erstwhile friend and admirer. It appeared, curiously enough, in an essay opposing "the new school of Wild Women," by which Linton meant feminists, whose agenda she summarized as "topsyturvyism and . . . universal license." Isabel exhibited one of the most troubling features of the "Wild Women," a "mental absolutism" that sought to "confine the area of men's excursions to the limits of their own." Linton charged that she had brought "dishonour on the memory of the man who had systematically preached a doctrine so adverse to her own," thereby belittling "the grandeur of [his] intellect."[36] While Isabel had never expressed support for the feminist cause, Linton interpreted her actions after Richard's death as demonstrative of its misguided presumption.[37] Another prominent woman writer who had been a close friend of the Burtons, the novelist Ouida (Maria Louise Ramé), was equally outraged, refusing to speak to Isabel ever again.[38] W. H. Wilkins, Isabel's biographer, reports that she was "publicly vilified and privately abused, pursued with obscene, anonymous, and insulting letters until the day of her death."[39]

What Isabel had inadvertently set in motion was a scramble to lay claim to Burton's memory, a struggle to define the terms of his intellectual patrimony. Her controversial actions ensured that the debate was initially framed around the issue of religious orthodoxy versus free thought. It was inflamed by a deeply ingrained tradition of anti-Catholicism in England, making allies of conventional Anglicans like the Stisteds and bohemian agnostics like Swinburne, who shared the conviction that Burton represented an intellectual and spiritual independence that was inimical to the ritualism and submissiveness of Popery. It was impossible, however, to contain the struggle over Burton's legacy to any single set of contending positions, as Linton's efforts to turn the focus of debate in the direction of gender made abundantly clear. The problem—although it might more accurately be considered an opportunity—was that Burton's career and writings were so rich and varied that they supplied the basis for a bewildering range of interpretations. Different observers found different meanings in his life, and those meanings proliferated over time.

✦

Isabel made the first sustained bid to set the terms by which Richard Burton would be remembered in perpetuity, by publishing an adoring biography of her husband in 1893. A massive tome, it was the story of a great man, brave, steady, and blessed with many gifts, true to himself and faithful to his wife and friends, unwavering in his service to his nation even in the face of its neglect and betrayal. For all its hagiographic qualities, the biography was surprisingly frank and free of sanctimony in its assessment of Burton's religious views. Isabel still maintained that her husband had edged closer to Catholicism in his final years, but she also acknowledged his contentious engagement with Christianity and his abiding interest in Sufism and other systems of belief.

These concessions did not prevent Georgiana Stisted, who had never forgiven her aunt for her actions when Richard died, from lambasting her in *The True Life of Capt. Sir Richard F. Burton,* published only a few months after Isabel's death. The distinguishing intent of this biography was to wrench the memory of Georgiana's uncle from the clutches of his widow, a woman she described as suffering from a "fatal want of tact and judgment," and, by extension, from the Catholic Church, which she regarded as a haven of "human folly and superstition." (Stisted also noted the contradiction between Isabel's "theatrical destruction of the 'Scented Garden'" and her subsequent decision to permit the reissue of a largely unexpurgated *Nights*.)[40] In what was otherwise represented as an exemplary life, Burton's great mistake was judged by Stisted to be his decision to marry Isabel. This harsh assessment brought a rejoinder of its own when W. H. Wilkins published *The Romance of Isabel Lady Burton* a year later. Begun in collaboration with Isabel in the final year or so of her life, this biography presented the marriage of Richard and Isabel as one of the great love stories of the age.[41]

What had become in many respects a family quarrel quieted as the key protagonists disappeared from the scene, and Burton's spiritual legacy was gradually disentangled from its associations with Catholicism. By the early twentieth century attention had began to turn much more directly to Burton the freethinker, mainly as a result of the rediscovery of *The Kasîdah*. The original edition of *The Kasîdah* had been a financial failure, with less than a hundred copies sold.[42] Isabel Burton sought to revive the work, but her edition of 1894 appears to have met with little interest. The agnostic elegy received a warmer reception, however, when a London publishing house reprinted it in 1900, leading to further English editions in 1914, 1925, 1927, and 1933. Interest also grew in the United States. The first American edition of *The Kasîdah* appeared in 1896 under the imprint of Thomas B. Moser of Portland, Maine, a specialty publisher who produced high-quality, limited-edition works. By 1923, Moser had issued at least fifteen editions of the poem. Other publishers in Massachusetts, New York, Pennsylvania, Connecticut, Kansas, and California produced their own editions in 1918, 1919, 1921, 1924, 1926, 1929, 1931, and 1937. Although it is difficult to be sure what attracted readers to the work, its eloquent yet bracing rejection of religious faith no doubt spoke to the sentiments of the growing number of Americans and Britons who were struggling with spiritual doubts of their own. From the late 1930s onward, however, the frequency with which new editions of *The Kasîdah* were issued began to diminish, which suggests that the poem's popularity was waning. The agnosticism it advocated most likely came to be seen as no less reflective of the Victorians' old-fashioned philosophical earnestness than the religiosity it opposed.

Insofar as Burton's reputation as a freethinker has endured into our own era, the improbable agent of its survival has been a science fiction novel, Philip José Farmer's popular *To Your Scattered Bodies Go* (1971), which presents Burton as its main character. Using Burton's doubts about an afterlife as the narrative's point of departure, Farmer has his hero resurrected after his fatal heart attack—though not by God, but rather by unseen aliens, who place him in a strange world for mysterious purposes that Burton is determined to uncover. This premise gives new life to Burton, both figuratively and literally, providing some serious reflections on his spiritual quest as the thematic underpinning to this adventure fantasy.[43]

Yet the popular memory of Burton would come to rest far more firmly on his associations with adventure than on his attitudes toward religion. These associations were cemented almost immediately after his death through the actions of Madame Tussaud's Wax Museum. Noting that "a great Englishman had just passed away," the museum's management quickly crafted a wax likeness to put on display, a move that marked an important stage in Burton's posthumous elevation into the pantheon of national heroes. The constraints of the medium and the interests of the audience worked together to ensure that his multifaceted career was reduced to a single iconic image, one that the public could identify as his most memorable accomplishment. What was it? Burton disguised in Arab garb, making the pilgrimage to Mecca. (Isabel supplied Madame Tussaud's with what she claimed to be the robes Richard wore on the journey.) It is both ironic and appropriate that Burton's reputation as a "great Englishman" would be staged in such a way that his Englishness was shrouded in otherness.[44]

The adventurous man of action would become the most popular and enduring of the many representations of Burton. It sustained a steady stream of biographies, supplying vicarious thrills for those who sought imaginative release from the monotonous confines of modern urban society. The first of this genre was *The Real Richard Burton* (1907), tellingly dedicated to Theodore Roosevelt as a "record of a strenuous life."[45] The association that Ma-

Madame Tussaud's effigy of Burton. The decision by Madame Tussaud's Wax Museum to place this effigy of Burton on display soon after his death confirmed his reputation as a national hero. But by portraying him in disguise on his pilgrimage to Mecca, it unwittingly acknowledged the ambiguous nature of his identity. From Thomas Wright, *The Life of Sir Richard Burton* (New York: G. P. Putnam's Sons, 1906).

dame Tussaud's had established between Burton and the Arab world would persist with biographies that sported the titles *Burton: Arabian Nights Adventurer* (1931), *The Arabian Knight* (1936), and *Death Rides a Camel* (1963).[46] These works tapped into the romantic appeal that Arabia held for the Western imagination, which reached its height in the interwar years with the celebrity of Lawrence of Arabia and the success of Hollywood films such as *The Sheikh* and *The Thief of Baghdad*. The title of another biography of the same vintage—*Richard Burton, Explorer* (1936)—signaled by its descriptor the broader frame of reference within which his life assumed its popular identity.[47] Burton the intrepid explorer inspired a wide array of works, including novels, fictionalized biographies, and children's books.[48] The expedition into East Africa, however, gradually came to supplant the pilgrimage to Mecca as the emblematic experience in his life of adventure. The success of Alan Moorehead's *White Nile* (1960), followed by the BBC production "The Search for the Nile" (1971), sparked renewed interest in Burton's role in the larger story of the European search for the source of the Nile. This interest generated another spate of biographies, as well as a historical novel, *Burton and Speke* (1982), and *Mountains of the Moon* (1989), a Hollywood feature film adapted from the novel.[49] Burton's tortured relationship with Speke took center stage in the novel, the film, and many of the biographies, supplying the highly charged human-interest story that transformed this remarkably full and complicated life into popular entertainment.

Burton the adventurer also has served as an inspiration and model for a number of individuals hungry to experience the kinds of dangers and discomforts he endured in his explorations. I have already noted his influence on several generations of British Arabists. Harry St. John Philby sought to model himself after Burton, whom he viewed as "the greatest of all British explorers."[50]

Wilfred Thesiger "allowed himself to imagine he was back in Burton's days" during his travels through Arabia.[51] More recently, the Canadian financier and philanthropist Christopher Ondaatje and the English novelist and travel writer Bruce Chatwin have drawn inspiration from Burton in their efforts to conjoin authorship and adventure. Ondaatje has made two journeys that follow in Burton's footsteps, the first through South Asia, the second through East Africa. In both instances, Ondaatje has written books that mix the genres of popular biography, *National Geographic*–style pictorial, and travel essay.[52] The late Bruce Chatwin, who as a youth was fascinated by Burton, evinced his influence in a less literal, but more artistically memorable fashion. After publishing a highly successful account of his trip through Patagonia, he made subsequent journeys to Australia, Afghanistan, Benin (Dahomey), Brazil, and elsewhere, using them as inspiration for a series of striking and innovative works of fiction. His biographer described him as "the literate adventurer" whose taste for travel, ambitions as a writer, and unease in English society bore a notable resemblance to the characteristics of Burton.[53]

Chatwin resembled Burton in another important respect—his unabashed interest in sexual experiences, which for Chatwin found expression in promiscuous sex with other men. Whether Burton himself had homosexual leanings will continue to provoke speculation and debate, but, whatever his personal proclivities may have been, it is evident that his frank inquiries into "pederasty" encouraged others to regard their own same-sex longings with less shame and to seek their gratification in travels abroad. Aleister Crowley credited Burton as an important inspiration for his decision to carry out occult homosexual experiments in the Algerian desert.[54] It may be going too far to suggest, as one scholar recently has done, that Burton was responsible for turning North Africa into a popular site for sex tourism by European homosexuals, but his contribution to this dubious cross-cultural exchange cannot be entirely discounted.[55]

Perhaps the most striking development in the posthumous career of Richard Burton has been the renewed attention his writings on sexuality have received, which has led in turn to his emergence in the public mind as something of an apostle of sexual knowledge. Although the "Terminal Essay," the *Kama Sutra,* and his other works on sexual customs and techniques had circulated for years in privately printed editions, their distribution was limited to a small set of cognoscenti.[56] This changed with the liberalization of obscenity laws in Britain and the United States in the 1960s. Commercial presses soon began to publish anthologies of Burton's writings on sex, as well as reprints of his and Arbuthnot's original English-language edition of the *Kama Sutra.*[57] As one commentator from this period wrote, Burton was "the unique Virgil, the essential guide" to a frank discussion of sexuality.[58] As ever more explicit sexual material entered an increasingly unregulated market, Burton's writings gradually lost their novelty value (not to mention their erotic charge), but this did not drive Burton the sexologist into obscurity, as might have been expected. On the contrary, the *Kama Sutra* came to acquire an iconic status as the ur-text of this new sexual freedom and Burton assumed the guise of its sage.

The *Kama Sutra* as a "brand" is more popular today than it has ever been, with over a hundred books currently in print that sport the term in their titles. These include several modern translations of the original text by Vatsyayana, as well as many more works that simply use *Kama Sutra* as a mantra for sexual enlightenment.[59] Yet the Burton-Arbuthnot translation, however quaint and euphemistic it may seem to modern readers, continues to serve as the basis for a remarkably large number of editions of the *Kama Sutra,* many of which blazon Burton's (though rarely

Arbuthnot's) name on their covers as evidence of their authenticity. This association between Burton and the *Kama Sutra* also figures prominently in a recent best-selling biography of Burton, which misleadingly proclaims in its subtitle that he was the man who "discovered the *Kama Sutra.*"[60] It was perhaps inevitable that this interest would give rise to a pornographic novel purporting to be the secret sex diaries of Burton, "the Victorian explorer and noted cocksman."[61] In addition, a comic novel by Lee Siegel satirizes this fascination with Burton and the *Kama Sutra.* It is about a professor of Sanskrit studies whose efforts to complete a new translation of the now ubiquitous work become entangled with his own messy love life. The shadow of Burton, whom the professor "liked to compare himself to," looms large over the story, serving as an ironic commentary on the unlikely way his memory has been kept alive in modern Western culture.[62]

It also should be noted that Burton's translation of the tales of the Arabian Nights retains its staying power. Despite its archaic diction and embroidered rendering of the Arabic original, it remains the standard English-language version of the work. Selections from the sixteen volumes of tales that Burton issued to subscribers at such personal risk in the 1880s are currently available in various editions,[63] and more recent translations have made little headway against Burton's versions.

Other aspects of Burton's life and thought, however, have been largely ignored or forgotten. His admiration for the Islamic faith has received little or no attention from his many British and American fans. Indeed, his ecumenical interest in religions of all sorts reflects a sensibility that seems to have lost favor in our own age. Most of his biographers have minimized his disdain for Africans and fulminations against Jews. Although he appears in some histories of colonial Africa as a prominent exponent of mid-nineteenth-century racism toward Africans, his anti-

Semitic sentiments were almost entirely forgotten until the recent effort to auction off his manuscript "Human Sacrifice among the Sephardine or Eastern Jews" generated a brief flurry of public attention.[64]

What memory of Burton remains in those non-Western societies that were the principal objects of his attention? Does his reputation survive in the countless countries where he spent so much of his life? And, if so, what sort of reputation did he leave behind? Though it is impossible to give an adequate answer to these questions, some impressionistic observations may be in order. It is worth noting, for example, that Burton's books about his South Asian experiences have been reprinted in multiple facsimile editions by Indian and Pakistani publishing houses, which indicates a continued interest in his work among the English-speaking elites of these countries. Moreover, the publication in 1976 of a Sindhi translation of Burton's *Sindh, and the Races That Inhabit the Valley of the Indus,* which Christopher Ondaatje reported to be in use as a school textbook in Karachi when he traveled through the province, provides an even more telling testament to the respect his work evidently elicits from some of the descendents of the peoples he wrote about in the 1840s.[65]

In Somalia, too, the memory of Burton seems to have survived, though with much more ambivalence. Emphasis is given to Burton's failure to maintain his disguise as a Muslim during his journey to Harar. A British colonial official writing about Somalia in the early twentieth century makes a reference to Burton that must have come from Somali informants, since it diverges in key respects from the account Burton himself supplied. He states that Burton was obliged to flee Harar because his deception was exposed *while* he was in the city, implying anger on the part of the Somalis and desperation on his part.[66] A modern historian of Somalia gives a rather different, yet equally intriguing, glimpse into his local reputation, reporting that "Burton is still remembered . . . with a mixture of amusement and admiration as 'Haji Abdallah.'"[67] One may assume that the amusement derived from Burton's failure to fool the Somalis. There is neither admiration nor amusement, however, in the way the Somali writer Faarax Cawl represents Burton. In his novel *Ignorance Is the Enemy of Love* (1982), Burton appears as a "swindler," an "infidel," and a "hypocrite," an agent of British imperialism whose efforts to disguise his true identity are exposed by a learned Somali cleric, forcing him to flee the country.[68] Although non-Western perceptions of Burton are no more likely to strike a single chord than those in the West, the views expressed by Cawl remind us that those who were the victims of the man's deception and the objects of his gaze would have had reason to regard him very differently than would those who were not. For many Somalis and others whose societies were deeply scarred and profoundly changed by colonial subjugation, Burton must seem first and foremost a duplicitous agent of imperial ambitions.

⌇✣⌇✣⌇✣⌇

My own contribution to this ongoing process of representing and reinterpreting Burton has been informed by the belief that the man cannot be fully understood or appreciated without framing his life and thought in the context of the larger array of forces that transformed the world in the nineteenth century. This is in some sense little more than a historical platitude, but it deserves to be enunciated in this case because so much of the biographical literature on Burton represents him as a man so original and so oversized that he succeeded in breaking free from the orbit of his own age. The problem with this perspective is twofold. First, it prevents us from attaining more than a highly personalized, entirely subjective sense of why he did what he did and thought what he thought. Second, it prevents us from learning more from his life than the mere sum of its parts. A life lived as fully as Burton lived his can tell us something of importance about the wider world within which he navigated, which in turn helps to place him in a fresh light. For all his determination to chart an independent course for himself, he was inextricably caught in the currents of his time, influenced by its ideas, values, institutions, opportunities, challenges, and constraints. By reconnecting him to his social, cultural, and intellectual moorings, we can better determine who he was, what he represented, and why he held such purchase on the imaginations of his contemporaries—and retains so much appeal to the present day.

Burton's life and thought can best be viewed through the prism of difference, which both fascinated and disoriented the Victorians. The unprecedented expansion of British influence across the globe in the nineteenth century brought in its wake an equally unprecedented array of encounters with peoples who differed in readily apparent ways from the British themselves. For the traders, soldiers, officials, missionaries, planters, and others whose economic, military, political, religious, and other interests took them to the far corners of the globe, a kaleidoscope of human differences confronted them—differences of speech, of dress, of custom, of faith, of appearance, and much more. The great intellectual challenge of the nineteenth century was to make epistemological sense of this world of difference.

Burton was intimately involved in this enterprise, an involvement that illuminates the broader terms by which the Victorians made meaningful the manifold variations among humankind. He brought to the task a distinctive set of traits and talents. His personal sense of difference, nurtured in his youth as an expatriate and honed in his unhappy experience in Oxford, kept him from succumbing to the emotional inducements of English nativism.

His natural genius for languages, nourished by the professional approbation of the army and exercised through direct encounters with South Asians, gave him the means to move beyond a superficial knowledge of other societies and cultures. His theatrical affinity for impersonation, acted out in a series of high-risk performances in Arabia and Somalia and rewarded with public acclaim in Britain, allowed him, to some degree at least, to break through the barriers of difference itself.

Still, were Burton to have done nothing more than demonstrate an uncommon ability to cross cultural boundaries, he would have remained a mere footnote in the history of the Victorian encounter with difference, a minor figure resembling a number of others who operated at the intersection of cultures. What set him apart was his restless determination to extend the reach of his experience to ever more diverse pockets of humanity and to draw insights from those increasingly varied encounters in order to advance the larger epistemological quest to understand, explain, and classify difference. The vast corpus of written work he produced during his lifetime constitutes a remarkable monument to that quest. It testifies to the range and depth of his inquiry, which entailed an active engagement in issues of language, religion, race, sex, and other criteria of difference. It also testifies to the shifts, the inconsistencies, the contradictions, and the occasional malice that marred his efforts to establish a stable and coherent taxonomy of difference. He mirrored the interests, concerns, and prejudices of his age in these respects, as, indeed, he mirrors some of our own. The racism and anti-Semitism he articulated were among the most prevalent and troubling of the nineteenth century's applications of difference to the interpretation of human diversity. Yet his use of difference in order to articulate a relativist stance was one of its most surprising and productive applications. The fact that such divergent uses of difference assumed such prominence in Burton's thought speaks to both the instability and the dynamism of his endeavor.

The experiential and intellectual odyssey of Richard Burton presents us with a number of insights into the ways the Victorians came to conceive of difference and the influence it had on their society and self-perceptions. His life gives us an indication of how thoroughly the theoretical debate about difference was enmeshed in the empirical encounter with other peoples and cultures. The realms of meaning and experience operated in tandem for Burton, as indeed they did for many more of his contemporaries than the conventional image of the Victorians has prepared us to recognize. Only recently have we begun to appreciate the degree to which the Victorians' mental map of themselves and their own society was produced through the encounters that so many of them had with other peoples across the globe as a result of leisure travel, military service, missionary work, merchant enterprise, and more. The Victorian world was in this sense a genuinely transnational and transcultural world, drawing inspiration and insight from wide-ranging, often unexpected sources. However much the intellectual tradition known as Orientalism was colored by the concerns of imperial authority, for example, it had its origins in the effort to understand the complex array of societies and traditions that stretched from the Near East to the Far East and to transmit their systems of knowledge to an interested audience in Britain and elsewhere in Europe, where their effects were impossible to contain within any officially sanctioned channel. The same unpredictable outcomes arose from encounters with other peoples and beliefs. The imperial networks that sustained British economic and political interests in the nineteenth century made possible the global circulation of ideas, and even though we have only begun to track their effects on the Victorians themselves, Burton gives us some sense of where this inquiry might lead.

The contentiousness that characterized Burton's efforts to understand difference, especially as it related to religion, race, and sexuality, also reminds us that there was far less consensus among Victorians than we tend to suppose; their debates strayed across so many of the boundaries we take for granted that the exchanges can seem disorienting and contradictory. We need to recognize that they were engaged in a great struggle to work out where to draw the line between religion and science, language and race, sexuality and morality, even life and death. So are we, of course, but insofar as our own debates are framed for or against the distinctions that gained predominance as a result of the Victorians' culture wars, we tend to forget that there were plenty of alternative views vying for victory, with the outcome far less apparent at the time than it appears in retrospect. Moreover, we often fail to appreciate the surprising associations that arose out of this intellectual ferment. The move that Burton made from racism to relativism is an especially telling demonstration of what could occur.

Finally, Burton's prolific array of interests points to the importance of placing Victorians' inquiries into various forms of difference within the same analytical field. However tentative and inconsistent his efforts, Burton approached race and gender and religion and language and other markers of human identity as mutually constitutive categories, alike in their epistemological meaning and often overlapping in their rhetorical and instrumental purposes. He was hardly alone in this regard; we now have a substantial body of scholarship tracing the discursive connections that the Victorians made between race, class, and gender. What we need now is to move beyond the mere acknowledgement of these associations and contemplate the uses they served in the increasingly intense and varied encounters that characterized the Victorian world of difference. Here again Burton provides us with a useful case study, both because his experiences extended to so many corners of the globe and because his efforts to draw meaning from those experiences involved him in so many of the leading controversies of his day. The sheer variety of his interests and the intensity with which they were pursued force us to move beyond the deceptive stereotypes that have so often shaped popular perceptions of the Victorians.

For all these reasons, then, Burton helps us to understand the wide-ranging set of concerns that characterized the Victorian engagement with difference. By tracing the ways Burton's curiosity about the world and its diverse inhabitants intersected with the interests of his contemporaries, we acquire a richer understanding of the man and his age. At the same time, we gain a glimpse of the closet continuities between the Victorians' preoccupations and our own. We pride ourselves on our cosmopolitanism, our appreciation of the multivalent, interconnected world we inhabit, but it can be said on the one hand that the Victorians adopted much the same stance toward the global system they confronted, while it should be acknowledged on the other hand that the categories we apply to our world bear more than a passing resemblance to those that flourished in the nineteenth century. Whether the subject is sexuality, multiculturalism, globalization, the clash of civilizations, or some other formulation of our current condition, we employ conceptions of differences that Burton and his contemporaries would have understood and would have found equally contentious.

A Note on Sources

I have dispensed with a standard bibliography for two main reasons. First, I have drawn on so many different sorts of primary and secondary material in order to set Burton's wide-ranging career and writings in their varied contexts that a complete bibliographical listing would be unwieldy and unhelpful. For those who wish to follow up on the issues I have addressed in this book, I have provided detailed references to the sources in my notes. Second, there is no dearth of bibliographical information about Burton himself. Every good biography of Burton appends a list of the many books he wrote. Nearly all of Burton's published writings—his books, journal articles, reviews, and ephemera—appear in James A. Casada's *Sir Richard F. Burton: A Biobliographical Study* (London: Mansell, 1990), as does a listing of all but one of the archives that hold his unpublished letters and manuscripts. Published items that managed to escape the notice of Casada—most of them pseudonymous articles and letters to the editors of newspaper and other periodicals—have been brought to light by Burke E. Casari, whose meticulous detective work is summarized in his essay in Alan H. Jutzi, ed., *In Search of Sir Richard Burton* (San Marino, Calif.: Huntington Library, 1993) and detailed in his privately printed *Additions to Richard F. Burton's Published Works, 1848–1888* (no date). There is no need for me to replicate these bibliographic labors.

I shall, however, try to provide an overview of those sources that have been particularly helpful to me in researching this book. Any study of Burton must rely first and foremost on his own voluminous writings, which consist of some fifty distinct works and run to more than eighty volumes. Nearly half of his books are

275

currently in print in various editions, a testament to the continued interest in his life and work. Norman M. Penzer's *Annotated Bibliography of Sir Richard Burton* (New York: Burt Franklin, 1923), though supplanted by Casada's work in some respects, remains an essential source of information about the complicated early publication history of Burton's books.

Manuscript material by and about Burton is scattered among a wide array of public institutions and private collectors. The single largest collection is available at the Huntington Library in San Marino, California, which has Burton's letters to and from various correspondents, several book and lecture manuscripts, some photographs, and other ephemera. The Huntington also owns Burton's extensive personal library, which is listed in B. J. Kirkpatrick, ed., *A Catalogue of the Library of Sir Richard Burton* (London: Royal Anthropological Society, 1978). The library speaks volumes (forgive the pun) about Burton's remarkably varied interests, and a great deal can be learned about his own thinking from the marginalia found in many of these books.

A second major manuscript collection came to public notice after Casada published his bibliography. The Wiltshire Record Office in Trowbridge, Wiltshire, possesses a large body of material that Isabel Burton left with her family upon her death, including an extensive array of letters, newspaper clippings, legal documents, photographs, and much more. It is especially enlightening about Richard's mining ventures and Isabel's activities after his death.

Other important sources of archival material by and about Burton include the Public Record Office (Kew), the Royal Geographical Society (London), the Royal Asiatic Society (London), the British Library (London), the Trinity College Library (Cambridge), and the Bodleian Library (Oxford). The John Speke and James Grant papers in the National Library of Scotland (Edin burgh) add insight into Burton's activities as an explorer. The Orleans House Gallery (Twickenham) is the main repository for the photographs, paintings, and ephemera that Isabel Burton left upon her death. The closest thing to a collected edition of Burton's letters is Donald A. Young, "The Selected Correspondence of Sir Richard Burton, 1848–1890" (M.A. thesis, University of Nebraska, Lincoln, 1979), a valuable work that reproduces letters from a number of public archives, as well as from the private collection of the late Quentin Keynes. Young also assisted Keynes in the preparation of *The Search for the Source of the Nile* (London: The Roxburghe Club, 1999), which makes available Keynes's interesting cache of letters by Burton, Speke, and others involved in the Nile controversy. Unfortunately, a large quantity of Burton material remains in the hands of private collectors, many of them far less forthcoming about their holdings than Keynes has been. Michael Hastings notes in his biography, *Richard Burton* (New York: Coward, McCann, and Geoghegan, 1978), p. 275, that he is aware of the existence of several privately owned Burton manuscripts that scholars have never seen. Many collections of Burton material become known only when they are placed on the market. In 2001 a good deal of public attention surrounded Christie's unsuccessful attempt to auction off Burton's anti-Semitic "Human Sacrifice among the Sephardine or Eastern Jews," which had been locked in the vaults of the Board of Deputies of British Jews for nearly a hundred years (where it has since been returned). Far less notice surrounded a rare book dealer's recent announcement of the sale of an extensive collection of letters by Burton to the publisher and bookseller Bernard Quaritch. Though it is unlikely that access to these and other items in private hands would significantly alter what we know about Burton, there can be little doubt that they would enrich our understanding of the man.

As it is, Burton's published writings and the available archival evidence have served as the basis for literally dozens of biographies. In addition to English-language books, French, Italian, and German studies have been written about Burton, as have several dissertations. The most impressively researched and reliable life of Burton is the most recent, Mary S. Lovell's *A Rage to Live: A Biography of Richard and Isabel Burton* (New York: W. W. Norton, 1998). Fawn M. Brodie's *The Devil Drives: A Life of Sir Richard Burton* (New York: W. W. Norton, 1967) still holds up remarkably well. Also worth reading are Frank McLynn, *Burton: Snow upon the Desert* (London: John Murray, 1990), and Donald Paul Nurse, "An Amateur Barbarian: The Life and Career of Sir Richard Burton, 1821–1890" (Ph.D. diss., University of Toronto, 1999). The best treatment of Burton's intellectual engagement with the issues of his age is Jean-François Gournay, *L'appel du proche-orient: Richard Francis Burton et son temps, 1821–1890* (Paris: Didier-Erudition, 1983). Burton's published writings have been the subject of a thoughtful literary analysis by Glenn S. Burne, *Richard F. Burton* (Boston: Twayne, 1985). Casada supplies a lengthy list of books and articles that discuss Burton, including biographies, reminiscences, and fictional representations. Since Casada's bibliography was published in 1990, there have been at least four new biographies of Burton and countless articles that address one or another aspect of his career. Several websites and an on-line discussion group also are devoted to Burton.

Far too much of the interest in Burton is myopic in character, magnifying the man while blurring the background that gave his life its shape and direction. Because Burton's activities and interests ranged so widely across countries and cultures, this myopia is by no means easy to correct, but the failure to do so leaves us with a distorted image of who he was and what he achieved. In this book I have drawn on several rich bodies of literature in order to rectify this imbalance. While it would be futile to single out particular works by name, many aspects of Burton's life and thought make a good deal more sense when set in the context of historical scholarship on the various lands and peoples that served as the backdrops for his career and the objects of his curiosity. The study of Burton also benefits from reading recent theoretically informed work on cross-cultural encounters and the epistemology of colonial knowledge. In the text I discuss some of the books and articles that I found especially helpful or provocative, and the rest are cited in my notes.

Notes

1. I especially admire Mary S. Lovell, *A Rage to Live: A Biography of Richard and Isabel Burton* (New York: W. W. Norton, 1998), and Fawn M. Brodie, *The Devil Drives: A Life of Sir Richard Burton* (New York: W. W. Norton, 1967). For further discussion of biographical treatments of Burton, see Chapter VIII and A Note on Sources.

2. These divisions continue to exist in much of the survey literature. Recent works on Victorian Britain that give little attention to the wider world include David Newsome, *The Victorian World Picture* (London: Fontana, 1998); K. Theodore Hoppen, *The Mid-Victorian Generation, 1846–1886* (Oxford: Clarendon Press, 1998); and A. N. Wilson, *The Victorians* (New York: W. W. Norton, 2003). By the same token, little notice is paid to the empire's effects on Britain in Andrew Porter, ed., *The Oxford History of the British Empire: The Nineteenth Century* (Oxford: Oxford University Press, 1999).

3. The literature on this subject has grown far too extensive to list in full, but some especially noteworthy examples include Linda Colley, *Britons: Forging the Nation, 1707–1837* (New Haven: Yale University Press, 1992); Antoinette Burton, *Burdens of History: British Feminists, Indian Women, and Imperial Culture, 1865–1915* (Chapel Hill: University of North Carolina Press, 1994); Anne McClintock, *Imperial Leather: Race, Gender, and Sexuality in the Colonial Context* (New York: Routledge, 1995); Jonathan Schneer, *London, 1900: The Imperial Metropolis* (New Haven: Yale University Press, 1999); Peter van der Veer, *Imperial Encounters: Religion and Modernity in India and Britain* (Princeton: Princeton University Press, 2001); Catherine Hall, *Civilising Subjects: Metropole and Colony in the English Imagination, 1830–1867* (Chicago: University of Chicago Press, 2002); Kathleen Wilson, *The Island Race: Englishness, Empire, and Gender in the Eighteenth Century* (New York: Routledge, 2003); and Philippa Levine, *Prostitution, Race, and Politics: Policing Venereal Disease in the British Empire* (New York: Routledge, 2003).

4. The key work that set scholars on this line of inquiry was Edward W. Said, *Orientalism* (New York: Random House, 1978), which was followed up by his *Culture and Imperialism* (New York: Alfred A. Knopf, 1993). Other noteworthy contributions to this subject include Timothy Mitch-

ell, *Colonizing Egypt* (Berkeley: University of California Press, 1988); Partha Chatterjee, *The Nation and Its Fragments: Colonial and Postcolonial Histories* (Princeton: Princeton University Press, 1993); Carol A. Breckenridge and Peter van der Veer, eds., *Orientalism and the Postcolonial Predicament* (Philadelphia: University of Pennsylvania Press, 1993); Robert J. C. Young, *Colonial Desire: Hybridity in Theory, Culture, and Race* (New York: Routledge, 1995); and Ann Laura Stoler, *Race and the Education of Desire: Foucault's History of Sexuality and the Colonial Order of Things* (Durham: Duke University Press, 1995).

5. This tension is addressed most explicitly by Thomas R. Metcalf, *Ideologies of the Raj* (Cambridge: Cambridge University Press, 1994); Anne Laura Stoler and Frederick Cooper, eds., *Tensions of Empire: Colonial Cultures in a Bourgeois World* (Berkeley: University of California Press, 1997); and Catherine Hall, ed., *Cultures of Empire* (New York: Routledge, 2002). Its origins in liberal thought are considered by Lynn Zastoupil, *John Stuart Mill and India* (Stanford: Stanford University Press, 1994), and Uday Singh Mehta, *Liberalism and Empire: A Study in Nineteenth-Century British Liberal Thought* (Chicago: University of Chicago Press, 1999)

6. Thomas Richards, *The Imperial Archive: Knowledge and the Fantasy of Empire* (London: Verso, 1993); Tony Ballantyne, "Empire, Knowledge, and Culture: From Proto-Globalization to Modern Globalization," in *Globalization in World History*, ed. A. G. Hopkins (New York: W. W. Norton, 2002), pp. 116–140.

1. THE GYPSY

1. This caption appears on the copy of the photograph recently sold as part of the estate of the late Quentin Keynes. See the Christie's sales catalogue, *The Quentin Keynes Collection, Part I: Important Travel Books and Manuscripts* (April 7, 2004), p. 191. The photography also is reproduced as the frontispiece to Quentin Keynes and Donald Young, eds., *The Search for the Source of the Nile* (London: The Roxburghe Club, 1999). The Royal Geographical Society owns a print of the photograph without the caption. Another photograph from the same sitting, which shows Burton in a slightly different pose, appears in Thomas Wright, *The Life of Sir Richard Burton* (London: Everett, 1906), opposite p. 122, and *The Quentin Keynes Collection*, p. 203.

2. *The Times*, Oct. 21, 1890, p. 8, col. 1.

3. Thomas Lloyd, "Sir Richard Burton," *The Bookman*, 30, no. 176 (May 1906): 55.

4. Alfred Bates Richards, Andrew Wilson, and St. Clair Baddeley, *A Sketch of the Career of Richard F. Burton* (London: Waterlow and Sons, 1886), p. 10, quoted by Isabel Burton, *The Life of Captain Sir Richard F. Burton* (London: Chapman and Hall, 1893), vol. 1, p. 16. Another early biography written during Burton's life and sanctioned by the Burtons also makes reference to suspicions of Gypsy blood in his ancestry. Francis Hitchman, *Richard F. Burton, K.C.M.G.: His Early, Private, and Public Life with an Account of His Travels and Explorations* (London: Sampson Low, Marston, Searle and Rivington, 1887), p. 20.

5. Isabel Burton, *Life*, vol. 1, pp. 251–252. In a later passage she suggests that Richard did have Gypsy blood, which accounted for "his fluency of languages, his wild and daring spirit, his Agnosticism, his melancholy pathos, his mysticism, his superstition . . . , his divination, his magician-like foresight into events, his insight, or reading of men through like a pane of glass, his restless wandering, his poetry" (p. 396). Also see Isabel Burton, "An Episode from the Life of Sir Richard Burton," *Journal of the Gypsy Lore Society*, 2, no. 6 (April 1891): 365–367.

6. W. H. Wilkins, *The Romance of Isabel, Lady Burton: The Story of Her Life Told in Part by Herself* (New York: Dodd Mead, 1897), vol. 1, pp. 22, 80–81.

7. Mary S. Lovell, *A Rage to Live: A Biography of Richard and Isabel Burton* (New York: W. W. Norton, 1998), p. 658.

8. Wilkins, *Romance*, vol. 1, pp. 53–54.

9. "I was enthusiastic about gypsies, Bedawin Arabs, and everything Eastern and mystic, and especially about a wild and lawless life," Isabel declares about her youthful interests. Wilkins, *Romance*, vol. 1, p. 21.

10. Arthur Symons, *Dramatis Personae* (Indianapolis: Bobbs-Merrill, 1923), pp. 242, 249.

11. Wilfred Scawen Blunt, *My Diaries*, Part 2 (London: Martin Secker, 1921), pp. 130, 132.

12. Stanley Lane-Poole, "Sir Richard Francis Burton," in *Encyclopaedia Britannica*, 11th ed. (1910), vol. 6, p. 864.

13. Richard F. Burton, "Indian Affinities of the Gypsies," *The Academy*, 7 (1875): 324–325. The unpublished essay appeared posthumously in *The Jew, the Gypsy, and El Islam*, ed. W. H. Wilkins (London: Hutchinson, 1898).

14. Founded in 1888, the Society published the *Journal of the Gypsy Lore Society* from its beginnings until 1892, when financial problems forced it to shut down.

15. See Michele H. Champagne, "'This Wild Gypsy Dream': The Gypsy

in the Nineteenth-Century British Imagination" (Ph.D. diss., University of Michigan, 2002), and George K. Behlmer, "The Gypsy Problem in Victorian England," *Victorian Studies*, 28, no. 2 (Winter 1985): 231–253.

16. Champagne, "'This Wild Gypsy Dream,'" p. 7.

17. B. C. Smark and H. T. Crofton, *The Dialect of the English Gypsies*, 2nd ed. (London: Asher, 1875), p. xvi, quoted in Behlmer, "The Gypsy Problem," p. 239.

18. Almost everything we know about Burton's early life comes from his autobiographical reflections, which constitute the first half-dozen chapters of Isabel Burton's *Life*. See also "Notes on the Burton Geneology, Collected at Different Times, by Isabel," in the Burton Papers, 2667/26, Box 1, Wiltshire Record Office, Trowbridge, Wiltshire.

19. John Pemble, *The Mediterranean Passion: Victorians and Edwardians in the South* (Oxford: Oxford University Press, 1988).

20. Isabel Burton, *Life*, vol. 1, pp. 17–18.

21. Joseph Burton to Walter Scott, July 1846, Scott Papers, ff. 121–122, MS 3867, National Library of Scotland.

22. Isabel Burton, *Life*, vol. 1, p. 32.

23. Alan H. Jutzi, "Burton and His Library," in Jutzi, ed., *In Search of Sir Richard Burton: Papers from a Huntington Library Symposium* (San Marino, Calif.: Huntington Library, 1993), p. 85.

24. Isabel Burton, *Life*, vol. 1, p. 92.

25. See Burton's cadet application, L/MIL/9/201, f. 42–46, Oriental and India Collection, British Library. John Maitland, a family friend, made the nomination on his behalf. According to the application form, appointments by purchase were prohibited, but Burton claims that his family paid £500 for the commission.

26. Different sources give different counts, ranging from twenty-five to twenty-nine, with the issue further complicated by uncertainty about what qualifies as a language. Burton is said to have told one person that he knew twenty-seven languages, though "I include different dialects of the same language in the twenty-seven." "Mr. Smalley on Capt. Burton," *The Critic*, 358 (Nov. 8, 1890): 240.

27. Burton describes his technique for learning a language in Isabel Burton, *Life*, vol., p. 81.

28. Although Victorians differed over the essential elements of civilization, they generally agreed that their own society marked its high tide. For one canonical statement on the meaning of civilization, see John Stuart Mill, "Civilization," *The Westminster Review*, 25 (April 1836): 1–28, reprinted in

George Levine, ed., *The Emergence of Victorian Consciousness: The Spirit of the Age* (New York: Free Press, 1967): 87–111.

29. Richard F. Burton, *Personal Narrative of a Pilgrimage to Al-Madinah and Meccah,* memorial ed. (1893; reprint New York: Dover, 1964), vol. 1, p. 151.

30. Richard F. Burton, *The Gold-Mines of Midian and the Ruined Midianite Cities* (1878, reprint New York: Oleander Press, 1979), p. 1. Among other relevant passages, Burton sketched out an essay near the end of his life entitled the "Drawbacks of High Civilization" in response to a request by the editor of *The Forum.* The notes can be found in his copy of Winwood Reade, *The Martyrdom of Man,* 12th ed. (London: Trubner, 1887), BL 295, Huntington Library.

2. THE ORIENTALIST

1. A classic study is David Kopf, *British Orientalism and the Bengal Renaissance: The Dynamics of Indian Modernization, 1773–1835* (Berkeley: University of California Press, 1969). Two excellent recent studies that revisit Indian Orientalism and its intellectual heritage are Thomas R. Trautmann, *Aryans and British India* (Berkeley: University of California Press, 1997), and Tony Ballantyne, *Orientalism and Race: Aryanism in the British Empire* (New York: Palgrave, 2002).

2. Edward W. Said, *Orientalism* (New York: Vintage Books, 1979), p. 3.

3. Said's influence on the scholarship about British India is so extensive it defies summary, but a few representative examples include Ronald Inden, *Imagining India* (Oxford: Blackwell, 1990); Javed Majeed, *Ungoverned Imaginings: James Mill's "The History of British India" and Orientalism* (Oxford: Oxford University Press, 1992); and Kate Teltscher, *India Inscribed: Europe and British Writing on India, 1600–1800* (Delhi: Oxford University Press, 1995). Major critiques of Said include Aijaz Ahmad, *In Theory: Classes, Nations, Literatures* (London: Verso, 1992), esp. chap. 5; John M. MacKenzie, *Orientalism: History, Theory, and the Arts* (Manchester: Manchester University Press, 1995); and Sumit Sarkar, "Orientalism Revisited: Saidian Frameworks in the Writing of Modern Indian History," *Oxford Literary Review,* 16, nos. 1–2 (1994): 205–224.

4. Richard F. Burton, *Sindh and the Races That Inhabit the Valley of the Indus* (1851; reprint Karachi: Oxford University Press, 1973), p. xxi.

5. The phrase and information come from Douglas M. Peers, *Between Mars and Mammon: Colonial Armies and the Garrison State in India, 1819–1835* (London: I. B. Tauris, 1995).

6. Peter Stanley, *White Mutiny: British Military Culture in India* (New York: New York University Press, 1998), pp. 22–28; P. J. Marshall, "British So-

ciety in India under the East India Company," *Modern Asian Studies*, 31, no. 1 (1997): 96, 98. See Patrick Cadell, *History of the Bombay Army* (London: Longman, Green, 1938), for a conventional military history of the Bombay army.

7. Quoted in Vincent A. Smith, *The Oxford History of India*, 4th ed. (Delhi: Oxford University Press, 1958), p. 609.

8. For two views by contemporaries, see Lieutenant-General Sir William Napier, *History of General Sir Charles Napier's Administration of Scinde, and the Campaign in the Cutchee Hills* (London: Chapman and Hall, 1851), who defends Napier, and Arthur F. Scott, ed., *Scinde in the Forties: Being the Journal and Letters of Colonel Keith Young, C.B.* (London: Constable, 1912), who attacks him.

9. Richard F. Burton, *Scinde; or, The Unhappy Valley* (London: Richard Bentley, 1851), vol. 2, p. 92.

10. Napier's character and policies receive repeated praise in Richard F. Burton, *Sind Revisited: With Notices of the Anglo-Indian Army; Railroads; Past, Present, and Future, etc.* (London: Richard Bentley, 1877), vol. 1, p. 114, vol. 2, pp. 38–42, and Isabel Burton, *The Life of Captain Sir Richard F. Burton* (London: Chapman and Hall, 1893), vol. 1, pp. 116–118, 140. A sketch of Napier on horseback, leading a charge into battle, can be found in the Burton Papers, 26667/26, Wiltshire Record Office. Burton also sent Napier a courtesy copy of his sword exercise manual: see the letter from Burton in the Napier Papers, Add. MS 49117, f. 214, British Library. In a characteristic declaration of his support for military government, Burton states: "a race of warriors must be ruled by the sword. They would themselves prefer military law to all the blessings of a plebiscite." Richard F. Burton, *Wanderings in West Africa* (1863; reprint New York: Dover, 1991), vol. 1, p. 155. Responding to remarks such as these, Frank McLynn calls Burton a "fascist" in *Burton: Snow upon the Desert* (London: John Murray, 1990), p. 71. Other biographers are more forgiving, and it should be noted that even the great Victorian liberal John Stuart Mill believed that "despotism is a legitimate mode of government in dealing with barbarians, provided the end be their improvement." Quoted by Richard Drayton, *Nature's Government: Science, Imperial Britain, and the 'Improvement' of the World* (New Haven: Yale University Press, 2000), p. 94.

11. Christopher Ondaatje rightly observes in his book, *Sindh Revisited: A Journey in the Footsteps of Captain Sir Richard Francis Burton* (Toronto: HarperCollins, 1996), that "many critically important clues to understanding Burton lay in India and the seven years he spent there" (p. 19),

though those clues receive little scrutiny in his travelogue. Edward Rice, *Captain Sir Richard Francis Burton* (New York: Charles Scribner's Sons, 1990), gives the lengthiest account of Burton's Indian career, but the most reliable and well researched is Mary S. Lovell, *A Rage to Live: A Biography of Richard and Isabel Burton* (New York: W. W. Norton, 1998).

12. Georgiana Stisted, *The True Life of Captain Sir Richard F. Burton* (London: H. S. Nichols, 1896); Rice, *Captain Sir Richard Francis Burton;* McLynn, *Burton;* Byron Farwell, *Burton* (New York: Avon Books, 1965). Farwell's chapter title alludes to the one-word dispatch Napier is said to have sent his superiors upon his victory in Sind: "Peccavi" (Latin for "I have sinned").

13. Richard F. Burton, *The Book of the Thousand Nights and a Night* (Benares: Kamashastra Society, 1886), vol. 10, pp. 205–206.

14. Nearly all of Burton's biographers accept without question his claims about the Karachi report and its effects on his career. One notable exception is James A. Casada, *Sir Richard F. Burton: A Biobibliographical Study* (London: Mansell, 1990), p. 29.

15. Richard Burton's Service Army List, L/MIL/12/73, ff. 115–116, Oriental and India Office Collection (hereafter cited as OIOC), British Library.

16. *The East-India Register and Directory* (London: Wm. H. Allen, 1843–1862). He was finally struck from the rolls when he was appointed British consul at Fernando Po.

17. Isabel Burton, *Life,* vol. 1, pp. 108, 109; General Sir James Simpson, quoted by Lovell, *A Rage to Live,* p. 73. Sexual relations between British officers and Indian women are discussed by Kenneth Ballhatchet, *Race, Sex, and Class under the Raj: Imperial Attitudes and Policies and Their Critics, 1793–1905* (New York: St. Martin's Press, 1980); Douglas M. Peers, "Privates Off Parade: Regimental Sexuality in the Nineteenth-Century Indian Empire," *The International History Review,* 20, no. 4 (Dec. 1998): 823–854; and E. M. Collingham, *Imperial Bodies: The Physical Experience of the Raj, c. 1800–1947* (Cambridge: Polity Press, 2001). For general examinations of the subject, see Ronald Hyam, *Empire and Sexuality: The British Experience* (Manchester: Manchester University Press, 1990), and Philippa Levine, *Prostitution, Race, and Politics: Policing Venereal Disease in the British Empire* (New York: Routledge, 2003).

18. Isabel Burton, *Life,* vol. 1, p. 107.

19. Richard F. Burton, *A Complete System of Bayonet Exercise* (London: William Clowes and Sons, 1853); Richard F. Burton, *A New System of Sword Exercise for Infantry* (London: William Clowes and Sons, 1876); Richard F. Burton, *The Book of the Sword* (London: Chatto and Windus, 1884).

20. Burton, *Scinde,* vol. 1, p. 40. Also see Stanley, *White Mutiny,* p. 46.
21. Richard F. Burton, *Falconry in the Valley of the Indus* (1852; reprint Karachi: Oxford University Press, 1997), p. 62.
22. C. A. Bayly, *Empire and Information: Intelligence Gathering and Social Communication in India, 1780–1870* (Cambridge: Cambridge University Press, 1996).
23. Peers, *Between Mars and Mammon,* p. 12; idem, "Colonial Armies and Colonial Knowledge in India, c. 1750–c. 1850" (unpublished ms.); idem, "'Those Noble Exemplars of the True Military Tradition': Constructions of the Indian Army in the Mid-Victorian Press," *Modern Asian Studies,* 31, no. 1 (1997): 109–142.
24. Bayly, *Empire and Information,* pp. 157–158.
25. *Bombay Times and Journal of Commerce,* Nov. 6, 1847, pp. 880–881. I am grateful to Burke Casari for bringing this reference to my attention.
26. Isabel Burton, *Life,* vol. 1, pp. 109, 135.
27. Bayly, *Empire and Information,* pp. 55, 94, 178, stresses the loss of this knowledge as the British placed restrictions on liaisons with native women, but these restrictions clearly did not apply in Sindh during Burton's years of service. For a perceptive comparative study of this issue, see Lynn Zastoupil, "Intimacy and Colonial Knowledge," *Journal of Colonialism and Colonial History,* 3, no. 2 (2002), an e-journal at http://muse.jhu.edu/journals.
28. Joseph Burton to Walter Scott, July 7, 1846, MS 3867, ff. 121–122, General Walter Scott Papers, MS 3867, National Library of Scotland (hereafter cited as NLS).
29. Francis Hitchman, *Richard F. Burton, K.C.M.G.: His Early, Private, and Public Life* (London: Sampson Low, Marston, Searle, and Rivington, 1887), vol. 1, p. 148.
30. Burton's Service Army List, L/MIL/12/73, ff. 115–116, OIOC.
31. Isabel Burton, *Life,* vol. 1, pp. 149, 159.
32. Burton's interest in languages was so intense and indiscriminate that he directed it toward the monkeys he kept as pets in his Baroda cantonment, claiming to have made some progress in decoding their speech. Isabel Burton, *Life,* vol. 1, p. 160.
33. *Bombay Times and Journal of Commerce,* Feb. 19, 1848, pp. 147–148. Burton personalizes this complaint in *Falconry,* p. 63. It was common for Company officers to voice their complaints in letters to the newspapers, according to Stanley, *White Mutiny,* p. 53.
34. *Bombay Times,* Feb. 23, 1848, p. 158; March 1, 1848, p. 179; March 14, 1848, p. 187.

35. "He succeeded at last, it is true, but, to use a classical expression, another such triumph would fairly have ruined him." *Bombay Times,* Feb. 19, 1848, p. 148.

36. Bernard S. Cohn, "The Command of Language and the Language of Command," in Ranajit Guha, ed., *Subaltern Studies,* vol. 4 (Delhi: Oxford University Press), pp.276–329, reprinted in Cohn, *Colonialism and Its Forms of Knowledge* (Princeton: Princeton University Press, 1996).

37. Lieutenant Burton, "A Grammar of the Jataki or Belochki Dialect," *The Journal of the Bombay Branch of the Royal Asiatic Society,* 3, part 1, no. 12 (Jan. 1849): 90; idem, "Notes and Remarks on Dr. Dorn's Chrestomathy of the Pushtu or Affghan Language," ibid., p. 61.

38. Burton, *Sindh,* p. 364.

39. Burton, *Sindh,* p. 80.

40. R. F. Burton, "Alhlak I Hindi or a Translation of the Hindustani version of Pilpay's Fables" (ms. written in Bombay, 1847), pp. 1, 47n, BL104 (a & b), Huntington Library. Burton's translation has recently been published as *Pilpay's Fables* (Tucson: Asian Ethnographer Society Press, 1997).

41. Lovell, *A Rage to Live,* p. 42. For an interesting account of Scott's contribution to the Romantic interest in folkways and its Orientalists associations, see Saree Makdisi, *Romantic Imperialism: Universal Empire and the Culture of Modernity* (Cambridge: Cambridge University Press, 1998), chap. 3.

42. See Lynn Zastoupil and Martin Moir, eds., *The Great Indian Education Debate* (Richmond, Surrey: Curzon Press, 1999).

43. Burton, *Sindh,* pp. 151–155, 364.

44. The story of this administrative debate and Burton's role in it is told by Hamida Khuhro, *The Making of Modern Sindh: British Policy and Social Change in the Nineteenth Century* (Oxford: Oxford University Press, 1999), chap. 6.

45. Lachman M. Khubchandani, "Sir Richard Burton and Sindhi Language," *Annals of the Bhandarkar Oriental Research Unit,* 66 (1985): 261. I am again grateful to Burke Casari for bringing this item to my attention.

46. William Napier (ADC to General Napier) to Walter Scott, Aug. 19, [1844], Scott Papers, MS 3867, f. 95, NLS.

47. Matthew H. Edney, *Mapping an Empire: The Geographical Construction of British India, 1765–1843* (Chicago: University of Chicago Press, 1997), p. 36. The same point has been made more succinctly by Anne McClintock, who terms mapping "a technology of possession." McClintock, *Imperial Leather: Race, Gender, and Sexuality in the Colonial Contest* (New York: Routledge, 1995), p. 28.

48. Khuhro, *Modern Sindh*, chap. 4.
49. Lt.-Col. Walter Scott, *Report on the Management of Canals and Forests in Sinde* (Bombay: printed for the Government, 1853), p. 8, MF 1/1003, OIOC.
50. Napier to Scott, Aug. 10, 1846, Scott Papers, MS 3867, ff. 123–124, NLS.
51. Lt. R. F. Burton, "Notes Relative to the Population of Sind; and the Customs, Languages, and Literature of the People," in *Selections from the Records of the Bombay Government*, vol. 17, n.s. (Bombay: Bombay Education Society's Press, 1855), pp. 637–657; Lt. R. F. Burton and J. E. Stocks, "Brief Notes Relative to the Division of Time, and the Articles of Cultivation in Sind; to which are appended Remarks on the Modes of Intoxication in that Province," in *Selections from the Records of the Bombay Government*, vol. 17, n.s. (Bombay: Bombay Education Society's Press, 1855), pp. 613–636. These papers also were collected in *Accounts and Papers: East India, Scinde*, Jan.31–Aug. 12, 1854, vol. 49 (1854). I am again grateful to Burke Casari for bringing this rare source to my attention.
52. In the course of revising the book for a second edition (which never appeared), Burton revealed that the Company had suppressed unidentified passages. See his marginal note in the copy of *Sindh*, p. 55, in the Burton Collection, BL3, Huntington Library. The information on the Company's decision to purchase copies of the book comes from Burton's Service Army List, L/MIL/12/73, OIOC.
53. Burton, *Sindh*, p. xxii.
54. Burton, *Sind Revisited*, vol. 2, p. 21.
55. Burton, *Falconry*, p. 1.
56. Burton, *Scinde, or, The Unhappy Valley*, vol. 2, p. 33. In *Sind Revisited*, vol. 2, pp. 26–27, Burton claimed that the British community in India had become more censorious of Englishmen who dressed in native garb by the 1870s, condemning "our 'morbid propensities' and our 'contemptible sacrifice of nationality in aping Asiatics.'"
57. Burton, *Falconry*, p. 65.
58. Burton, *Falconry*, pp. 65–66.
59. For an entertaining account of their exploits, see Karl Meyer and Shareen Brysac, *Tournament of Shadows: The Great Game and the Race for Empire in Asia* (London: Abacus, 2001).
60. Michael Silvestri, "The Thrill of 'Simply Dressing Up': The Indian Police, Disguise, and Intelligence Work in Colonial India," *Journal of Colonialism and Colonial History*, 2, no. 2 (2001), an e-journal at http:muse .jhu.edu/journals.
61. Burton, *Sindh*, p. 35.

62. "To maintain as much as possible the equality of these great divisions [between Hindu and Muslim], is to serve our own interest." Burton, *Sindh,* p. 362–363.

63. Burton, *Scinde,* vol. 1, p. 246.

64. See Sarah F. D. Ausari, *Sufi Saints and State Power: The Pirs of Sind, 1843–1947* (Cambridge: Cambridge University Press, 1992).

65. *Athenaeum,* 1225 (April 19, 1851): 423.

66. Burton, *Sind Revisited,* vol. 2, p. 104.

67. See George E. Marcus and Michael M. J. Fischer, *Anthropology as Cultural Critique: An Experimental Moment in the Human Sciences* (Chicago: University of Chicago Press, 1986).

68. Richard F. Burton, *Goa, and the Blue Mountains: Or, Six Months of Sick Leave* (1851; reprint Berkeley: University of California Press, 1991), pp. 226–227, 242; Burton, *Scinde,* vol. 1, pp. 248–249, vol. 2, pp. 168–169.

69. Burton, *Scinde,* vol. 2, pp. 125, 192.

70. Burton, *Sindh,* p. 283; Burton, *Scinde,* vol. 2, p. 276.

71. Burton, *Scinde,* vol. 2, pp. 270–271. He was hardly alone in this regard. See, for example, Philip Francis's reference to Indian *banyans* (commercial agents) as the "Jews of Bengal." Quoted by T. Robert Travers, "Country Whiggism Goes to Bengal: The Case of Philip Francis," paper presented to the North American Conference on British Studies, Baltimore, Nov. 2002.

72. Burton, *Sindh,* chap. 13.

73. Burton, *Sindh,* p. 283.

74. See Trautmann, *Aryans and British India.*

75. James Cowles Prichard, *The Natural History of Man* (London: Hippolyte Bailliere, 1848), notes facing p. 1, Burton Collection, BL281, HL. Burton wrote marginal notes in his copy of Prichard on two occasions, once in pen, once in pencil. The notes I refer to in this context were written in pen, and they differ so substantially from the penciled notes in their perspective on race that it appears likely that they were written first, probably toward the end of Burton's years in India or shortly thereafter. I will address the shift of attitude evident from the two sets of notes in Chapters IV and V.

76. See, for example, Richard F. Burton, *Vikram and the Vampire or Tales of Hindu Devilry* (London: Longman, Green, 1870), preface.

77. Opposite the title page of Prichard's *Natural History,* Burton wrote a lengthy outline of "Divisions," which include categories for skin complexion, skull shapes, and pelvis shapes. His annotations to Culver included comments on the relationship between skin color and climate:

Baron George Cuvier, *The Animal Kingdom* (London: Wm. S. Orr, 1849), notes on list of plates page, Burton Collection, BL273, HL. The inscription "R. F. Burton, Bombay 1854" indicates the approximate date of the marginalia.

78. Burton, *Goa*, pp. 45, 97.

79. Mark Harrison, *Climates and Constitutions: Health, Race, Environment, and British Imperialism in India, 1600–1850* (Delhi: Oxford University Press, 1999), examines British notions of race and climate in India.

80. Burton, *Goa*, pp. 156, 88.

81. Burton, *Scinde*, vol. 1, p. 271. This passage reappears in *Sind Revisited*, vol. 1, p. 317.

82. Isabel Burton, *Life*, vol, 1, pp. 123, 144.

83. Joseph Burton to Walter Scott, July 1846, Scott Papers, MS 3867, ff. 121–122, NLS.

84. Isabel Burton, *Life*, vol. 1, p. 104.

85. Richard Burton to Grattan Geary, July 13, 1877, Metcalf Collection, vol. 4, Huntington Library.

86. Burton, *Goa*, p. 289. For the social history of Ootacamund and other hill stations in British India, see Dane Kennedy, *The Magic Mountains: Hill Stations and the British Raj* (Berkeley: University of California Press, 1996).

87. For a fuller analysis of *Goa*, see my introduction to the University of California reprint of the book.

88. Parama Roy, *Indian Traffic: Identities in Question in Colonial and Postcolonial India* (Berkeley: University of California Press, 1998), pp. 29–30.

89. Burton, *Goa*, pp. 127–130, 65–67. In a forlorn attempt at farce, Burton also tells the story in *Goa* of a British officer—a thinly disguised version of himself—who tries to kidnap a young woman from a convent.

90. Burton, *Scinde*, vol. 1, pp. 72–78.

91. For a shrewd analysis of the rhetorical strategies that Burton uses in his authorial relationship with readers, see Tim Youngs, *Travellers in Africa: British Travelogues, 1850–1900* (Manchester: Manchester University Press, 1994), p. 96.

92. Burton, *Scinde*, vol. 1, pp. 1, 195; vol. 2, pp. 242, 309.

3. THE IMPERSONATOR

1. Burton to James C. Melvile, Secretary, India House, Nov. 6, 1852, L/PJ/1/318, Oriental and India Office Collection (hereafter cited as OIOC), British Library.

2. For a meticulous examination of the circumstances that led to the pil-

grimage, see Jon R. Godsall, "Fact and Fiction in Richard Burton's Personal Narrative of the Pilgrimage to El-Medinah and Meccah (1855–6)," *Journal of the Royal Asiatic Society*, 3rd ser., 3, part 3 (November 1993): 331–351.

3. This summary draws mainly on Kathryn Tidrick, *Heart-Beguiling Araby* (London: I. B. Tauris, 1989). See also Thomas J. Assad, *Three Victorian Travellers: Burton, Blunt, Doughty* (London: Routledge and Kegan Paul, 1964).

4. In W. H. Wilkins, *The Romance of Isabel Lady Burton: The Story of Her Life* (New York: Dodd Mead, 1897), p. 19, Isabel refers to *Tancred*, "with its glamour of the East," as one of the favorite books of her youth, though she probably read the novel later than she indicates in her memoirs; that is, after she had met Richard and he had made the pilgrimage. Her copy of *Tancred* is inscribed: "Isabel Arundell from her attached Mother Eliza Arundell, 20th March 1854," in BL845, Burton Collection, Huntington Library.

5. This paragraph and the following one are drawn largely from Jason Thompson, *Sir Gardner Wilkinson and His Circle* (Austin: University of Texas Press, 1992); Lynne Withey, *Grand Tours and Cook's Tours: A History of Leisure Travel, 1750–1915* (New York: William Morrow, 1997), chap. 8; Debra N. Mancoff, *David Roberts: Travels in Egypt and the Holy Land* (San Francisco: Pomegranate, 1999). and John Barrell, "Death on the Nile: Fantasy and the Literature of Tourism, 1840–60," in Catherine Hall, ed., *Cultures of Empire* (London: Routledge, 2000), pp. 187–206.

6. Burton to Norton Shaw, Nov. 16, 1853, Burton Correspondence, Royal Geographical Society.

7. See Jason Thompson, "Osman Effendi: A Scottish Convert to Islam in Early Nineteenth-Century Egypt," *Journal of World History*, 5, no. 1 (1994): 99–123. For earlier British contact with the region, which provides a context for the experience of Osman Effendi and suggests that there were many others much like him, see Linda Colley, *Captives: Britain, Empire, and the World, 1600–1850* (New York: Pantheon Books, 2002), part 1.

8. Richard Trench, *Arabian Travellers* (London: Macmillan, 1986), chaps. 1–3.

9. See Amira K. Bennison, "Muslim Universalism and Western Globalization," in A. G. Hopkins, ed., *Globalization in World History* (New York: W. W. Norton, 2002), pp. 73–98.

10. Salih, "Burton at Damascus," *The Bookman*, October 1891, p. 24. Much

the same point is made by Wilfred Scawen Blunt, *My Diaries* (London: Martin Seeker, 1921), part 1, p. 132.

11. By way of example, consider the case of Richard Clifford Kennedy, a lieutenant in the 2nd Bombay Light Cavalry, who became the subject of an official investigation in 1859 when a press report claimed that he had voiced objections to British rule in India. The investigation found that he had taken residence in Damascus, where he wore Turkish dress and had a Muslim wife. Kennedy claimed that he had merely disguised himself as a Muslim in order "the more easily to be admitted into the society of the inhabitants," citing in his defense the example of Burton's pilgrimage to Mecca. The authorities were not persuaded, and he was discharged from the army. See the collection of documents about the case compiled by Rob Van Craenenburg for the Victorian Web: http://65.107 .211.206/history/empire/kennedy/kennedy1–18. I am grateful to Burke Casari for bringing this material to my attention.

12. Terry Castle, *Masquerade and Civilization: The Carnivalesque in Eighteenth-Century English Culture and Fiction* (Stanford: Stanford University Press, 1986); Tracy C. Davis, "The Actress in Victorian Pornography," in Kristine Ottesen Garrigan, ed., *Victorian Scandals: Representations of Gender and Class* (Athens: Ohio University Press, 1992), pp. 99–133.

13. See Nina Auerbach, *Private Theatricals: The Lives of the Victorians* (Cambridge: Harvard University Press, 1990).

14. Quoted in Tidrick, *Heart-Beguiling Araby*, p. 66.

15. Fawn M. Brodie, *The Devil Drives: A Life of Sir Richard Burton* (New York: W. W. Norton, 1967), p. 107.

16. For an important analysis of the role of performance in eighteenth-century British imperial culture, see Kathleen Wilson, *The Island Race: Englishness, Empire, and Gender in the Eighteenth Century* (London: Routledge, 2003), esp. chap. 4.

17. F. Grenfell Baker, "Sir Richard F. Burton as I Knew Him," *Cornhill Magazine*, 304 (October 1921), 417. The connections between the multiple identities Burton assumed over the course of his career and the roles of an actor are addressed by Jonathan Bishop, "The Identities of Sir Richard Burton: The Explorer as Actor," *Victorian Studies*, 1, no. 2 (December 1957): 119–135.

18. See Homi K. Bhabha, *The Location of Culture* (London: Routledge, 1994).

19. Anne McClintock, *Imperial Leather: Race, Gender, and Sexuality in the Colonial Contest* (New York: Routledge, 1995), p. 69.

20. Richard F. Burton, *Personal Narrative of a Pilgrimage to Al-Madinah and Meccah*, Memorial Edition (1893; reprint New York: Dover, 1964), vol. 1, p. 114.

21. Kaja Silverman, "White Skin, Brown Masks: The Double Mimesis, or with Lawrence in Arabia," *Differences*, 1, no. 3 (1989), p. 19.

22. Edward Said, *Orientalism* (New York: Vintage Books, 1979): 195, 196.

23. Parama Roy, *Indian Traffic: Identities in Question in Colonial and Postcolonial India* (Berkeley: University of California Press, 1998), p. 26. Also see Patrick Brantlinger, *Rule of Darkness: British Literature and Imperialism, 1830–1914* (Ithaca: Cornell University Press, 1988), pp. 163–164.

24. Burton, *Personal Narrative*, vol. 1, pp. 5, 6. Evidence that the Turk saw through Burton's disguise is presented by Mary S. Lovell, *A Rage to Live: A Biography of Richard and Isabel Burton* (New York: W. W. Norton, 1998), p. 121. For an amusing indication of the ease with which a Briton in the guise of a "native" could deceive fellow countrymen, consider the improbable case of Virginia Woolf, the novelist, who in 1910 blackened her face, put on a false beard, and obtained a tour of the battleship *Dreadnought* from naval officials who were led to believe that she was an Abyssinian prince on an official visit to England. See Panthea Reid, "Virginia Woolf, Leslie Stephen, Julia Margaret Cameron, and the Prince of Abyssinia: An Inquiry into Certain Colonialist Representations," *Biography*, 22, no. 3 (Summer 1999): 322–355.

25. Isabel Burton, *The Life of Captain Sir Richard F. Burton* (London: Chapman and Hall, 1893), vol. 2, p. 162.

26. Osman Effendi also acquired "a more intimate knowledge of Egyptian life" by dispensing medical advice to locals. Thompson, "Osman Effendi," p. 105.

27. Burton, *Personal Narrative*, vol. 1, pp. 13, 14, 15. He reproduces a copy of the diploma as Appendix III in *Personal Narrative*, vol. 2, but with his name omitted. In his subsequent book, an account of his journey to Harar in Ethiopia, he refers to "my diploma as a master Sufi." Richard Burton, *First Footsteps in East Africa* (1856; reprint New York: Frederick A. Praeger, 1966), p. 209.

28. Roy, *Indian Traffic*, p. 8.

29. For a fascinating analysis of the modernizing forces at work in Egypt in the nineteenth century, see Timothy Mitchell, *Colonizing Egypt* (Berkeley: University of California Press, 1988).

30. Burton, *Personal Narrative*, vol. 1, pp. 216–217, 240–241, 152, 167. Burton gives a somewhat different account of this event in a lecture he gave in Brazil on the pilgrimage. Here he implies that Mohammed's discovery of

the sextant complicated his efforts to obtain a passport from authorities, obliging him to prove himself by lecturing on Muslim theology. Richard Burton, "Burton's Pilgrimage to Mecca; An Unpublished Ms. of the Late Sir Richard F. Burton, F.R.S.L.," *Transactions of the Royal Society of Literature*, 20, part 3, 2nd ser. (1899): 201.

31. Burton, *Personal Narrative*, vol. 1, pp. 165–167.

32. In addition to the *Personal Narrative*, Burton wrote two reports on the journey for the Royal Geographical Society, published as "Journey to Medina, with Route from Yambu," *Journal of the Royal Geographical Society*, 24 (1854): 208–225, and "A Journey from El-Medina to Mecca down the 'Darb el Sharki' on the Eastern Road (hitherto unvisited by Europeans) in September 1853," *Journal of the Royal Geographical Society*, 25 (1855): 121–136.

33. Burton, *Personal Narrative*, vol. 1, pp. 150, 287; vol. 2, pp. 86, 118, 119. I am aware of the clever revisionist thesis by Ter Ellingson, *The Myth of the Noble Savage* (Berkeley: University of California Press, 2001), which claims that the concept of the noble savage was the invention of the British ethnographer John Crawfurd in 1859, but I think his argument is too rigid in its determination of the ways the terms "noble" and "savage" were joined together as an analytic category.

34. Burton, *Personal Narrative*, vol. 1, p. 428; vol. 2, p. 237; vol. 1, p. 109–110n; vol. 2, p. 92. Also see John Hayman, ed., *Sir Richard Burton's Travels in Arabia and Africa: Four Lectures from a Huntington Library Manuscript* (San Marino: Huntington Library, 1990), p. 40.

35. See Antoinette Burton, *Burdens of History: British Feminists, Indian Women, and Imperial Culture, 1865–1915* (Chapel Hill: University of North Carolina Press, 1994).

36. Burton, *Personal Narrative*, vol. 2, p. 90.

37. R. F. Burton, "Notes on Waitz's Anthropology," *The Anthropology Review*, 2, no. 7 (November 1864): 249.

38. Burton, *Personal Narrative*, vol. 2, p. 91; vol. 1, p. 229n, 175n. In a footnote written in Latin so as to escape British censors, Burton also notes that female circumcision is widespread in North Africa and Arabia, though he makes no editorial comment on a practice that has become the focal point of criticism by Western feminists in recent decades. See *Personal Narrative*, vol. 2, p. 19n.

39. Rana Kabbani, *Europe's Myths of Orient* (London: Macmillan, 1986), p. 48.

40. Richard F. Burton, *Two Trips to Gorilla Land and the Cataracts of the*

Congo (London: Sampson Low, Marston, Low, and Searle, 1876), vol. 1, p. 80.

41. Richard F. Burton, *The City of the Saints and across the Rocky Mountains to California* (1862: reprint Niwot: University Press of Colorado, 1990), p. 8. For a shrewd analysis of Burton's view of Mormonism, see Scott Dransfield, "'Orientalizing' the American West: Sir Richard Burton's 'City of the Saints,'" *Nineteenth-Century Prose,* 23, no. 1 (Spring 1996): 40–53.

42. Burton, *City of the Saints,* pp. 428–441. Also see Burton, "Waitz's Anthropology," p. 240.

43. Richard F. Burton, *Wanderings in West Africa* (1863: reprint New York: Dover, 1991), vol. 1, pp. 180–181.

44. Richard F. Burton, *Explorations of the Highlands of the Brazil* (London: Tinsley Brothers, 1869), vol. 1, p. 374n.

45. Richard F. Burton, *The Book of the Thousand Nights and a Night* (Benares: printed for the Kamashastra Society, 1885–1886), vol. 10, pp. 195, 199.

46. Burton, *Personal Narrative,* vol. 1, pp. 161, 226, xxiii.

47. Burton, *First Footsteps,* p. 54.

48. Richard F. Burton, *The Guide-Book: A Pictorial Pilgrimage to Mecca and Medina* (London: printed for the author by William Clowes, 1865), p. 17.

49. Hayman, ed., *Burton's Travels,* p. 18.

50. Burton, "Waitz's Anthropology," pp. 240, 248, 249.

51. Sir Richard F. Burton, *The Jew, the Gypsy, and El Islam* (London: Hutchinson, 1898), p. 337.

52. *Anthropological Review,* 3 (1865): ccxi.

53. *London Review,* Jan. 16, 1863; Isabel Burton, "Preface," *Highlands of the Brazil,* vol. 1, p. viii; *The Echo,* Aug. 19, 1870; *The Spectator,* no. 1489 (Nov. 27, 1875); *Saturday Review,* May 25, 1878; unidentified review essay on *Abeokuta* and *Mission to Gelele,* bound in a volume of pamphlets in the Burton Library, BL228. Burton assiduously collected reviews of his books, and many of them, including those cited above, were clipped and inserted in his copies of the books under review.

54. Carl W. Ernst, *The Shambhala Guide to Sufism* (Boston: Shambhala, 1997), p. 9.

55. Isabel Burton, *Life,* vol. 1, p. 360; Richard Burton to Richard Monckton Milnes, March 24, 1864, Lord Houghton Collection, 228/27, Trinity College Library, Cambridge University.

56. Bertrand Russell and Patricia Russell, eds., *The Amberley Papers* (New York: Simon and Schuster, 1937), vol. 1, p. 347.

57. Isabel Burton, *Life,* vol. 1, p. 123.

58. Burton, *City of the Saints,* p. 301.

59. Richard Burton, *A Mission to Gelele, King of Dahome* (1864; reprint London: Routledge and Kegan Paul, 1996), pp. 292, 293.

60. Peter van der Veer, *Imperial Encounters: Religion and Modernity in India and Britain* (Princeton: Princeton University Press, 2001), p. 63.

61. Burton, *Highlands of Brazil,* vol. 1, p. 227.

62. Isabel Burton, *Life,* vol. 1, pp. 545–546. She makes much the same point in *Life,* vol. 2, p. 137.

63. Richard Burton to Norton Shaw, Oct. 16, 1854 [1853], and Nov. 16, 1853, Burton Correspondence, Royal Geographical Society (hereafter cited as RGS), London.

64. Burton to Shaw, Dec. 15, 1853, RGS.

65. This was the goal, for example, of Mansfield Parkyns, who spent several years in Ethiopia and Sudan in the 1840s. See Duncan Cumming, *The Gentleman Savage: The Life of Mansfield Parkyns, 1823–1894* (London: Century, 1987).

66. John Hanning Speke, *What Led to the Discovery of the Source of the Nile* (Edinburgh: William Blackwood and Sons, 1864), p. 23; Richard F. Burton, *Zanzibar; City, Island, and Coast* (London: Tinsley Brothers, 1872), vol. 2, p. 383.

67. Richard Burton, *First Footsteps in East Africa, or, An Exploration of Harar,* Memorial Edition (1894; reprint New York: Dover, 1987), vol. 1, pp. 163–164.

68. Burton, *First Footsteps,* vol. 1, pp. 166, 197. Also see his "A Trip to Harar," *Journal of the Royal Geographical Society,* 25 (1855): 136–150, and Hayman, ed., *Travels in Arabia and Africa,* lecture 3.

69. At the time the Turks and Egyptians were the most aggressive imperialists in the region. When Mansfield Parkyns entered the Sudan in 1844, he was suspected of being a Turkish or Egyptian spy. Cumming, *Gentleman Savage,* pp. 112, 128.

70. Burton was treated by the acting civil surgeon at Aden, who reports that the javelin pierced his palate and destroyed several molars. He also notes that Burton was suffering from secondary syphilis. Acting Civil Surgeon to Acting Political Resident, Aden, April 22, 1855, R.P. 2173, Manuscripts Department, British Library.

71. Gordon Waterfield included the official correspondence and reports on the Berbera incident as chap. 12 of the edition of *First Footsteps in East Africa* (New York: Frederick A. Praeger, 1966) that he edited.

72. Burton, *First Footsteps,* vol. 1, p. 35.

73. Burton to Albert Tootal, May 16, 1870, Metcalf Collection of Burton Manuscripts, vol. 3, Huntington Library.

74. Consul General Eldridge to Ambassador Elliott, Nov. 18, 1870, FO78/2259, Public Record Office; Lovell, *A Rage to Live,* pp. 489–499, 543.

75. Isabel Burton, *Life,* vol. 1, p. 481.

76. Salih, "Burton at Damascus," p. 24.

77. Isabel Burton, *Life,* vol. 1, p. 474. Among the more notable Western women who dressed as Arab men were the famous free spirit Jane Digby, a friend of the Burtons who resided in the Lebanon with her Arab husband, and the French writer Isabelle Eberhardt, who was married to an Algerian man. See Lesley Blanch, *The Wilder Shores of Love* (New York: Carroll and Graf, 1983), and Billie Melman, *Women's Orients: English Women and the Middle East, 1718–1918* (London: Macmillan, 1992), p. 13.

78. See, for example, the discussion of the relationship between Arthur Munby and Hannah Cullwick by McClintock, *Imperial Leather,* chaps. 2 and 3.

79. Burton, *Personal Narrative,* vol. 1, p. 150.

80. Richard F. Burton, *The Gold-Mines of Midian and the Ruined Midianite Cities* (1878; reprint New York: Oleander Press, 1979), p. 1.

81. See Tidrick, *Heart-Beguiling Araby;* John M. MacKenzie, *Orientalism: History, Theory, and the Arts* (Manchester: Manchester University Press, 1995), p. 59; and Hsu-Ming Teo, "Clean Spaces, Dirty Bodies: The Middle Eastern Desert in British Women's Travel Writing, 1890–1914," in Patricia Grimshaw and Diane Kirkby, eds., *Dealing with Difference: Essays in Gender, Culture, and History* (Melbourne: University of Melbourne Press, 1997), pp. 23–33, which argues that the desert was especially liberating to British women.

4. THE EXPLORER

1. For reflections on the explorer as imperial hero, see John M. MacKenzie, "Heroic Myths of Empire," in John M. MacKenzie, ed., *Popular Imperialism and the Military 1850–1950* (Manchester: Manchester University Press, 1992), pp. 109–138.

2. The novel is William Harrison, *Burton and Speke* (New York: St. Martin's Press, 1982), which served as the basis for the film *Mountains of the Moon* (directed by Bob Rafelson, 1989). Among the many narrative histories that recount the Burton/Speke expedition and its repercussions, see Alan Moorehead, *The White Nile* (London: Hamish Hamilton,

1960), and Christopher Hibbert, *Africa Explored: Europeans in the Dark Continent, 1769–1889* (London: Allan Lane, 1982). A useful recent book on the expedition that draws extensively from Quentin Keynes's private collection of letters by Burton and Speke is Donald Young, ed., *The Search for the Source of the Nile* (London: The Roxburghe Club, 1999).

3. Richard F. Burton, "The Lake Region of Central Equatorial Africa, with Notices of the Lunar Mountains and the Sources of the White Nile," *Journal of the Royal Geographical Society*, 29 (1859): 6.

4. Mary Louise Pratt, *Imperial Eyes: Travel Writing and Transculturation* (London: Routledge, 1992). Also see Tony Ballantyne, "Empire, Knowledge, and Culture: From Proto-Globalization to Modern Globalization," in A. G. Hopkins, ed., *Globalization in World History* (New York: W. W. Norton, 2002), pp. 116–140, who refers to the rise of a "cartographic consciousness" (p. 124).

5. Robert A. Stafford, *Scientist of Empire: Sir Roderick Murchison, Scientific Exploration, and Victorian Imperialism* (Cambridge: Cambridge University Press, 1989), p. 22.

6. See Stafford, *Scientist of Empire*. David Mackay, *In the Wake of Cook: Exploration, Science, and Empire, 1780–1801* (New York: St. Martin's Press, 1985), shows that this emphasis on empirical observation had its roots in the naval explorations of the late eighteenth century and was connected with the development of more precise scientific instrumentation.

7. For an insightful analysis of these guidebooks and their role in establishing scientific standards of exploration, see Felix Driver, *Geography Militant: Cultures of Exploration and Empire* (Oxford: Blackwell, 2001), chap. 3.

8. Francis Galton, *Memories of My Life*, 2nd ed. (London: Methuen, 1908), p. 199.

9. Nicholas Wright Gillham, *A Life of Sir Francis Galton: From African Exploration to the Birth of Eugenics* (New York: Oxford University Press, 2001), p. 98.

10. Burton's copies of Sir Francis Galton, *The Art of Travel: or, Shifts and Contrivances Available in Wild Countries*, 2nd ed. (London: John Murray, 1856), Colonel J. R. Jackson, *What to Observe; or, the Traveller's Reminiscencer*, 2nd ed. (London: Madden and Malcolm, 1845), and Sir John F. W. Herschel, ed., *A Manual of Scientific Enquiry*, 2nd ed. (London: John Murray, 1851), are in the Huntington Library's Burton collection, BL1360. Burton recommended the works by Galton and Jackson/Shaw in the edition of a guidebook for travelers in the American West that he edited and annotated: Randolph B. Marcy, *The Prairie Traveler:*

A Hand-Book for Overland Expeditions (London: Trübner and Co., 1863), p. 53.

11. Richard F. Burton and J. H. Speke, "A Coasting Voyage from Mombasa to the Pangani River; Visit to Sultan Kimwere; and Progress of the Expedition into the Interior," *Journal of the Royal Geographical Society,* 28 (1858): 226.

12. Richard F. Burton, *The Lake Regions of Central Africa* (1860; reprint New York: Dover Publications, 1995), pp. 117, 546. Although the Royal Geographical Society shipped a case of instruments to Zanzibar for the expedition, it failed to arrive. Burton obtained replacements from the Bombay Geographical Society and other sources in Bombay.

13. Burton and Speke, "A Coasting Voyage," pp. 221, 222, 224.

14. Galton, *Memories,* pp. 171–172.

15. Burton, "Lake Regions," pp. 20–21.

16. Richard F. Burton, "Narrative of a Trip to Harar," *Journal of the Royal Geographical Society,* 25 (1855): 138.

17. Burton to Norton Shaw, April 9, 1856, Burton Correspondence, Royal Geographical Society.

18. Burton, "Lake Regions," p. 20.

19. For an excellent analysis of the role that science and technology played in Western claims of superiority, see Michael Adas, *Machines as the Measure of Men: Science, Technology, and Ideologies of Western Dominance* (Ithaca: Cornell University Press, 1989).

20. Richard F. Burton, *Zanzibar: City, Island, and Coast,* vol. 2 (London: Tinsley Brothers, 1872), p. 137.

21. Richard F. Burton, trans., *Os Lusiadas (The Lusiads),* 2 vols. (London: Bernard Quaritch, 1880); Richard F. Burton, *Camoens: His Life and His Lusiads,* 2 vols. (London: Bernard Quaritch, 1881); and Richard F. Burton, trans., *Camoens, The Lyricks,* 2 vols. (London: Bernard Quaritch, 1884). Burton was not the only nineteenth-century British explorer to become fascinated by Camoes. Sir Thomas Livingston Mitchell, who explored and surveyed portions of Australia, also published a translation of Camoes's *Lusiads.* Paul Carter, *The Road to Botany Bay* (London: Faber and Faber, 1987), p. 122.

22. Burton, *Zanzibar,* vol. 2, pp. 222–223.

23. Driver, *Geography Militant,* p. 12; Stafford, *Scientist of Empire,* pp. 38, 194–195.

24. Galton to James Grant, Nov. 24, 1864, Grant Papers, MS 17909, ff. 93–94, National Library of Scotland (hereafter cited as NLS).

25. Speke to William Blackwood, no date [1863], Blackwood Papers, MS 4185, ff. 282–283, NLS. Stanley to Clement Markham, Sept. 5, 1872, Sir Francis Galton Papers, 76, University College, London.

26. Richard F. Burton, *The Jew, The Gypsy, and El Islam* (London: Hutchinson, 1898), p. 164. Burton, *Lake Regions,* p. vii.

27. Burton, *Lake Regions,* pp. 365–366. Comments correcting Cooley also appear in Burton's lengthy official report on the expedition. The sharp-tongued Burton was unable to resist referring to one of Cooley's publications as "a most able paper which wanted nothing but the solid basis of accurate data." Quoted by J. N. L. Baker, "Sir Richard Burton and the Nile Sources," *The English Historical Review,* 59, no. 233 (January 1944): 61.

28. W. D. Cooley, *The Memoir on the Lake Regions of East Africa, Reviewed* (London: Edward Stanford, 1864). For a summary of Cooley's career, see "William Desborough Cooley," *Dictionary of National Biography,* vol. 12 (London: Smith, Elder, 1887), pp. 107–108. Burton responded to Cooley's pamphlet in a letter to the *Athenaeum,* 1899 (March 19, 1864): 407–408, to which Cooley wrote a rejoinder. Eager to have the last word, Burton drafted an attack on Cooley that he sought to attach as an appendix to his translation of *The Lands of Cazembe: Lacerda's Journey to Cazembe in 1798* (London: John Murray, 1873), but the Royal Geographical Society, which sponsored the publication, rejected it. He issued it himself in *Supplementary Papers to the Mwata Cazembe* (Trieste: privately printed, 1873), BL217/43, Huntington Library.

29. Much the same point is made by Alexander Maitland, *Speke* (London: Constable, 1971), p. 99.

30. See W. H. Wilkins, *The Romance of Isabel Lady Burton: The Story of Her Life* (New York: Dodd Mead, 1897), vol. 1, pp. 144, 152; Mary S. Lovell, *A Rage to Live: A Biography of Richard and Isabel Burton* (New York: W. W. Norton, 1998), pp. 317–318.

31. See Mrs. Charles E. B. Russell, ed., *General Rigby, Zanzibar, and the Slave Trade* (London: George Allen and Unwin, 1935), pp. 234–273. The Indian government chastised Burton, who was so stung by its judgment that he published an exchange of correspondence on the subject as an appendix to the *Lake Regions* in hopes of defusing the controversy.

32. Gillham, *Galton,* pp. 114, 131–133; Driver, *Geography Militant,* p. 129.

33. Burton to Lord Houghton, Sept. 23, 1872, Lord Houghton Collection, Trinity College Library, Cambridge University.

34. This discussion of the East African caravan trade draws on Jonathon Glassman, *Feasts and Riot: Revelry, Rebellion, and Popular Consciousness*

on the Swahili Coast, 1856–1888 (Portsmouth, N.H.: Heinemann, 1995), chap. 2, and Stephen J. Rockel, "'A Nation of Porters': The Nyamwezi and the Labour Market in Nineteenth-Century Tanzania," *Journal of African History,* 41 (2000): 173–195.

35. For information on the Beluchis of East Africa (alternative spellings include Baluchis and Balochis), see http://www.baloch2000.org/people/africa.htm. I am grateful to Jan-Georg Deutsch for bringing this source to my attention.

36. Burton, "Lake Regions," p. 12; Burton and Speke, "A Coasting Voyage," p. 224; Burton, *Lake Regions,* p. 434.

37. Richard Burton to Norton Shaw, Feb. 25, 1855, Burton Correspondence, Royal Geographical Society, London. Burton, *Zanzibar,* vol. 2, p. 225.

38. Driver, *Geography Militant,* chap. 6.

39. Johannes Fabian, *Out of Our Minds: Reason and Madness in the Exploration of Central Africa* (Berkeley: University of California Press, 2000).

40. Burton, *Lake Regions,* p. 74. The same point is made by Isabel Burton, *The Life of Captain Sir Richard F. Burton* (London: Chapman and Hall, 1893), vol 1, p. 281.

41. Richard F. Burton, *Abeokuta and the Cameroons Mountains* (London: Tinsley Brothers, 1863), vol. 1, p. 5; vol. 2, p. 173.

42. Burton, *Zanzibar,* vol. 2, pp. 387, 396.

43. Burton made similar complaints about Henry Morton Stanley. His review of Stanley's *How I Found Livingstone in Central Africa* stressed that it was littered with linguistic errors and concluded rather snidely that Stanley "wants only study and discipline to make him a first-rate traveler." Burton, *Supplementary Papers to the Mwata Cazembe,* p. xxviii.

44. Burton, *Lake Regions,* p. 390. Also see Isabel Burton, *Life,* vol. 1, pp. 290, 309, 315, 316.

45. Burton, *Zanzibar,* vol. 1, p. 438; Burton, *Lake Region,* p. 406.

46. Bombay was a Yao African from the region near Lake Nyasa who had been enslaved at the age of twelve, transported to Zanzibar, and sold to an Arab merchant who took him to Bombay, whence he acquired his knowledge of Hindustani and his names Bombay and Sidi (or Seedy: an Indian term for Muslims of black African descent). He subsequently spent some time as a sailor and soldier before making himself indispensable to a series of European explorers in East Africa. See Donald Simpson, *Dark Companions: The African Contribution to European Exploration* (New York: Barnes and Noble, 1976), p. 12, and Henry Yule and A. C. Burnell, *Hobson-Jobson* (1886; reprint Calcutta: Rupa, 1986), p. 806.

47. Roy C. Bridges, "John Hanning Speke: Negotiating a Way to the Nile,"

in Robert I. Rotberg, ed., *Africa and Its Explorers* (Cambridge: Harvard University Press, 1970), p. 106.

48. Burton, *Lake Region*, pp. 411–412.

49. John Hanning Speke, *What Led to the Discovery of the Source of the Nile* (Edinburgh: William Blackwood and Sons, 1864), pp. 202–203.

50. Speke told Rigby that the Royal Geographical Society had selected him to lead a second expedition "in consequence of my having done the scientific part of the last one." Speke to Christopher Rigby, Sept. 3, 1859, ff. 82–83, Grant Papers, MS 17910, NLS.

51. Speke to William Blackwood, Nov. 5, 1859, Blackwood papers, MS 4143, ff. 134–135, NLS.

52. Speke to Christopher Rigby, [no month], 22, 1860, Grant Papers, MS 17910, ff. 96–97, NLS. Rigby shared Speke's distrust of Burton's intellectual ability, describing him as an "untrustworthy concocter of books." Rigby, manuscript comments on Burton's book on Zanzibar (no date), Grant Papers, MS 17922, f. 107.

53. Speke to Christopher Rigby, Oct. 6, 1860, in Russell, ed., *General Rigby,* p. 236.

54. Isabel Burton, *Life,* vol. 1, p. 290.

55. Greg Garrett draws a similar distinction between the views of Speke and Burton on the value of Africans as a "potential source of knowledge" in his essay "Relocating Burton: Public and Private Writings on Africa," *The Journal of African Travel-Writing,* 2 (March 1997): 70.

56. Sean Redmond, "Speke's Journal," *The Journal of African Travel-Writing,* 3 (September 1997): 90.

57. Speke, *What Led to the Discovery,* pp. 198, 314. Outraged by this statement, Burton quotes it as evidence of Speke's ignorance in his *Lake Regions,* p. 412. Speke also declared in his *Journal of the Discovery of the Source of the Nile* (1868) that he had "made up my mind never to sit upon the ground as the natives and Arabs are obliged to do, nor to make my obeisance in any other manner than is customary in England." Quoted in Redmond, "Speke's Journal," p. 89.

58. Speke, *What Led to the Discovery,* pp. 285, 277.

59. Burton, *Lake Regions,* pp. 359–360.

60. The disconcerting effects of this reversal of the ethnographic gaze on Europeans in Africa has been noted by Timothy Burke, *Lifebouy Men, Lux Women: Commodification, Consumption, and Cleanliness in Modern Zimbabwe* (Durham, N.C.: Duke University Press, 1996), p. 32, and Fabian, *Out of Our Minds,* p. 186.

61. Burton, *Zanzibar,* vol. 2, pp. 3–4.

62. Leaves from Burton's 1860 notebook, Add. MS 49380, f. 54, British Library.

63. Richard F. Burton, *The City of the Saints and across the Rocky Mountains to California* (1862; reprint Niwoto: University Press of Colorado, 1990), p. 42.

64. See, for example, Elliott West, *The Contested Plains: Indians, Goldseekers, and the Rush to Colorado* (Lawrence: University Press of Kansas, 1998), chap. 9.

65. Randolph B. Marcy, *The Prairie Traveler: A Hand-Book for Overland Expeditions*, ed. Richard F. Burton (London: Trubner, 1863). The original edition was published in New York in 1859. On Marcy, see William H. Goetzmann, *Exploration and Empire: The Explorer and the Scientist in the Winning of the American West* (New York: Vintage Books, 1966), pp. 271–274.

66. Marcy, *Prairie Traveler,* pp. 154–160. Burton also discusses the use of Indian sign language in *City of the Saints,* pp. 123–130.

67. Richard F. Burton, *Abeokuta and the Cameroons Mountains: An Exploration* (London: Tinsley Brothers, 1863), vol. 2, p. 109.

68. Burton's experiment in sign language was reflective of a broader effort in the nineteenth century to devise a global lingua franca, which inspired, for example, the invention of Esperanto. See T. N. Harper, "Empire, Diaspora, and the Languages of Globalism, 1850–1914," in A. G. Hopkins, ed., *Globalization in World History* (New York: W. W. Norton, 2002), pp. 141–166.

69. The most critical stance is taken by Frank McLynn, *Burton: Snow upon the Desert* (London: John Murray, 1990), chap. 13, who claims that Richard was trapped into marriage by a scheming Isabel.

70. The fullest and fairest biographical treatment of Isabel is to be found in Lovell, *A Rage to Live.* Also see Wilkins, *Romance;* Jean Burton, *Sir Richard Burton's Wife* (New York: Alfred A. Knopf, 1941); and Lesley Branch, *The Wilder Shores of Love* (New York: Simon and Schuster, 1954), chap. 1.

71. Richard F. Burton, *The Land of Midian (Revisited)* (London: C. Kegan Paul, 1879), vol. 2, p. 177. Some of the reviewers of these later books were withering in their criticisms. Writing about Burton's *Gold-Mines of Midian* (1878), the reviewer for *Mayfair,* May 7, 1878, complained that "we have vainly tried to read his book . . . one of the most striking instances of padding ever witnessed." This review, along with many others, was clipped and inserted in Burton's copy of *Gold-Mines* (BL 60) in the Huntington Library's Burton Library. Burton was sensitive to these criticisms, addressing them in his last travel book: "We travelers often find

ourselves in a serious dilemma. If we do not draw our landscapes some-what in pre-Raphaelite fashion, they do not impress the reader; if we do, critics tell us that they are wearisome *longueurs,* and that the half would be better than the whole." Richard F. Burton and Verney Lovett Cameron, *To the Gold Coast for Gold* (London: Chatto and Windus, 1883), vol. 1, p. x.

72. Richard F. Burton, *Two Trips to Gorilla Land and the Cataracts of the Congo* (London: Sampson Low, Marston, Low, and Searle, 1876), vol. 2, p. 199; Burton and Cameron, *To the Gold Coast,* vol. 2, pp. 108, 181–182, and appendices.

73. Richard F. Burton and Charles F. Tyrwhitt Drake, *Unexplored Syria* (London: Tinsley Brothers, 1872), vol. 1, appendix 1.

74. He acquired a particular interest in archeology, which became a major preoccupation in his books on Midian and Syria and the central focus of *Etruscan Bologna: A Study* (London: Smith Elder, 1876) and numerous articles. He also kept in touch with archeologists in England and conti-nental Europe. See A. H. Sayce, *Reminiscences* (London: Macmillan, 1923), pp. 27, 216–217, 235, 243.

75. See Maitland, *Speke,* and Bridges, "John Hanning Speke."

76. Burton, *Zanzibar,* vol. 2, pp. 390–391.

77. *The Times,* Sept. 14, 1864, p. 10.

78. A forceful case for accidental death is made by Maitland, *Speke,* chap. 10, but the immense pressures on Speke and the unfortunate timing of his demise make it impossible to dismiss suspicions of suicide.

79. *The Times,* Sept. 19, 1864, p. 6.

80. *The Times,* Sept. 23, 1864, p. 8.

81. Richard F. Burton and James Macqueen, *The Nile Basin* (London: Tins-ley Brothers, 1864).

82. See, for example, the letter from Speke's mother to James Grant, Dec. 27, 1864, Grant Papers, MS 17931, ff. 81–82, NLS.

83. See Baker, "Burton and the Nile Sources," and Tim Jeal, *Livingstone* (New York: G. P. Putnam's Sons, 1973), pp. 284–287, 299.

84. See W. P. Morrell, *The Gold Rushes* (London: Adam and Charles Black, 1940).

85. Richard F. Burton, *Exploration of the Highlands of Brazil* (London: Tins-ley Brothers, 1869), vol. 1, p. 184.

86. Isabel Burton, *Life,* vol. 1, pp. 453, 455.

87. Richard F. Burton, *Ultima Thule; or, A Summer in Iceland,* 2 vols. (Lon-don: William P. Nimmo, 1975); Lovell, *A Rage to Live,* pp. 580, 584–586.

88. Isabel Burton, *AEI Arabia Egypt India* (London: William Mullan, 1879),

chap. 9. This chapter, which is devoted to diamonds in India, was written by Richard, not Isabel.

89. Burton, *The Gold-Mines of Midian;* Burton, *The Land of Midian.* Optimistic reports about Burton's prospects of discovering valuable mineral deposits in Midian appeared in *The Times, The Standard, The Illustrated London News, The Morning Post,* and other newspapers. Remarkably, Midian Limited, the company created in anticipation of the success of Burton's prospecting expeditions, was still in existence in 1925, when it joined forces with another company to seek oil and other mineral resources in the region. Anthony Cave Brown, *Treason in the Blood: H. St. John Philby, Kim Philby, and the Spy Case of the Century* (Boston: Houghton Mifflin, 1994), pp. 85–86.

90. Burton and Cameron, *To the Gold Coast.* Isabel Burton reprints some of Richard's letters on mining in her *Life,* vol. 2, pp. 230–250.

91. Alfred G. Lock to Isabel Burton, Jan. 29, 1875, Burton Papers, 2667/26, Box 2, Wiltshire Record Office, Trowbridge. Lock tried in the same letter to solicit Isabel's aid in persuading her relative Lord Arundel to lend his support to the enterprise with a publicly announced investment of £1,000, which Lock promised to reimburse secretly. We do not know Isabel's response to this proposal.

92. See the bundle of letters concerning the Littai Lead and Cinnabar Mine, dated 1880–81, in the Burton Papers, 2667/26, Box 2, Wiltshire Record Office.

93. Isabel Burton, *Life,* vol. 2, pp. 227–228.

94. Raymond E. Dumett, *El Dorado in West Africa: The Gold-Mining Frontier, African Labor, and Colonial Capitalism in the Gold Coast, 1875–1900* (Athens: Ohio University Press, 1998), pp. 113, 116, 115. The scale of Burton's involvement in this venture is evident from the voluminous correspondence he carried on with Irvine. See the Huntington Library's Metcalf collection of Burton manuscripts, Box 10, envelopes 3–5, and Box 11, envelope 3; Wiltshire Record Office, Burton Papers, Box 2; and British Library, Manuscripts Department, R.P. 1950.

95. Robert A. Stafford, "Scientific Exploration and Empire," in Andrew Porter, ed., *The Oxford History of the British Empire,* vol. 3: *The Nineteenth Century* (Oxford: Oxford University Press, 1999), p. 300.

96. See Adam Hochschild, *King Leopold's Ghost* (Boston: Houghton Mifflin, 1998).

97. Burton, *Ultima Thule,* vol. 1, p. xi; Burton and Drake, *Unexplored Syria,* vol. 1, pp. 115, 138; Richard F. Burton, *The Gold-Mines of Midian* (1878; reprint New York: Oleander Press, 1979), p. 139; Richard F. Burton, *Etrus-*

can Bologna (London: Smith, Elder, 1876), p. 3; Richard F. Burton, *A Glance at the "Passion Play"* (London: W. H. Harrison, 1881), p. 50.

98. *Punch,* May 13, 1882.

5. THE RACIST

1. Christine Bolt, *Victorian Attitudes to Race* (London: Routledge and Kegan Paul, 1971).

2. The first sustained analysis of these associations between race and class was made by Douglas A. Lorimer, *Colour, Class, and the Victorians: English Attitudes to the Negro in the Mid-Nineteenth Century* (New York: Holmes and Meier, 1978). More recently, Catherine Hall has probed the impact of these associations on the midcentury debate about democracy in *Civilising Subjects: Metropole and Colony in the English Imagination, 1830–67* (Chicago: University of Chicago Press, 2002).

3. Nancy Stepan, *The Idea of Race in Science: Great Britain, 1800–1960* (Hamden, Conn.: Archon, 1982).

4. Both of the best biographies are disappointing in this regard: Fawn M. Brodie, *The Devil Drives: A Life of Sir Richard Burton* (New York: W. W. Norton, 1967), and Mary S. Lovell, *A Rage to Live: A Biography of Richard and Isabel Burton* (New York: W. W. Norton, 1998). Frank McLynn, *Burton: Snow upon the Desert* (London: John Murray, 1990), does a better job of confronting Burton's racism, but the strongest analysis of the subject is to be found in Donald Paul Nurse, "An Amateur Barbarian: The Life and Career of Sir Richard Francis Burton, 1821–1890" (Ph.D. diss., University of Toronto, 1999), pp. 235–255.

5. See, for example, the remarks on Burton in Dorothy Hammond and Alta Jablow, *The Myth of Africa* (New York: Library of Social Science, 1977), pp. 58–59, 63–66, and by Robert O. Collins in his "Introduction" to Richard F. Burton, *The Nile Basin* (1864; reprint New York: DaCapo, 1967).

6. Richard F. Burton, *The Lake Regions of Central Africa* (1860; reprint New York: Dovere Publications,1995),pp. 490, 499, 490, 489.

7. Richard Burton, "Ethnological Notes on M. du Chaillu's 'Explorations and Adventures in Equatorial Africa,'" *Transactions of the Ethnological Society of London,* 1861, p. 316. For his earlier views on the impact of slavery in East Africa, see Burton, *Lake Regions,* pp. 514–522.

8. Richard F. Burton, *Wanderings in West Africa* (1865; reprint New York: Dover, 1991), vol. 1, p. 208; vol. 2, pp. 35, 86.

9. Richard F. Burton, *Zanzibar; City, Island, and Coast* (London: Tinsley Brothers, 1872), vol. 1, p. 409. It should be noted that elsewhere he explained this odor as the product of oily lotions (smearing), bad food, and

poor hygiene, not as an innate characteristic of Africans as a race: "Even amongst Europeans in the tropics the transpiratory secretion often becomes acrid." Richard F. Burton, *Abeokuta and the Cameroons Mountains: An Exploration* (London: Tinsley Brothers, 1863), vol. 1, pp. 111–112.

10. Burton, *Wanderings*, vol. 2, p. 283; Richard F. Burton, *Two Trips to Gorilla Land and the Cataracts of the Congo* (London: Sampson Low, Marston, Low, and Searle, 1876), vol. 1, p. 217.

11. Burton, *Wanderings*, vol. 1, pp. 175, 178.

12. The origins of the Anthropological Society and the intellectual environment from which it arose have been examined by J. W. Burrow, *Evolution and Society: A Study in Victorian Social Theory* (Cambridge: Cambridge University Press, 1970), chap. 4; Ronald Rainger, "Race, Politics, and Science: The Anthropological Society of London in the 1860s," *Victorian Studies*, 22, no. 1 (Autumn 1978): 51–70; Stepan, *Idea of Race*, chaps. 1–3; George W. Stocking, Jr., *Victorian Anthropology* (New York: Free Press, 1987), esp. chap. 8; and Ter Ellingson, *The Myth of the Noble Savage* (Berkeley: University of California Press, 2001), chaps. 13–19.

13. *Farewell Public Dinner to Captain R. F. Burton Given by the Anthropological Society of London, April 4th, 1865,* reprint from the *Anthropological Review* (London: Trübner, 1865), p. 7.

14. In one instance, the publisher of his *First Footsteps in East Africa* had refused to include an appendix he had written on infibulation among the Somali. See Gordon Waterfield's preface to the reprint of *First Footsteps* (New York: Frederick A. Praeger, 1966), p. x.

15. Richard F. Burton, "Notes on Certain Matters Connected with the Dahoman," *Memoirs Read before the Anthropological Society of London*, 1 (1863–64): 308–321.

16. Richard F. Burton, "Notes on Waitz's Anthropology," *Anthropological Review*, 2, no. 7 (November 1864): 237. Also see the passages on African sexuality that were left out of the published version of *Zanzibar*. Burton's handwritten remarks can be found inserted in his copy of *Abeokuta and the Cameroons Mountains*, vol. 2, BL13, Huntington Library.

17. Richard F. Burton, "A Day among the Fans," *Anthropological Review*, 1 (1863): 43–54; Richard F. Burton, "Notes on Scalping," *Anthropological Review*, 2 (1864): 49–52.

18. Burton's prurient curiosity was not as strange as it might seem. The study of human freaks played an important role in the rise of German anthropology as a social science, according to Andrew Zimmerman, *Anthropology and Antihumanism in Imperial Germany* (Chicago: University of Chicago Press, 2001), chap. 3.

19. Burton, *Lake Regions,* p. 457; Burton and C. Carter Blake, "On Skulls from Annabom in the West African Seas," *Anthropological Review,* 2 (1864): ccxxx; Burton and Blake, "On Anthropological Collections from the Holy Lands, with Notes on the Human Remains," *Journal of the Anthropological Institute,* 1 (1871–72): 300–363; Burton and Blake, "On Human Remains and Other Articles from Iceland," *Journal of the Anthropological Institute,* 2 (1872–73): 342–347; Burton and Blake, "Stones and Bones from Egypt and Midian," *Journal of the Anthropological Institutes,* 7 (1878–79): 290–319.

20. His most sustained "scientific" treatment of the subject appears in Richard F. Burton, *Etruscan Bologna* (London: Smith, Elder, 1876), esp. pp. 175–186, 187–211, where he demonstrates a good deal of familiarity with continental research on skulls and race.

21. See, for example, Stephen Jay Gould, *The Mismeasure of Man* (New York: W. W. Norton, 1981), and David Hurst Thomas, *Skull Wars* (New York: Basic Books, 2000).

22. Dr. Paul Broca, *On the Phenomena of Hybridity in the Genus Homo* (London: Longman, Green, Longman, and Roberts, 1864); Georges Pouchet, *The Plurality of the Human Race* (London: Longman, Green, Longman, and Roberts, 1864); Dr. Carl Vogt, *Lectures on Man: His Place in Creation, and in the History of the Earth* (London: Longman, Green, Longman, and Roberts, 1864); Theodor Waitz, *The Anthropology of Primitive Peoples* (London: Longman, Green, Longman, and Roberts, 1864); Johann Friedrich Blumenbach, *Anthropological Treatises* (London: Longman, Green, Longman, and Roberts, 1865).

23. Burton, "Waitz's Anthropology"; Burton, *Etruscan Bologna,* p. 177.

24. Stocking, *Victorian Anthropology,* p. 248.

25. Ellington, *Myth of the Noble Savage,* p. 303.

26. Adrian Desmond, *Huxley: From Devil's Disciple to Evolution's High Priest* (Reading, Mass.: Persus, 1997), p. 326.

27. Stepan, *Idea of Race,* p. 4.

28. Footnote by Burton in Randolph B. Marcy, *The Prairie Traveler: A Hand-Book for Overland Expeditions,* ed. Richard F. Burton (London: Trübner, 1863), p. 140.

29. Lorimer, *Colour, Class, and the Victorians,* pp. 137–138, 158, notes that the midcentury racists tended to be religious skeptics as well.

30. James Hunt, *On the Negro's Place in Nature* (London: Trübner, 1863), pp. vi–vii. Richard F. Burton, *A Mission to Gelele, King of Dahome,* vol. 2 (London: Tinsley, 1864), p. 203.

31. The most recent study of the subject is R. J. M. Blackett, *Divided Hearts:*

Britain and the American Civil War (Baton Rouge: Louisiana State University Press, 2001), which notes Hotz's role in the Society (p. 41).

32. See Hall, Civilising Subjects.

33. Burton, "Waitz's Anthropology," p. 246.

34. John Hayman, ed., Sir Richard Burton's Travels in Arabia and Africa: Four Lectures from a Huntington Library Manuscript (San Marino, Calif.: Huntington Library, 1990), p. 109. He gave the lecture from which this statement is drawn to a Brazilian audience in 1866.

35. Burton, Mission to Gelele, vol. 2, pp. 204–205.

36. Burton, Wanderings, vol. 1, p. 270n.

37. Burton, Mission to Gelele, vol. 2, pp. 197, 193, 203.

38. Burton, comments at the meeting of Nov. 1, 1864, in Journal of the Anthropological Society, 3 (1865): xi.

39. Richard F. Burton, Two Trips to Gorilla Land and the Cataracts of the Congo (London: Sampson Low, Marston, Low, and Searle, 1876), vol. 2, p. 41.

40. Burton, Zanzibar, vol. 1, pp. 414–415. Also see his description of the Wanyika in vol. 2, pp. 82–83.

41. Burton, Wanderings, vol. 1, p. 188.

42. Burton, Zanzibar, vol. 1, p. 25.

43. Richard F. Burton, The City of the Saints and across the Rocky Mountains to California (1862: reprint Niwot: University Press of Colorado, 1990), p. 82.

44. Richard F. Burton, Exploration of the Highlands of the Brazil (London: Tinsley, 1869), vol. 1, p. 39n.

45. Burton, Explorations, vol. 1, pp. 241–242.

46. Burton, City of the Saints, pp. 80, 36, 51, 37.

47. Burton, Explorations, vol. 1, p. 390.

48. See, for example, H. L. Malchow, Gothic Images of Race in Nineteenth-Century Britain (Stanford: Stanford University Press, 1996), and Kenan Malik, The Meaning of Race: Race, History, and Culture in Western Society (New York: New York University Press, 1996).

49. Parliamentary Papers, Report From the Select Committee Appointed to Consider the State of the British Establishment on the Western Coast of Africa, 412 (1865).Burton's testimony appears on pp. 87–107. The classic account of the British encounter with West Africa is Philip D. Curtin, The Image of Africa: British Ideas and Action, 1780–1850 (Madison: University of Wisconsin Press, 1964).

50. Alexander Bryson, Report on the Climate and Physical Disease of the African Station (London: Clowes, 1847), p. 22, quoted by David Arnold, "In-

troduction," *Warm Climates and Western Medicine* (Amsterdam: Rodopi, 1996), p. 10. "A consulate on the West Coast of Africa was defined as a corrugated iron case with a dead consul inside," according to D. C. M. Platt, *The Cinderella Service: British Consuls since 1825* (London: Longman, 1971), p. 28.

51. Burton, *Wanderings,* vol. 2, p. 295. Fernando Po's role in the West African economy is examined by Ibrahim K. Sundiata, *From Slaving to Neoslavery: The Bight of Biafra and Fernando Po in the Era of Abolition, 1827–1930* (Madison: University of Wisconsin Press, 1996).

52. Burton to Earl Russell, Jan. 14, 1862, FO2/42, Public Record Office (herafter cited as PRO). James Grant, who accompanied John Speke on his follow-up expedition to confirm that the White Nile originated in Lake Victoria, was offered the consulship at Fernando Po when Burton moved on to Brazil. When he declined, the position went to David Livingstone's brother, Charles. This suggests that the Foreign Office regarded African explorers as specially suited for the post. Robert A. Stafford, *Scientist of Empire: Sir Roderick Murchison, Scientific Exploration, and Victorian Imperialism* (Cambridge: Cambridge University Press, 1989), pp. 170, 181.

53. He made the case for the Cameroon highlands as a site for a sanitarium in his book *Abeokuta and the Cameroons Mountains.*

54. Initialed minute, Sept., 7, 1864, FO84/1221, PRO.

55. See Platt, *The Cinderella Service,* chap. 2.

56. The Equity Court regulations that Burton instituted are reproduced in C. W. Newbury, ed., *British Policy Towards West Africa: Select Documents, 1786–1874* (Oxford: Clarendon Press, 1965), pp. 396–399. Burton's official correspondence and reports from West Africa can be found in the files of the Foreign Office (FO2/42, 97/438, 84/1176, 84/1203, 84/1221) and Colonial Office (CO147/2), PRO.

57. Burton, testimony in *Report from the Select Committee,* p. 89.

58. Burton, extract from a letter to Mr. Wylde, May 6, 1863, FO84/1203/301.

59. Burton to Lord Russell, Jan. 14, 1862, FO84/1176/50.

60. Burton, testimony in *Report from the Select Committee,* p. 90.

61. Burton to Lord Russell, April 15, 1864, FO84/1221/193, 201. It was true, as Burton's reference to the missionaries' "mechanic origins" indicates, that most British missionaries came from working-class and lower-middle-class backgrounds. See Jean and John Comaroff, *Of Revelation and Revolution: Christianity, Colonialism, and Consciousness in South Africa* (Chicago: University of Chicago Press, 1991), vol. 1, p. 85.

62. See Leo Spitzer, *The Creoles of Sierra Leone: Responses to Colonialism,*

1870–1945 (Madison: University of Wisconsin Press, 1974), and Philip S. Zachernuk, *Colonial Subjects: An African Intelligentsia and Atlantic Ideas* (Charlottesville: University Press of Virginia, 2000).

63. *Anthropological Review,* 3 (1865): clxxiii. Burton also acknowledged the assistance he received in his travels through West Africa from men like Mr. Wilhelm, an Egba convert and Christian Missionary Society missionary. Burton, *Abeokuta,* vol. 1, p. 139.

64. F.R.G.S. (Richard Burton), "My Wanderings in West Africa: A Visit to the Renowned Cities of Wari and Benin," *Fraser's Magazine,* 67 (February 1863): 157.

65. Burton, *Wanderings,* vol. 1, p. 239, 276.

66. Burton to Lord Russell, April 15, 1864, FO84/1221/195.

67. Burton, *Wanderings,* vol. 1, p. 211.

68. William Rainy, *The Censor Censured: or, the Calumnies of Captain Burton (Late Her Majesty's Consul at Fernando Po) on the Africans of Sierra Leone* (London: printed for the author, 1865), p. 5, passim. Rainy was a West Indian from Dominica who was recruited for government service in Sierra Leone. He resigned to study for the law at the Inner Temple in London, and upon his return to Sierra Leone he mixed a legal career with journalism, publishing a newspaper and conducting a polemical war against Burton and other racists. See Nemata Blyden, *West Indians in West Africa, 1808–1880: The African Diaspora in Reverse* (Rochester, N.Y.: University of Rochester Press, 2000), chap. 7.

69. Rigby to Grant, Feb. 12, 1866, and June 17, 1866, Grant Papers, MS 17910, ff. 52–55, National Library of Scotland.

70. See the correspondence concerning the estate of Wm. Johnson, especially the report by Charles Robinson, Nov. 12, 1866, in FO97/438.

71. Burton to Lord Stanley, June 5, 1867, FO97/438/181–187; and Foreign Office to Burton, Jan. 31, 1867, FO13/450.

72. Richard F. Burton and Verney Lovett Cameron, *To the Gold Coast for Gold* (London: Chatto and Windus, 1883), vol. 2, p. 17.

73. See Christopher Fyfe, *Africanus Horton: West African Scientist and Patriot* (New York: Oxford University Press, 1972).

74. James Africanus Horton, *West African Countries and Peoples* (1868; reprint Edinburgh: Edinburgh University Press, 1969), p. vi.

75. Burton and Cameron, *To the Gold Coast,* vol. 2, p. 1. Burton's comments on Horton appear on p. 115.

76. Burton, *Mission to Gelele,* vol. 2, pp. 232, 313. Burton took much the same stance in his official report to the Foreign Office. See Burton to Lord Russell, March 23, 1864, FO84/1221/224–283.

77. Burton to Richard Monckton Milnes, May 31, 1863, Lord Houghton Collection, Trinity College Library, Cambridge.

78. Burton, *Mission to Gelele*, vol. 2, p. 254.

79. Burton, *Mission to Gelele*, vol. 1, p. 159; vol. 2, p. 292; vol. 1, p. 150. These assessments of Burton's book come from Melville J. Herskovitz, *Dahomey, an Ancient West African Kingdom* (New York: J. J. Augustin, 1938); and C. W. Newbury, "Introduction" to *A Mission to Gelele* (London: Routledge and Kegan Paul, 1966), pp. 1–39.

80. Burton to Milnes, May 7, 1863, and Nov. 5, 1873, Houghton Collection. See also Burton to Albert Tootal, March 2, 1874, Metcalf Collection, Huntington Library; and marginalia in Burton's copy of *Wanderings in West Africa*, p. 177, BL18, Huntington Library. Burton also wrote an unpublished manuscript about the British-Asanti wars that disappeared after Isabel's death. See the list of the contents of Isabel Burton's Baker Street residence in the Burton Papers, 2667/26, Box 1, Wiltshire Record Office, Trowbridge, Wiltshire.

81. Richard F. Burton, *Wit and Wisdom from West Africa; or, A Book of Proverbial Philosophy, Idioms, Enigmas, and Laconisms* (London: Tinsley Brothers, 1865), pp. xii, xii, xxiv–xv, xxvii–xxviii. Burton makes similar observations about African proverbs in *Two Trips*, vol. 1, pp. 111, 186.

82. Burton to Lord Russell, April 15, 1864, FO84/1221/193.

83. Burton, *Two Trips to Gorilla Land*, vol. 1, pp. 185–186.

84. Verney Lovett Cameron, Burton's friend and fellow African explorer, makes much the same point in "Burton as I Knew Him," *Fortnightly Review*, 288 (December 1, 1890): 879–880.

85. Burton, *Wanderings*, vol. 1, p. 161.

86. Burton and Cameron, *To the Gold Coast*, vol. 2, p. 63. Also see Lovell, *A Rage to Live*, pp. 387–388.

87. Burton, "Waitz's Anthropology," pp. 248–249.

88. Richard F. Burton, "The Present State of Dahome," *Transactions of the Ethnological Society of London*, 1865, p. 408.

89. Robert J. C. Young argues in his *Colonial Desire: Hybridity in Theory, Culture, and Race* (London: Routledge, 1995) that the polygenist position was associated with the rise of the concept of culture, and that "culture was invented for difference" (p. 49). Burton's engagement with these ideas supports this contention. I should add, however, that whereas Young's intent is to show how the concept of culture carried the stain of racism, mine is in some sense the inverse.

90. Burton, *Gelele*, vol. 2, p. 207. Burton, *Abeokuta*, vol. 2, pp. 102–103.

91. Stocking, *Victorian Anthropology*, p. 253.

92. My discussion of Reade relies heavily on the insightful analysis by Felix Driver, *Geography Militant: Cultures of Exploration and Empire* (Oxford: Blackwell, 2001), chap. 5. Also see J. D. Hargreaves, "Winwoode Reade and the Discovery of Africa," *African Affairs*, 56 (1957): 306–316. Reade's books on West Africa are *Savage Africa* (London: Smith, Elder, 1863) and *The African Sketch-book*, 2 vols. (London: Smith, Elder, 1873).

93. See Winwood Reade, "Efforts of Missionaries among Savages," *Anthropological Review*, 3 (1865: clxiii–clxviii), and the transcript of the discussion that followed (pp. clxx–clxxxiii), which includes extended remarks by Burton in defense of Reade's views on the failures of missionaries in West Africa.

94. Warren Sylvester Smith, *The London Heretics, 1870–1914* (New York: Dodd, Mead, 1968), p. 5.

95. Burton and Cameron, *To the Gold Coast*, vol. 2, p. 49.

96. Winwoode Reade, *The Martyrdom of Man* (London: Trübner, 1872), p. xlvii. Driver notes that Reade originally contemplated titling his book *Africa's Place in History.*

97. Burton to Gerald Massey, April 7 and April 22, 1881, in Donald Young, "The Selected Correspondence of Sir Richard Burton, 1848–1890" (M.A. thesis, University of Nebraska, Lincoln, 1879), pp. 221–222.

98. Katherine Frank, *A Voyager Out: The Life of Mary Kingsley* (Boston: Houghton Mifflin, 1986), p. 30.

99. Frank, *A Voyager Out*, p. 112.

100. Various historians have stressed Kingsley's importance to the rise of a relativist understanding of cultural difference in British thought. See Jonathan Schneer, *London 1900: The Imperial Metropolis* (New Haven: Yale University Press, 1999), pp. 148–158; Paul B. Rich, *Race and Empire in British Politics* (Cambridge: Cambridge University Press, 1986), chap. 2; Bernard Porter, *Critics of Empire: British Radical Attitudes to Colonialism in Africa, 1895–1914* (London: Macmillan, 1968), pp. 149–155.

101. Hollis R. Lynch, *Edward Wilmot Blyden: Pan-Negro Patriot, 1832–1912* (London: Oxford University Press, 1967), p. 59.

102. Other Westernized Africans in the region, among them Richard Blaize, editor of the *Lagos Times,* shared Blyden's anxiety about the dangers of African degeneration under European influence. See Annie E. Coombes, *Reinventing Africa: Museums, Material Culture, and Popular Imagination in Late Victorian and Edwardian England* (New Haven: Yale University Press, 1994), pp. 39–40.

103. Edward W. Blyden, *Christianity, Islam, and the Negro Race* (London: W. B. Whittingham, 1887), pp. 12, 14.

104. V. Y. Mudimbe, *The Invention of Africa: Gnosis, Philosophy, and the Order of Knowledge* (Bloomington: Indiana University Press, 1988), p. 110.

105. Burton and Cameron, *To the Gold Coast,* vol. 2, p. 54.

6. THE RELATIVIST

1. Marilyn R. Brown, *Gypsies and Other Bohemians: The Myth of the Artist in Nineteenth-Century France* (Ann Arbor, Mich.: UMI Research, 1985); Christopher A. Kent, "The Idea of Bohemia in Mid-Victorian England," in *On Bohemia: The Code of the Self-Exiled* (New Brunswick, N.J.: Transaction, 1990), pp. 158–167.

2. Justin McCarthy, *Reminiscences* (New York: Harper and Brothers, 1899), vol. 1, p. 271.

3. McCarthy, *Reminiscences,* pp. 285, 288. Also see Justin McCarthy, *Portraits of the Sixties* (London: T. Fisher Unwin, 1903), chap. 13. The publisher William Tinsley also recalls that Burton often could be found on "the Strand with a few Bohemian friends." William Tinsley, *Random Recollections of an Old Publisher* (London: Simpkin, Marshall, Hamilton, Kent, 1890), p. 144.

4. Handwritten notes on Burton, Francis Galton Papers, 75B, University College, London. Burton's acquaintants often noted his pleasure in shocking others. See, for example, Edwin De Leon, *Thirty Years of My Life on Three Continents* (London: Ward and Downey, 1890), vol. 2, pp. 103–107; Lord Redesdale, *Memories* (New York: E. P. Dutton, 1916), vol. 2, p. 574.

5. See the Lord Houghton Collection, 228/11–50, Trinity College Library, Cambridge University; James Pope-Hennessy, *Monckton Milnes: The Flight of Youth, 1851–1885* (New York: Farrar, Straus and Cudahy, 1951).

6. See, for example, Swinburne to Burton, Jan. 11, 1867, in Algernon Charles Swinburne, *Letters to Sir Richard Burton and Other Correspondents* (London: printed for private circulation, 1912), pp. 5–9, and Burton to Swinburne, April 5, 1867, Ashley MS 297, British Library.

7. Swinburne relates Burton's remarks in a letter to Milnes, Aug. 8, 1867, in Cecil Y. Lang, ed., *The Swinburne Letters,* 6 vols. (New Haven: Yale University Press, 1959), vol. 1, p. 259. As one of Swinburne's biographers explains, *Poems and Ballads* "sent ripples of sexual and religious rebellion far and wide . . . it challenged Victorian culture's repressive attitudes to the body, to sex, to the value of sensual life, and struck a blow for artistic expression." Ricky Rooksby, *A. C. Swinburne: A Poet's Life* (Aldershot, Eng.: Scolar Press, 1997), p. 135.

8. Swinburne to Milnes, July 11? 1865, in Lang, vol. 1, p. 124.

9. Lang, vol. 1, p. 288n; Mary S. Lovell, *A Rage to Live: A Biography of Richard and Isabel Burton* (New York: W. W. Norton, 1998), p. 413.

10. Kent, "Idea of Bohemia," p. 162. In 1864 Thomas Huxley organized the X-Club, a dining club consisting of men who were "all of a mind on Darwinism and Colensoism." Adrian Desmond, *Huxley: From Devil's Disciple to Evolution's High Priest* (Reading, Mass.: Perseus, 1997), p. 327.

11. McCarthy, *Portraits*, p. 246.

12. Lisa Z. Sigel, *Governing Pleasures: Pornography and Social Change in England, 1815–1914* (New Brunswick, N.J.: Rutgers University Press, 2002), pp. 50, 51.

13. Algernon Charles Swinburne, *The Cannibal Catechism* (London: printed for private circulation, 1913), p. 7. The poem is full of fire and brimstone, envisioning the damned being roasted in hell as food for God's cannibal adherents.

14. See Margot K. Louis, *Swinburne and His Gods: The Roots and Growth of an Agnostic Poetry* (Montreal: McGill-Queen's University Press, 1990).

15. Humphrey Hare, *Swinburne* (London: H. F. & G. Witherby, 1949), p. 112; Smith, *London Heretics,* pp. 55–57. The description of *The Reader* comes from a brochure advertising its new ownership in the Francis Galton Papers, 119/1, University College, London.

16. Frank Baker (Richard Burton), *Stone Talk: Marvellous Sayings of a Petral Portion of Fleet Street, London* (London: Robert Hardwicke, 1865).

17. Burton to Swinburne, April 5, 1867, Ashley MS 297, British Library.

18. Isabel Burton, *The Life of Captain Sir Richard F. Burton* (London: Chapman and Hall, 1893), vol. 1, p. 393. Isabel was so successful in her efforts to suppress the work that no mention of it is made in the biographies of Burton by Edward Rice, *Captain Sir Richard Francis Burton* (New York: Charles Scribner's Sons, 1990), or Byron Farwell, *Burton* (New York: Avon, 1965).

19. While touring India in 1876, the Burtons visited the grave of the great French traveler Victor Jacquemont, "a fellow Bohemian," in order to pay "tribute to his memory." Isabel Burton, *AEI Arabia Egypt India* (London: William Mullan, 1879), p. 226.

20. In a footnote, Burton endorses Robert Chambers's *Vestiges of the Natural History of Creation* (first ed., 1844), the controversial book that presented the first sustained scientific assault on the biblical story of creation.

21. Burton adds a footnote to clarify that the stone does not mean "the Genesetic Adam, but the first human 'produced of aggregation and fit apposition of matter.'" *Stone Talk,* p. 20.

22. Sycee refers to Chinese silver bullion, which was drained from the country to pay for opium imports.

23. Fanqui was a derogatory Chinese term for a European, meaning "foreign demon."

24. A simoom is a fierce dust storm.

25. A lakh (lac) is an Indian numerical designation for one hundred thousand.

26. Magdalen refers to a house of incarceration for unwed mothers and prostitutes.

27. See Ruth Richardson, *Death, Dissection, and the Destitute* (London: Penguin, 1989).

28. Starting in 1860, Burton saw into print *The Lake Regions of Central Africa*, 2 vols. (1860), *The City of the Saints* (1861), *Abeokuta and the Cameroons Mountains*, 2 vols. (1863), *Wanderings in West Africa*, 2 vols. (1863), *The Prairie Traveller* (1863), *A Mission to Gelele, King of Dahome*, 2 vols. (1864), *The Nile Basin* (1864), and *Wit and Wisdom from West Africa* (1865).

29. Inserted in Burton's copy of *Stone Talk* is a list of thirty-five newspapers and journals that were sent review copies, as well as a letter to Burton from his publisher, Robert Hardwicke (April 28, 1865), lamenting the lack of reviews. Hardwicke figured that "people are afraid to tackle it" and suggested that Burton find someone to "pitch into it hot and strong." *Stone Talk,* BL26, Huntington Library.

30. Burton's South American experience is the subject of two studies: Frank McLynn, *From the Sierras to the Pampas: Richard Burton's Travels in the Americas, 1860–69* (London: Century, 1991), and Alfredo Cordiviola, *Richard Burton, a Traveller in Brazil, 1865–1868* (Lewiston, Maine: Edwin Mellen Press, 2001).

31. This journey is recounted in Richard F. Burton, *Explorations of the Highlands of Brazil*, 2 vols. (London: Tinsley Brothers, 1869).

32. For his observations on the war, see Richard F. Burton, *Letters From the Battle-fields of Paraguay* (London: Tinsely Brothers, 1870).

33. Burton to Swinburne, April 5, 1867, Ashley MS 297, British Library..

34. Wilfred Scawen Blunt, *My Diaries* (London: Martin Seeker, 1921), part 2, p. 131.

35. Elliot to Stanley, May 3, 1869, FO78/2259 (FO; hereafter cited as Foreign Office), Public Record Office.

36. See the minute of June 16, 1869, and the draft memo of June 19, 1869, FO78/2259.

37. See Philip S. Khoury, *Urban Notables and Arab Nationalism: The Politics of Damascus, 1860–1920* (Cambridge: Cambridge University Press, 1983). Isabel Burton gives her own Catholic slant to these ethnic and religious

tensions in *The Inner Life of Syria, Palestine, and the Holy Land* (London: Henry S. King, 1875), vol. 1, esp. chap. 8.

38. Burton's unsuitability for the Damascus post is acknowledged by various friends and acquaintances. See Redesdale, *Memories,* vol. 2, p. 563; Tinsley, *Random Recollections,* p. 149; Blunt, *My Diaries,* part 2, p. 132.

39. For a detailed but flawed treatment of the subject, see Andrew Vincent, "The Jew, the Gipsy, and El-Islam: An Examination of Richard Burton's Consulship in Damascus and His Premature Recall, 1868–1871," *Journal of the Royal Asiatic Society,* 2 (1985): 155–173.

40. Burton to Elliot, July 11, 1870, FO78/2150.

41. See the correspondence of October through November 1870 in FO78/2259; the defense of Burton's actions by E. H. Palmer and C. F. Tyrwhitt Drake in a letter to *The Times* (Oct. 27, 1870), and the reply in *The Times* (Nov. 2, 1870) by Sir Moses Montefiore; and the confidential print "The Case of Captain Burton, Late H.B.M.'s Consul at Damascus" (1872), in FO78/2260. Also see L. Lowe, ed., *Diaries of Sir Moses and Lady Montefiore* (Chicago: Belford-Clarke, 1890), vol. 2, pp. 233–235.

42. Elliott to Lord Granville, May 22, 1871, FO78/2259. Isabel Burton describes this alarm in *Inner Life of Syria,* vol. 1, chap. 20, arguing that her husband's actions were justified.

43. This explanation appears in Isabel Burton, *Inner Life,* vol. 2, chap. 29.

44. Like many Europeans who came in contact with them, Burton admired the Druze, considering them, in the words of his wife, a "fine, manly race." Isabel Burton, *Inner Life,* vol. 1, p. 346. On the romanticizing of the Druze by Europeans, see Ussama Makdisi, *The Culture of Sectarianism: Community, History, and Violence in Nineteenth-Century Ottoman Lebanon* (Berkeley: University of California Press, 2000), pp. 24–25. On Rasid Pasha, see Eugene L. Rogan, *Frontiers of the State in the Late Ottoman Empire: Transjordan, 1850–1921* (Cambridge: Cambridge University Press, 1999), pp. 48–49, who presents him as an efficient, reforming governor, not the corrupt and decadent figure portrayed by Burton.

45. Elliot to Granville, June 26, 1871, FO78/2259.

46. Unfortunately, the only biographer to give the subject scrutiny is Fawn M. Brodie, *The Devil Drives: A Life of Sir Richard Burton* (New York: W. W. Norton, 1967), pp. 265–266.

47. Burton, *Explorations of the Highlands of Brazil* vol. 1, p. 403. Although Brodie and others have quoted this remark, they invariably drop the subordinate clause, with its reference to the "white family."

48. This is the argument advanced by Vincent, "The Jew," and Brodie, *The Devil Drives.*

49. Jan Morris, *Trieste and the Meaning of Nowhere* (London: Faber and Faber, 2001), p. 89.

50. Isabel Burton, *AEI*, pp. 418–423. Although they were published under Isabel's name, Richard wrote these passages. Lovell, *A Rage to Live*, p. 644.

51. See the correspondence from Burton to Grattan Geary, 1876–1879, Metcalf Collection, vol. 4, Huntington Library. On May 12, 1877, Burton informed Geary: "I am ready to give you a long Pantillaria about the Jews which will cut up into two, but you must tell me that you want it, or rather that you are not afraid of it." Fawn Brodie interprets this statement as a reference to Burton's anti-Semitic tract on ritual murder among the Sephardim Jews, but this seems unlikely in light of the fact that Geary was interested in publishing Burton's views on the Balkans crisis. See Brodie, *The Devil Drives*, p. 363n7. Burton was not alone in charging that Disraeli's approach to the "Eastern Question" was motivated by his Jewish heritage. Humphrey Sandwith, one of the most prominent Liberal critics of the policy, wrote to Burton that the "Jewish Earl [Disraeli] has a positive sympathy with the Turks. After all these are only doing what his ancestors did in Canaan." Sandwith to Burton, Sept. 16, 1876, Metcalf Collection, Box 10, envelope 2, Huntington Library. Similarly, Edward Freeman, the Liberal historian who was also active in the campaign against Disraeli's policy, voiced intensely anti-Semitic views in his correspondence on the subject with Burton. See Freeman's letters to Burton, 1876–1881, in the Burton Papers, 2667/26, Box 2, Wiltshire Record Office. Only brief notice is paid to anti-Semitic views in the standard work on the Liberal campaign, Richard Shannon, *Gladstone and the Bulgarian Agitation 1876*, 2nd ed. (Hamden, Conn.: Archon Books, 1975), pp. 200–201.

52. Richard F. Burton, *The Jew, the Gypsy, and El Islam*, ed. W. H. Wilkins (London: Hutchinson, 1898), pp. 5–6.

53. The manuscript's strange history requires explanation. Burton evidently began work on it soon after his recall from Damascus. W. H. Wilkins, who later edited the manuscript and published a portion of it in *The Jew, the Gypsy, and El Islam*, states that he completed it in 1874 (p. viii). Fawn Brodie gives the date as 1877, but her evidence is the ambiguous letter to Geary cited in the earlier note. Whether Burton ever sought a publisher for the work is unclear, but it remained unpublished at his death. Isabel Burton left instructions with her sister, Elizabeth Fitzgerald, to have the manuscript burned after she died (see "Private instructions for my sister," undated, in Wiltshire Record Office, Burton Papers, 2667/26, Box 2). In-

stead, the manuscript came into the hands of Wilkins, Isabel's biographer, who announced his intention in 1897 to publish it. The Board of Deputies of British Jews filed a libel action to prevent publication. (See London Committee of Deputies of the British Jews to Mrs. E. M. R. Fitzgerald, March 15, 1897, and Wilkins to the London Committee, March 16, 1897, in Burton Papers, 2667/26, Box 2, Wiltshire Record Office.) Wilkins consequently altered his plans, extracting a portion of the manuscript, which he reconstituted as one of three Burton essays posthumously published as *The Jew, the Gypsy, and El Islam*. Wilkins evidently left the manuscript in the hands of his publisher, Hutchinson, who sold it in the early twentieth century to Henry Walpole Manners-Sutton for £31 10s. When Manners-Sutton sought to publish it, the Jewish Board of Deputies again launched a legal action and won control of the disputed manuscript (see "King's Bench Division: Human Sacrifices," *The Times*, March 28, 1911). The manuscript disappeared into the Board of Deputies' vaults until 2001, when the Board sought to sell it at auction through Christie's. When bids failed to reach the estimated value of £150,000–200,000, the manuscript was evidently returned to the Board's vaults.

54. This account is drawn from the description supplied by Christie's auction house when the manuscript was offered for sale in June 2001.

55. Burton, *The Jew*, pp. 9, 7, 8, 6, 30, 117.

56. The Oberammergau passion play remains a source of concern to the Jewish Anti-Defamation League, as its website (www.adl.org/Interfaith/Oberammergau) indicates.

57. Richard F. Burton, *A Glance at the "Passion Play"* (London: W. H. Harrison, 1881), pp. 13, 139, 157–158, 159.

58. Richard F. Burton, "Lord Beaconsfield: A Sketch" (pamphlet: no publisher, no date [1882]), pp. 4, 5, 3. Burton Collection, BL219(13), Huntington Library.

59. Burton believed that certain "pure" races possessed special powers of acclimatization that placed them at an advantage in the Darwinian struggle for survival. "The mixed Anglo-Saxon race wants those cosmopolitan powers of acclimatization which scatter pure races, like the Chinese and Turanians, the Jews and the Gipsies, unscathed over the habitable world. . . . Our melancholy task appears to be that of smoothing the way for a future and higher type of the initial genus and species—man." Richard F. Burton, *Abeokuta and the Cameroon Mountains* (London: Tinsley Brothers, 1863), p. 64.

60. See the article by Burton that is reprinted as appendix E in Isabel Bur-

ton, *The Life of Captain Sir Richard F. Burton* (London: Chapman and Hall, 1893), vol. 2, p. 549. The Burtons were made aware of efforts to establish a Jewish homeland in Palestine during their stay in Damascus. See Isabel Burton, *AEI,* p. 418.

61. Note should be paid, however, to the letter from an H. Graetz to Burton (Sept. 28, 1884), evidently responding to the latter's query about whether ancient Jews engaged in female circumcision. Graetz insists that they did not. The letter appears in an envelope inside the front cover of Burton's copy of the *Supplemental Nights,* vol.1, BL94a, Huntington Library.

62. Richard F. Burton, *Camoens: His Life and His Lusiads* (London: Bernard Quaritch, 1881), vol. 1, p. 1.

63. Burton, *Camoens,* vol. 1, pp. 52, 56, 59, 26, 27.

64. Isabel Burton, "The Reviewer Reviewed," in Burton, *Camoens,* vol. 2, p. 713.

65. Robert Bernard Martin, *With Friends Possessed: A Life of Edward Fitzgerald* (London: Faber and Faber, 1985), p. 219. Burton reportedly recited Fitzgerald's translation of the *Rubaiyat* to a distinguished group of houseguests at Milnes's Fryston estate in 1861. Lovell, *A Rage to Live,* p. 383. The Burton Library has copies of the third and fourth editions of Fitzgerald's edition of the *Rubaiyat* (1872 and 1879), as well as a lithograph edition of the Persian text, published in 1867. See B. J. Kirkpatrick, ed., *A Catalogue of the Library of Sir Richard Burton* (London: Royal Anthropological Institute, 1978), items 969, 970, and 971.

66. Justin Huntly McCarthy, trans., *Rubaiyat of Omar Khayyam* (London: David Nutt, 1889).

67. Martin, *With Friends Possessed,* p. 221. Also see Alfred McKinley Terhune, *The Life of Edward Fitzgerald* (New Haven: Yale University Press, 1947), and Thomas Wright, *The Life of Edward Fitzgerald,* 2 vols. (New York: Charles Scribner's Sons, 1904).

68. Anonymous, "A Great Poet of Denial and Revolt," *The Spectator,* March 11, 1876, p. 334. This reviewer goes on to charge that the *Rubaiyat* lacks "any moral sense," a deficiency he associates with its "Mohammedan" and "Oriental" character.

69. When the British consul-turned-Irish-revolutionary and religious freethinker Roger Casement was arrested by authorities on the eve of the Easter Rising, he was found with a copy of *The Rubaiyat* in his pocket. Adam Hochschild, *King Leopold's Ghost* (Boston: Houghton Mifflin, 1999), p. 285.

70. See John M. MacKenzie, *Orientalism: History, Theory, and the Arts* (Manchester: Manchester University Press, 1995), and Holly Edwards,

ed., *Noble Dreams, Wicked Pleasures: Orientalism in America, 1870–1930* (Princeton: Princeton University Press, 2000).

71. Leighton House Museum guidebook, Holland Park, London.

72. Burton to Albert Tootal, May 24, 1875, in vol. 3, Metcalf Collection, Huntington Library.

73. The fez and slippers can be found among the Burton memorabilia in the collection of the Orleans House Gallery, Twickenham.

74. See Thomas Wright, *The Life of Sir Richard Burton* (New York: G. P. Putnam's Sons, 1906), vol. 2, p. 20. Isabel Burton to Monckton Milnes, Dec. 3, 1876, Lord Houghton Collection, 4/207, Trinity College Library, Cambridge.

75. Isabel attempted to counter these criticisms by insisting that her husband had actually written the poem after his return from Mecca in 1853, years before *The Rubaiyat* was published, but the evidence—including the letter cited above—does not support this claim. Isabel Burton, "Preface" to Richard F. Burton, *The Kasîdah (Couplets) of Hâjî Abdû al-Yazdi* (London: H. S. Nichols, 1894), p. 4.

76. Isabel realized this when she finally saw the finished work, causing her to lament: "Richard will never be a thoroughly happy man till he believes in a *future*." Isabel Burton to Milnes, April 20, 1877, Lord Houghton Collection, 4/208.

77. Burton, *The Kasîdah*, p. 22.

78. Burton, *The Kasîdah*, pp. 23, 24, 25, 26, 28.

79. Burton, *The Kasîdah*, pp. 41, 36.

80. See Bernard Lightman, *The Origins of Agnosticism: Victorian Unbelief and the Limits of Knowledge* (Baltimore: Johns Hopkins University Press, 1987); Frank M. Turner, *Contesting Cultural Authority: Essays in Victorian Intellectual Life* (Cambridge: Cambridge University Press, 1993).

81. Christopher Herbert, *Victorian Relativity: Radical Thought and Scientific Discovery* (Chicago: University of Chicago Press, 2001). Relativism was arguably even more prevalent in eighteenth-century thought. See Sankar Muthu, *Enlightenment against Empire* (Princeton: Princeton University Press, 2003).

82. Though Christopher Herbert concedes that there is no necessary correlation between relativism and support for more representative political institutions, all of the figures he examines in *Victorian Relativity* shared that view—with the partial exception of Karl Pearson, whose move to the right in the latter stage of his career is dismissed by Herbert as an inexplicable anomaly.

83. Frank Harris, *Contemporary Portraits* (London: Methuen, 1915), p. 167.

84. Uday Singh Mehta, *Liberalism and Empire: A Study in Nineteenth-Century British Liberal Thought* (Chicago: University of Chicago Press, 1999); Lynn Zastoupil, *John Stuart Mill and India* (Stanford: Stanford University Press, 1994). Herbert, *Victorian Relativity,* says almost nothing about attitudes toward empire.

85. J. W. Burrow, *Evolution and Society: A Study in Victorian Social Theory* (Cambridge: Cambridge University Press, 1970).

7. THE SEXOLOGIST

1. Some examples of this scholarship are Antoinette Burton, *At the Heart of the Empire: Indians and the Colonial Encounter in Late-Victorian Britain* (Berkeley: University of California Press, 1998); Ruth H. Lindeborg, "The 'Asiatic' and the Boundaries of Victorian Englishmen," *Victorian Studies,* 37, no. 3 (Spring 1994): 381–404; Paul R. Deslandes, "'The Foreign Element': Newcomers and the Rhetoric of Race, Nation, and Empire in 'Oxbridge' Undergraduate Culture," *Journal of British Studies,* 37, no. 1 (January 1998): 54–90.

2. See Dane Kennedy, *Britain and Empire, 1880–1945* (London: Pearson, 2002).

3. Edward W. Said, *Orientalism* (New York: Vintage, 1979). The alternative uses of Orientalism are examined by John M. MacKenzie, *Orientalism: History, Theory, and the Arts* (Manchester: Manchester University Press, 1995), and Peter van der Veer, *Imperial Encounters: Religion and Modernity in India and Britain* (Princeton: Princeton University Press, 2001).

4. For a general consideration of Burton and Orientalism, see Jean-François Gournay, *L'appel du proche-orient: Richard Francis Burton et son temps, 1821–1890* (Paris: Didier-Erudition, 1983).

5. Richard F. Burton, *Sindh and the Races That Inhabit the Valley of the Indus* (1851; reprint Karachi: Oxford University Press, 1973), p. 163.

6. The most striking example came when the publisher of *First Footsteps in East Africa* (1856) removed Burton's appendix on infibulation among the Somali people. See Gordon Waterfield, "Preface," to Richard F. Burton, *First Footsteps in East Africa* (New York: Frederick A. Praeger, 1966), p. x. There is evidence that *Sindh and the Races That Inhabit the Valley of the Indus* (1851) and *Personal Narrative of a Pilgrimage to Al-Madinah and Meccah* (1855) also were bowdlerized.

7. James Pope-Hennessy, *Monckton Milnes: The Flight of Youth, 1851–1885* (New York: Farrar, Straus, and Cudahy, 1955), pp. 114–122.

8. See Ian Gibson, *The Erotomaniac: The Secret Life of Henry Spencer Ashbee* (Cambridge, Mass.: Da Capo Press, 2001).

9. Alec Craig, *The Banned Books of England* (London: George Allen and Unwin, 1937), pp. 23–24.

10. Burton to Milnes, May 31, 1863, Lord Houghton Collection, Trinity College Library, Cambridge. There is no evidence that Burton actually sought to meet Hankey's request. The comment about the *peau de femme* appears in the context of a passage that downplayed Dahomey's bloodthirsty reputation.

11. Lisa Z. Sigel, *Governing Pleasures: Pornography and Social Change in England, 1815–1914* (New Brunswick, N.J.: Rutgers University Press, 2002), p. 50. Earlier studies that offer valuable insights into the role of pornography in Victorian culture include Steven Marcus, *The Other Victorians: A Study of Sexuality and Pornography in Mid-Nineteenth Century England* (New York: Basic Books, 1964), and Walter Kendrick, *The Secret Museum: Pornography in Modern Culture* (New York: Viking, 1987).

12. Burton to Leonard Smithers, Nov. 14, 1888, Huntington Library, quoted by Mary S. Lovell, *A Rage to Live* (New York: W. W. Norton, 1998), p. 717. Burton did, however, recognize that some people got an erotic charge from sadistic practices. He arrived at the insight that all "passions are sisters" during his visit to Dahomey, where he observed the torture and execution of prisoners: "Seeing the host of women who find a morbid pleasure in attending the maimed and dying, I must think that it is a tribute paid to sexuality by those who object to the ordinary means." Richard F. Burton, *A Mission to Gelele, King of Dahome* (1864; reprint London: Routledge and Kegan Paul, 1966), pp. 259, 260.

13. Burton to Milnes, May 31, 1863, Houghton Collection. On the rape of white women as a metonym for colonial disorder and rebellion, see Jenny Sharpe, *Allegories of Empire: The Figure of Woman in the Colonial Text* (Minneapolis: University of Minnesota Press, 1993); Jock McCulloch, *Black Peril, White Virtue: Sexual Crime in Southern Rhodesia, 1902–1935* (Bloomington: Indiana University Press, 2000); and Nancy L. Paxton, *Writing under the Raj: Gender, Race, and Rape in the British Colonial Imagination, 1830–1947* (New Brunswick, N.J.: Rutgers University Press, 1999). On cross-racial pornography, see Malek Alloula, *The Colonial Harem* (Minneapolis: University of Minnesota Press, 1986).

14. Although Sigel does discuss the *Kama Sutra*, her analysis focuses on Ashbee's lengthy description of the work, not the translation itself or the correspondence by Burton that gives some evidence of his intentions. Sigel, *Governing Pleasures*, pp. 64–69.

15. Richard F. Burton, *Goa, and the Blue Mountains* (1851; reprint Berkeley: University of California Press, 1991), chap. 7.

16. Richard F. Burton, "The Lake Regions of Central Equatorial Africa, with Notices of the Lunar Mountains and the Sources of the White Nile," *Journal of the Royal Geographical Society,* 29 (1859): 163.

17. Book of medical prescriptions, Burton Papers, 2667/26, Box 3, Wiltshire Record Office.

18. Swinburne to Theodore Watts, Aug. 30, 1875, in Cecil Y. Lang, ed., *The Swinburne Letters* (New Haven: Yale University Press), vol. 3, p. 61. Edmund Gosse quotes William Rossetti as stating that Swinburne "seems to have conceived an excessive affection" for Burton. Lang, ed., *Letters,* vol. 6, p. 241.

19. See F. F. Arbuthnot, "Life and Labours of Mr. Edward Rehatsek," *Journal of the Royal Asiatic Society* (July 1892): 581–595, for an appreciation. Rehatsek is credited with translating *all* of the Kama Shastra Society publications except *The Perfumed Garden* and the *Nights* by Thomas Wright, *The Life of John Payne* (London: T. Fisher Unwin, 1919), p. 74. Although this claim exaggerates his importance, Rehatsek probably did play an undisclosed role in the early translations and he was responsible for translating the Society's final two publications, *The Beharistan (Abode of Spring)* (1887) and *The Gulistan or Rose Garden of Sa'di* (1887). See Norman M. Penzer, *An Annotated Bibliography of Sir Richard Burton* (New York: Burt Franklin, 1923), p. 162.

20. Lovell, *A Rage to Live,* p. 621.

21. Pisanus Fraxi, pseud. (Henry Spencer Ashbee), *Catena Librorium Tacendorum* (1885; reprint New York: Jack Brussel, 1962), p. 459. Wendy Doniger and Sudhir Kakar, who have prepared a new translation of the work, summarize the circumstances surrounding the Arbuthnot-Burton translation in their introduction to Vatsyayana Mallanaga, *Kamasutra* (Oxford: Oxford University Press, 2002).

22. *Athenaeum,* 2313 (February 24, 1872): 241–243. I am grateful to Burke Casari for bringing this letter to my attention.

23. Pisanus Fraxi, pseud. (Henry Spencer Ashbee), *Index Librorum Prohibitoru* (1877; reprint New York: Jack Brussel, 1962), p. 282.

24. Burton to John Payne, Aug. 5, 1882, Metcalf Collection, Box 11, envelope 2, Huntington Library

25. Arbuthnot is identified as the "chief translator" of the *Kama Sutra* in Fraxi, *Catena,* p. 457.

26. Burton to Payne, Dec. 23, 1882, and Jan. 15, 1883, Metcalf Collection. This name is virtually identical to the original title they gave to the *Ananga-Ranga* when they attempted to publish it in 1873: *Kama-Shastra; or, The Hindoo Art of Love (Ars Amoris Indica).*

27. Isabel Burton, "The Scented Garden," typewritten manuscript in Burton Papers, 2667/26, Box 2, Wiltshire Record Office.

28. *The Kama Sutra of Vatsyayana* (Cosmopoli: for the Kama Shastra Society of London and Benares, 1883); *Ananga-Ranga (Stage of the Bodiless One): or, The Hindu Art of Love,* translated from the Sanskrit by A.F.F. and B.F.R. (Cosmopoli: for the Kama Shastra Society of London and Benares, 1885); *The Perfumed Garden of the Cheikh Nefzaou:. A Manual of Arabian Erotology* (Cosmopoli: for the Kama Shastra Society of London and Benares, 1886).

29. For the background and context of the work, see Mary S. Lovell, "Introduction," *The Perfumed Garden of the Cheikh Nefzaoui,* trans. Richard F. Burton (New York: Signet Classic, 1999); and Jim Colville, "Introduction," to Muhammad ibn Muhammad al-Nafzawi, *The Perfumed Garden of Sensual Delight,* trans. Jim Colville (London: Kegan Paul, 1999). Colville complains that in "Burton's version, details were expanded, episodes introduced and whole sections incorporated from other, non-Arabic, sources. . . . The result is a consistently exaggerated and bizarre misrepresentation of the original" (p. xi). Since Burton relied on a French translation, these charges presumably apply to that text as well.

30. Judith R. Walkowitz, *City of Dreadful Delight: Narratives of Sexual Danger in Late-Victorian London* (Chicago: University of Chicago Press, 1992).

31. W. T. Stead, "The Maiden Tribute of Modern Babylon," *Pall Mall Gazette,* July 6, 7, 8, 10, 1885. This series of articles was reissued as *The Maiden Tribute of Modern Babylon* (Philadelphia: International Publishing Co., 1885).

32. In addition to Walkowitz's *City of Dreadful Delight,* see Trevor Fisher, *Scandal: The Sexual Politics of Late Victorian Britain* (Stroud, Gloustershire: Alan Sutton, 1995); Edward J. Bristow, *Vice and Vigilance: Purity Movements in Britain since 1700* (Totowa, N.J.: Rowman and Littlefield, 1977), part 2; Frank Mort, *Dangerous Sexualities: Medico-Moral Politics in England since 1800* (London: Routledge and Kegan Paul), part 3; Stefan Petrow, *Policing Morals: The Metropolitan Police and the Home Office, 1870–1914* (Oxford: Clarendon Press, 1994); and Craig, *Banned Books,* chap. 1.

33. Bristow, *Vice and Vigilance,* chaps. 5 and 9. Burton kept a close eye on the Vizitelly case, clipping news accounts of the trial and referring to it in letters.

34. The term evidently has its origins in Thomas Morton's play, *Speed the Plough* (1798), in which one of the characters makes repeated reference to a Mrs. Grundy as the arbiter of respectability.

35. Isabel Burton, *The Inner Life of Syria, Palestine, and the Holy Land* (London: Henry S. King, 1875), vol. 2, pp. 130–131.

36. Burton to Payne, June 3, 1882, Oct. 29, 1882, and May 22, 1883, Metcalf Collection.

37. Stead evoked the genres of melodrama, pornography, and fairy tales in his "Maiden Tribute" exposé, according to Walkowitz, *City of Dreadful Delight,* pp. 85–87. The key role played by women in the purity campaign is examined by Lucy Bland, *Banishing the Beast: Sexuality and the Early Feminists* (New York: New Press, 1995).

38. Richard F. Burton, trans., *The Book of the Thousand Nights and a Night* (Benares: Kama Shastra Society, 1885), vol. 1, pp. vii, viii, x, xv. In his foreword to vol. 1 of the *Nights,* Burton claims that he started his translation to 1879 (see p. ix), but in vol. 6 of the *Supplemental Nights to the Book of the Thousand Nigths and a Night* (Benares: Kamashasgtra Society, 1888), he identifies 1882 as the date of origin (see p. 390).

39. Burton, *Nights,* vol. 1, pp. xv, xvi, xvii.

40. For the historical background to the *Nights* and its reception in Britain, see Muhsin Mahdi, *Introduction and Indexes,* vol. 3 of *The Thousand and One Nights (Alf Layla wa-Layla) from the Earliest Known Sources* (Leiden: Brill, 1994); Robert Irwin, *The Arabian Nights: A Companion* (London: Penguin, 1994); Peter L. Caracciolo, ed., *The Arabian Nights in English Literature* (New York: St. Martin's, 1988); and Muhsin Jassim Ali, *Scheherazade in England: A Study in Nineteenth-Century English Criticism of the Arabian Nights* (Washington, D.C.: Three Continents, 1981).

41. Edward William Lane, trans., *The Thousand and One Nights,* 3 vols. (London: C. Knight, 1839–1841); and John Payne, *The Book of the Thousand Nights and One Night,* 9 vols. (London: printed for subscribers only, 1882–1884).

42. Burton to Payne, May 12, 1883, Metcalf Collection.

43. Lovell, *A Rage to Live,* p. 146.

44. Richard F. Burton, *First Footsteps in East Africa* (1856; reprint New York: Frederick A. Praeger, 1966), p. 59.

45. Comments by Mr. Roberts and James Hunt after Burton's address "Certain Matters Connected with Dahomey," in *Journal of the Anthropological Society of London,* 3 (1865): viii, ix.

46. Lord Redesdale, *Memories* (New York: E. P. Dutton, 1916), vol. 2, pp. 272–273.

47. For very different assessments of the relative strengths and weaknesses of Burton's translation, see Jorge Luis Borges, "The Translators of *The Thousand and One Nights,*" in *Selected Non-Fictions,* ed. Eliot Weinberger

(New York: Penguin Books, 1999), pp. 92–109, and Husain Haddawy, "Introduction," *The Arabian Nights,* trans. Husain Haddawy (New York: W. W. Norton, 1990), pp. ix–xxix.

48. Swinburne to Lord Houghton, Aug. 8, 1867, in Lang, ed., *Letters,* vol. 1, p. 259.

49. See the memorandum inserted in Burton's copy of the *Nights,* vol. 1, BL91(a), Huntington Library. This memorandum is a separate flier that was presumably sent to solicit subscribers.

50. Georgiana M. Stisted, *The True Life of Capt. Sir Richard F. Burton* (London: H. S. Nichols, 1896), p. 406.

51. *Printing Times and Lithographer,* Aug. 15, 1885. A clipping of this brief news item can be found in Burton's copy of the *Nights,* vol. 1, BL91(a), Huntington Library.

52. Richard Phillips, "Sexual Politics of Authorship: Rereading the Travels and Translations of Richard and Isabel Burton," *Gender, Place, and Culture,* 6, no. 3 (1999): 249.

53. *The Echo,* Oct. 12, 1885.

54. "The Arabian Nights," *Edinburgh Review,* 335 (July 1886): 183, 184.

55. Sigma (pseud.), "Pantagruelism or Pornography?" *Pall Mall Gazette,* 42, no. 6396 (September 14, 1885): 2; *Pall Mall Gazette,* 42, no. 6406 (September 25, 1885): 6; *Pall Mall Gazette,* no. 42, 6407 (September 27, 1885): 3; "Pantagruelism or Pornography?" p. 3; Sigma (pseud.), "The Ethics of the Dirt," *Pall Mall Gazette,* 42, no. 6409 (September 29, 1885): 2.

56. *The Standard,* Sept. 12, 1885, p. 5.

57. *The Morning Advertiser,* Sept. 15, 1885, p. 4.

58. Letter to the Editor, *Pall Mall Gazette,* 42, no. 6397 (September 15, 1885): 2; Letter to the Editor, *Pall Mall Gazette,* 42, no. 6405 (September 24, 1885): 6.

59. John Addington Symonds, "The Arabian Nights' Entertainments," *Academy,* 700 (October 3, 1885): 223. Also see Edward Peacock, "The Arabian Nights," *Academy,* 702 (October 17, 1885): 258.

60. Burton, *Nights,* vol. 1, p. xxiii. It should be noted in this context that Burton changed the subtitle of his work from "Notes on the Manners and Customs Described in *The Book of a Thousand Nights and a Night*" to "Notes on the Manners and Customs of Oriental Men," with "Oriental" replaced by "Moslem" when the volumes were in page proofs. See the proof sheets of the *Nights* in the Harry Ransom Research Center, University of Texas at Austin.

61. It was not the first time that the Burton employed this device. Appended to the second volume of *Camoens: His Life and His Lusiads* (London:

Bernard Quaritch, 1881), is "The Reviewer Reviewed" (pp. 709–727), a critique of Burton's critics purportedly written by his wife, Isabel. Is this another case of ventriloquism?

62. Richard F. Burton, "The Biography of the Book and Its Reviewers Reviewed," in Burton, trans., *Supplemental Nights,* vol. 6, pp. 403, 405, 431, 400.

63. Burton, "Biography of the Book," pp. 404, 431, 437, 438.

64. See Michael Mason, *The Making of Victorian Sexuality* (Oxford: Oxford University Press, 1994), and *The Making of Victorian Sexual Attitudes* (Oxford: Oxford University Press, 1994). In the epilogue to the latter volume, Mason observes that the campaigns of Josephine Butler and other late Victorian feminists had a strong antisensualist dimension to them.

65. Burton, *Supplemental Nights,* vol. 6, p. 438.

66. Burton to Payne, Sept. 9, 1884, where he proclaimed: "all the women of England will read it and half the men will cut me." Similarly, he announced to Payne on Oct. 21, 1882: "The fair sex appears wild to get at the Nights." Metcalf Collection.

67. Stisted, *True Life,* p. 402.

68. This is evident, for example, from Isabel Burton's correspondence with J. J. Fahie, MS Eng. misc. d. 187, Bodleian Library, Oxford University.

69. Isabel Burton to Leonard Smithers, July 17, 1892, Burton/Smithers Correspondence, Huntington Library.

70. Isabel Burton to Eliza Lynn Linton, June 9, 1885, letter in the private possession of Burke Casari.

71. Isabel's handwriting marks passages for deletion in a copy of the "Terminal Essay" (B159) in the Metcalf Collection.

72. Burton, *Supplemental Nights,* vol. 6, p. 439.

73. Burton, *Supplemental Nights,* vol. 6, p. 439.

74. Kathleen Wilson, *The Island Race: Englishness, Empire, and Gender in the Eighteenth Century* (London: Routledge, 2003), pp. 142, 155.

75. Burton, *Nights,* vol. 3, pp. 40, 241.

76. Rana Kabbani, *Europe's Myths of Orient* (London: Macmillan, 1986), pp. 7, 66.

77. Irwin, *The Arabian Nights,* p. 159.

78. Burton, *Nights,* vol. 10, pp. 195, 192, 199.

79. Burton, *Nights,* vol. 10, p. 200.

80. *The Kama Sutra of Vatsyayana,* trans. Richard Burton and F. F. Arbuthnot (1884; reprint New York: Berkley Books, 1963), pp. 119, 116; *Ananga-Ranga,* p. vii.

81. Jim Colville, "Introduction" to al-Nafzawi, *The Perfumed Garden,* p. xi.

82. Burton, *Supplemental Nights,* vol. 6, p. 404.

83. See Bram Dijkstra, *Idols of Perversity: Fantasies of Feminine Evil in Fin-de-Siècle Culture* (New York: Oxford University Press, 1986), and Elaine Showalter, *Sexual Anarchy: Gender and Culture at the Fin de Siècle* (New York: Viking, 1990).

84. Burton to Payne, May 22, 1883, Metcalf Collection.

85. Richard F. Burton, "Terminal Essay," in Burton, *Nights,* vol. 10, pp. 63–302.

86. Burton's study of pederasty has attracted a good deal of scholarly attention in recent years. See, for example, Chris White, "Hunting the Pederast: Richard Burton's Exotic Erotology," in Tim Youngs, ed. *Writing and Race* (London: Longman, 1997), pp. 191–215; Richard Phillips, "Writing Travel and Mapping Sexuality: Richard Burton's Sotadic Zone," in James Duncan and Derek Gregory, eds., *Writes of Passage: Reading Travel Writing* (London: Routledge, 1999), pp. 70–91; and Colette Colligan, "'A Race of Born Pederasts': Sir Richard Burton, Homosexuality, and the Arabs," *Nineteenth-Century Contexts,* 25, no. 1 (2003): 1–20. Burton's interest in homosexualty is framed in the larger imperial context by Robert Aldrich, *Colonialism and Homosexuality* (London: Routledge, 2003), pp. 29–34.

87. Burton, *Nights,* vol. 10, p. 204.

88. According to Brian Reade, Burton's "Terminal Essay" was "the first account in English of any length or breadth devoted entirely to this matter." See Reade, ed., *Sexual Heretics: Male Homosexuality in English Literature from 1850 to 1900* (London: Routledge and Kegan Paul, 1970), p. 30.

89. Burton, *Nights,* vol. 10, p. 205n.

90. Burton, *Nights,* vol. 10, pp. 207, 208, 248. Elsewhere, Burton suggested that Muslim invaders introduced sodomy to India. *Kama Sutra* (1963 ed.), p. 155.

91. Burton, *Nights,* vol. 10, pp. 204, 209.

92. Colligan, "A Race of Born Pederasts," argues that Burton plays to Orientalist stereotypes of Arabs as pederasts. On the other hand, Rudi C. Bleys insists that ethnographic evidence of homosexuality in other cultures helped to instill a sense of moral relativism that aided the cause of emancipation for homosexuals. See Bleys, *The Geography of Perversity: Male-to-Male Sexual Behavior outside the West and the Ethnographic Imagination, 1750–1918* (New York: New York University Press, 1995). Also see Stephen O. Murray, "Some Nineteenth-Century Reports of Islamic Homosexualities," in Stephen O. Murray and Will Roscoe, eds., *Islamic*

Homosexualities: Culture, History, and Literature (New York: New York University Press, 1997), pp. 204–221.

93. John Addington Symonds, *A Problem of Modern Ethics* (London: privately published, 1896), pp. 78, 80. Elsewhere, Symonds refers to Burton's "composing a treatise on what he calls 'the third sex..." Herbert M. Schueller and Robert L. Peters, eds., *The Letters of John Addington Symonds* (Detroit: Wayne State University Press, 1969), vol. 3, p. 500. In *The Intermediate Sex: A Study of Some Transitional Types of Men and Women* (London: S. Sonnenschein, 1909), Edward Carpenter would coin a strikingly similar term for homosexuals, referring to them as the "intermediate sex."

94. Burton to John Payne, quoted in Wright, *Life*, vol. 2, p. 198.

95. See Burton, *Nights*, vol. 10, BL91(a), Huntington Library. This copy is signed "Isabel Burton's copy," though the annotations are Richard's.

96. See the prospectus for Sir Richard F. Burton, *Terminal Essay to the Thousand and One Nights* (London, 1890), in the Burton Collection, Royal Asiatic Society Library, London.

97. Burton to A. G. Ellis, Feb. 12, 1890, in the Burton Collection, Royal Asiatic Society Library.

98. Burton to Payne, Jan. 28, 1890, Metcalf Collection. It is unclear how much of the original Arabic manuscript was devoted to homosexual love. A translation published in 1975 suggests that homosexuality was the main focus of the work, but a 1999 translation devotes almost no attention to the subject. See Shaykh Nafzawi (Umar ibn Muhammed al-Nafzawi), *The Glory of the Perfumed Garden: The Missing Flowers: An English Translation from the Arabic of the Second and Hitherto Unpublished Part of Shaykh Nafzawi's Perfumed Garden* (London: Neville Spearman, 1975), and Muhammad ibn Muhammad al-Nafzawi, *The Perfumed Garden of Sensual Delight*, trans. Jim Colville (London: Kegan Paul International, 1999).

99. Penzer, *Annotated Bibliography*, p. 176.

100. Redesdale, *Memories*, vol. 2, p. 573.

101. Jeffrey Weeks, *Sex, Politics, and Society: The Regulation of Sexuality since 1800* (London: Longman, 1981), chap. 6.

102. Havelock Ellis and John Addington Symonds, *Sexual Inversion* (London: Wilson and Macmillan, 1897). The next important English-language study of homosexuality was Edward Carpenter's *Intermediate Sex* (1909). For an introduction to the lives and work of Ellis and Carpenter, see Sheila Rowbotham and Jeffrey Weeks, *Socialism and the New Life: The Personal and Sexual Politics of Edward Carpenter and Havelock Ellis* (London: Pluto Press, 1977).

103. Phyllis Grosskurth, *Havelock Ellis: A Biography* (New York: Alfred A. Knopf, 1980), chaps. 11–12.
104. Ellis and Symonds, *Sexual Inversion,* pp. 3, 9, 22.
105. Ellis and Symonds, *Sexual Inversion,* p. 23n.
106. Ellis and Symonds, *Sexual Inversion,* p. vi.
107. Burton makes several references to the Cleveland Street scandal in letters to Leonard Smithers. See Burton to Smithers, Dec. 20, 1888, and Nov. 20, 1889, reproduced in Donald A. Young, "The Selected Correspondence of Sir Richard Burton, 1848–1890" (M.A. thesis, University of Nebraska, 1979), pp. 259, 287.
108. See James G. Nelson, *Publisher to the Decadents: Leonard Smithers in the Careers of Beardsley, Wilde, Dowson* (University Park, Penn.: Pennsylvania State University Press, 2000).
109. *Priapeia or the Sportive Epigrams of divers Poets on Priapus: the Latin Text now for the first time Englished in Verse and Prose (the Metrical Version by "Outidanos") with Introduction, Notes Explanatory and Illustrative, and Excursus by "Neaniskos"* (Cosmopoli: privately printed for the Erotika Biblion Society, 1890); *The Carmina of Caius Valerius Catullus, Now first completely Englished into Verse and Prose, the Metrical Part by Capt. Sir Richard F. Burton . . . and the Prose Portion, Introduction, and Notes Explanatory and Illustrative by Leonard C. Smithers* (London: privately printed, 1894).
110. See the remarkable correspondence between the Burtons and Smithers in the Huntington Library, which is examined in Kennedy and Casari, "Burnt Offerings". Sheffield, the city where Smithers resided, had an especially active National Vigilance Association chapter that worked closely with authorities to expose and prosecute individuals it deemed a threat to public morals. Mort, *Dangerous Sexualities,* p. 135.
111. Edward Carpenter, *Intermediate Types among Primitive Folk: A Study in Social Evolution* (London: George Allen and Unwin, 1919). Part 1 of this book originally appeared in several journals in 1911.
112. Alex Owen, "The Sorcerer and His Apprentice: Aleister Crowley and the Magical Exploration of Edwardian Subjectivity," *Journal of British Studies,* 36, no. 1 (January 1997): 113.
113. Nelson, *Publisher to the Decadents;* Thomas Jay Garbaty, "The French Coterie of the *Savoy* 1896," *PMLA,* 75, no. 5 (December 1960): 609–615.
114. See the bound copy of Burton's "Terminal Essay," p. 114, in the Huntington Library, Metcalf Collection, B159.
115. Ironically, in this regard Burton's motivation was not all that different from the self-proclaimed intent of our own era's postcolonial theorists,

who see themselves as engaged in "a critical ethnography of the West." Homi Bhabha, "The Postcolonial Critic," *Arena*, 96 (1991): 54, quoted in Robert J. C. Young, *Colonial Desire: Hybridity in Theory, Culture, and Race* (London: Routledge, 1995), p. 163.

8. THE AFTERLIFE

1. W. H. Wilkins, *The Romance of Isabel Lady Burton: The Story of Her Life* (New York: Dodd Mead, 1897), vol. 1, p. 54.

2. Alfred Bates Richards, Andrew Wilson, and St. Clair Baddeley, *A Sketch of the Career of Richard F. Burton* (London: Waterlow and Sons, 1886); Francis Hitchman, *Richard F. Burton, K.C.M.G.: His Early, Private, and Public Life with an Account of His Travels and Explorations*, 2 vols. (London: Sampson Low, Marston, Searle and Rivington, 1887).

3. Burton's library was well stocked with the major religions' sacred texts, as well as various other religious works written in an astonishing array of languages. In addition to a lengthy list of books related to orthodox Christianity, Judaism, and Islam, he had works on Hinduism, Buddhism, Mormonism, Spiritualism, Swedenborgism, ancient Egyptian mythology, and witchcraft and occultism. See B. J. Kirkpatrick, ed., *A Catalogue of the Library of Sir Richard Burton* (London: Royal Anthropological Society, 1978).

4. See, for example, Richard F. Burton, *Sindh and the Races That Inhabit the Valley of the Indus* (1851; reprint Karachi: Oxford University Press, 1973), pp. 174–194.

5. Richard F. Burton, *Personal Narrative of a Pilgrimage to Al-Madinah and Meccah*, memorial ed. (1893; reprint New York: Dover, 1964), vol. 1, p. 428.

6. See Alison Winter, *Mesmerized: Powers of Mind in Victorian Britain* (Chicago: University of Chicago Press, 1998).

7. Isabel Burton, *The Life of Captain Sir Richard F. Burton* (London: Chapman and Hall, 1893), vol. 1, p. 450. Isabel explained: "I did not like it, and used to resist it, but after a while I consented. . . . Once mesmerized, he had only to say, 'Talk,' and I used to tell everything I knew. . . . I often told him things that I would much rather keep to myself" (pp. 450–451). Given these sentiments, it is scarcely surprising that Isabel erupted into a rage of jealousy when she learned that on one occasion Richard had mesmerized another woman outside her presence. See Bertrand Russell and Patricia Russell, eds., *The Amberley Papers* (New York: Simon and Schuster, 1937), vol. 1, pp. 349–350. Men invariably were the mesmerizers, women the mesmerized, a situation that recapitulated traditional gender power relations. Wilfred Scawen Blunt remarked that Burton seemed to

possess a hypnotic control over his wife. Blunt, *My Diaries* (London: Martin Seeker, 1921), part 2, p. 129.

8. Richard F. Burton, *Explorations of the Highlands of Brazil* (London: Tinsley Brothers, 1869), vol. 1, p. 391n.

9. See Alex Owen, *The Darkened Room: Women, Power, and Spiritualism in Late Victorian England* (Philadelphia: University of Pennsylvania Press, 1990).

10. See Peter van der Veer, *Imperial Encounters: Religion and Modernity in India and Britain* (Princeton: Princeton University Press, 2001), chap. 3. Burton owned a copy of Madame Blavatsky's *Isis Unveiled: A Master-Key to the Mysteries of Ancient and Modern Science and Theology,* 2nd ed. (London: Bernard Quaritch, 1877).

11. Richard F. Burton, "Spiritualism in Eastern Lands," *The Humanitarian,* 10, no. 6 (June 1897): 409, 405. This is a reprint of an article that originally appeared in *The Spiritualist* in 1878. Also see Richard F. Burton, "Spirit Phenomena," *The Times,* Nov. 13, 1876, p. 7; and "Captain R. F. Burton's Experiences" in W. H. Harrison, ed., *Psychic Facts* (London: W. H. Harrison, 1880), pp. 70–79.

12. Isabel Burton, *Life,* vol. 2, pp. 120, 137. On this matter, as in many others regarding life after death, Isabel disagreed. Several years after Richard's death, she reported to a friend that she got "spiritual messages and signs from him." Isabel Burton to Alexander Wheelock Thayer, Jan. 5, 1894, Library of the Boston Athenaeum.

13. Burton's interest in electric telepathy is noted by Isabel Burton in a letter to J. J. Fahie, Jan. 12, 1885, MS Eng. misc. d. 187, Bodleian Library, Oxford.

14. Burton to Gerald Massey, May 28, 1881, in Donald A. Young, "The Selected Correspondence of Sir Richard Burton, 1848–1890" (M.A. thesis, University of Nebraska, 1979), p. 228.

15. Richard F. Burton, *A Glance at the "Passion Play"* (London: W. H. Harrison, 1881), pp. 165–168.

16. The fullest account of these events is given by Mary S. Lovell, *A Rage to Live: A Biography of Richard and Isabel Burton* (New York: W. W. Norton, 1998), pp. 731–733.

17. For a fascinating study of this issue, see George K. Behlmer, "Grave Doubts: Victorian Medicine, Moral Panic, and the Signs of Death," *Journal of British Studies,* 42, no. 2 (April 2003): 206–235.

18. Isabel Burton to Eliza "Dilly" Fitzgerald, Dec. 30, 1895, Burton Papers, 2667/26, Box 2, Wiltshire Record Office.

19. Last Will and Testament of Isabel Lady Burton, Dec. 28, 1895, in Alan

F. S. Mackenzie, "Captain Sir Richard F. Burton, K.C.M.G., and Lady Isabel (Arundell) Burton, His Wife: Vital Statistics" (typescript, 1971), X.705/153, British Library.

20. "Will and Last Wishes of Isabel Burton" (typescript), Burton Papers, 2667/26, Box 2, Wiltshire Record Office.

21. It was widely assumed that Isabel Burton burned all of Richard's private journals and correspondence, as well as most of his unfinished manuscripts, in a bonfire at her Trieste residence. But the Burton papers recently donated to the Wiltshire Record Office by the Arundell family conclusively demonstrate that much of the material thought to have been destroyed in that fire actually survived at least until Isabel's own death. See the handwritten inventory of the contents of Isabel's Baker Street residence and the typescript "Private Instructions for my Sister" (2667/26, Box 2). In a meticulous analysis of the Wiltshire papers and other evidence, Mary Lovell has concluded that what Isabel destroyed in Trieste was "The Scented Garden," an unnamed satiric poem critical of many of Burton's contemporaries, and a lot of useless paperwork. See Lovell, *A Rage to Live*, pp. 746–751.

22. The letter, which appeared in the *Morning Post* on June 19, 1891, is reprinted in Burton and Wilkins, *Romance*, vol. 2, pp. 723–726.

23. Isabel Burton, "Sir Richard Burton: An Explanation and a Defence," *The New Review*, 7, no. 42 (November 1892): 567.

24. Statement by Isabel Burton in a packet of letters labeled "Letchford," Burton Papers, 2667/26, Box 2, Wiltshire Record Office. Burton left a shockingly meager personal estate valued at only £188, which was further reduced by the cost of the funeral ceremony in Trieste and the expenses required to settle affairs there and ship possessions and Burton's body back to England. *The Times*, April 7, 1891, p. 10.

25. For a fuller treatment of the argument advanced in this paragraph and the following two, see Dane Kennedy and Burke E. Casari, "Burnt Offerings: Isabel Burton and 'The Scented Garden' Manuscript," *Journal of Victorian Culture*, 2, no. 2 (Autumn 1997): 229–244.

26. Isabel Burton to Leonard Smithers, July 21, 1891, in the Burton/Smithers correspondence, Huntington Library.

27. *The Carmina of Caius Valerius Catullus: Now First Completely Englished into Verse and Prose*, trans. Richard F. Burton and Leonard C. Smithers (London: printed for the translators, 1894); *Il Pentamerone; or, the Tale of Tales*, trans. Richard F. Burton (London: privately printed, 1894).

28. *Pall Mall Gazette*, March 7, 1894. This and other reviews of *Il Pen-*

tamerone can be found in a book of newspaper cuttings in the Burton Papers, 2667/26, Box 4, Wiltshire Record Office.

29. "Prospectus for the Memorial Edition of the Works of Sir Richard F. Burton," Burton Papers, Royal Asiatic Society, London.

30. See "Prospectus to the Library Edition in Twelve Volumes of Captain Sir R. F. Burton's Arabian Nights," Burton Papers, 2667/26, Box 2, Wiltshire Record Office, which states that it was the most complete edition "which can ever be published, the extreme grossness of the few passages excised absolutely precluding their appearance. These few alterations . . . enable it to be lifted from the shelf of pornography."

31. Isabel issued a public denial of any role in the publication of the Library Edition of the Nights. See the typescript letter to the editor of the *Whitehall Review* (no date), in Burton Papers, 2667/26, Box 2, Wiltshire Record Office. In an effort to prevent the publication of a fake copy of "The Scented Garden" and, it seems, to restore the luster of her reputation, Isabel decided shortly before her death to add the National Vigilance Society official William Coote as a trustee of her late husband's literary estate! If she was reunited with Richard in an afterlife, one wonders what sort of reception she received. Isabel Burton, "The Scented Garden," typed manuscript (no date), Burton Papers, 2667/26, Box 2. Also see William Alexander Coote, *A Romance of Philanthropy* (London: The National Vigilance Association, 1916), p. 111; and Lovell, *A Rage to Live,* p. 783.

32. Lovell, *A Rage to Live,* p. 788.

33. Cecil Y. Lang, ed., *The Swinburne Letters* (New Haven: Yale University Press, 1959), vol. 2, p. 336; vol. 6, p. 45.

34. Algernon Charles Swinburne, "Elegy," *Fortnightly Review,* 307, n.s. (July 1, 1892): 1–5.

35. Isabel Burton to Eliza Lynn Linton, June 9, 1885, letter in the private possession of Burke Casari.

36. E. Lynn Linton, "The Partisans of the Wild Women," *The Nineteenth Century,* 31 (March 1892): 455, 463, 461. See also Nancy Fix Anderson, *Women against Women in Victorian England: A Life of Eliza Lynn Linton* (Bloomington: Indiana University Press, 1987), esp. p. 202.

37. In *The Inner Life of Syria, Palestine, and the Holy Land* (London: Henry S. King, 1975), vol. 2, pp. 128–129, Isabel Burton refused to endorse women's suffrage, though she did express confidence that women would be a stabilizing, conservative force if granted the vote.

38. See Monica Stirling, *The Fine and the Wicked: The Life and Times of Ouida* (New York: Coward-McCann, 1958), pp. 49, 64.

39. Wilkins, *Romance,* vol. 2, p. 727.
40. Georgiana M. Stisted, *The True Life of Capt. Sir Richard F. Burton* (London: H. S. Nichols, 1896), pp. 275, 414, 403.
41. Isabel Burton has been the subject of several biographical treatments. In addition to Wilkins, *The Romance,* see Jean Burton, *Sir Richard Burton's Wife* (New York: Alfred A. Knopf, 1941); Lesley Branch, *The Wilder Shores of Love* (New York: Simon and Schuster, 1954), chap. 1; and the dual biography of Richard and Isabel by Mary Lovell, *A Rage to Live.*
42. Norman M. Penzer, *An Annotated Bibliography of Sir Richard Francis Burton* (New York: Burt Franklin, 1923), p. 98.
43. Philip Jose Farmer, *To Your Scattered Bodies Go* (1971; reprint New York: Ballantine Books, 1998). I am grateful to Michael Saler for bring this work to my attention.
44. John Theodore Tussaud, *The Romance of Madame Tussaud's* (New York: George H. Doran, 1920), pp. 205–206.
45. Walter Phelps Dodge, *The Real Sir Richard Burton* (London: T. Fisher Unwin, 1907).
46. Fairfax Downey, *Burton: Arabian Nights Adventurer* (New York: Charles Scribner's Sons, 1931); Seaton Deardon, *The Arabian Knight: A Study of Sir Richard Burton* (London: Arthur Barker, 1936); Allen Edwardes, *Death Rides a Camel: A Biography of Sir Richard Burton* (New York: Julian Press, 1963). Also see Achmed Abdullah and T. Compton Pakenham, *Dreamers of Empire* (New York: Frederick A. Stokes, 1929), which portrays Burton as one who had a special affinity for Arabs, and Thomas J. Assad, *Three Victorian Travellers: Burton, Blunt, Doughty* (London: Routledge and Kegan Paul, 1964), which focuses on Burton as an Arabian explorer.
47. Hugh Schonfield, *Richard Burton, Explorer* (London: Herbert Joseph, 1936).
48. Novels about Burton include William Rayner, *Trail to Bear Paw Mountain* (London: Collins, 1974), Win Blevins, *The Rock Child* (New York: Tom Doherty Associates, 1998), Farmer, *To Your Scattered Bodies Go,* and, most recently, John Dunning, *The Bookman's Promise* (New York: Scribner, 2004), a mystery framed around the discovery of an unknown Burton diary. Both Edwardes, *Death Rides a Camel,* and Alfred Bercovici, *That Blackguard Burton!* (Indianapolis: Bobbs-Merrill, 1962), invent scenes and dialogue for their "biographies" of Burton. Works for children and young adults include Charnan Simon, *Richard Burton: The World's Great Explorers* (Chicago: Children's Press, 1991), and Arthur Orrmont, *Fearless Adventurer: Sir Richard Burton* (New York: Julian Messner, 1969).

49. Alan Moorehead, *The White Nile* (London: Hamish Hamilton, 1960); British Broadcasting Corporation, "The Search for the Nile" (1971); William Harrison, *Burton and Speke* (New York: St. Martin's, 1982); Bob Rafelson, director, *The Mountains of the Moon* (Tri-Star Pictures, 1989). The relevant biographies are Byron Farwell, *Burton: A Biography of Sir Richard Francis Burton* (New York: Holt, Rinehart and Winston, 1963); Fawn M. Brodie, *The Devil Drives: A Life of Sir Richard Burton* (New York: W. W. Norton, 1967); and Michael Hastings, *Sir Richard Burton* (London: Hodder and Stoughton, 1978).

50. H. St. John B. Philby, *Arabian Days: An Autobiography* (London: Robert Hale, 1948), p. xvi.

51. Michael Asher, *Thesiger: A Biography* (London: Viking, 1994), p. 289. Seconded into service with the Druzes of Syria during World War II, Thesiger was well aware that Burton had spent time among the Druzes and admired them (p. 207).

52. Christopher Ondaatje, *Sindh Revisited: A Journey in the Footsteps of Captain Sir Richard Francis Burton* (Toronto: HarperCollins, 1996); Christopher Ondaatje, *Journey to the Source of the Nile: An Extraordinary Quest to Solve the Riddle of the World's Longest River* (New York: HarperCollins, 1998).

53. Nicholas Shakespeare, *Bruce Chatwin* (New York: Doubleday, 2000), p. 564. For references to Burton's influence on Chatwin, see pp. 58, 338, 350.

54. Alex Owen, "The Sorcerer and His Apprendice: Aleister Crowley and the Magical Exploration of Edwardian Subjectivity," *Journal of British Studies*, 36, no. 1 (January 1997): 113, 114. For Crowley's admiration for Burton more generally, see Lawrence Sutin, *Do What Thou Wilt: A Life of Aleister Crowley* (New York: St. Martin's, 2000), pp. 35, 51, 200.

55. Colette Colligan, "'A Race of Born Pederasts': Sir Richard Burton, Homosexuality, and the Arabs," *Nineteenth-Century Contexts*, 25, no. 1 (2003): 12–13.

56. In addition to English and American editions that were privately printed for subscribers, recent research by Deana Heath has found that Indian dealers were marketing English-language translations of the *Kama Sutra* to English buyers by mail. It is unclear whether these were pirated editions of the Burton-Arbuthnot translation or independent translations. According to Penzer, K. Rauguswami Iyengar published a complete English-language translation of the *Kama Sutra* in Lahore in 1921. Private communication by Deana Heath, Feb. 19, 2004, and Penzer, *Annotated Bibliography*, pp. 167–168.

57. Richard F. Burton, *Love, War, and Fancy: The Customs and Manners of the East, from Writings on the Arabian Nights,* ed. Kenneth Walker (London: W. Kimber, 1964); Richard F. Burton, *The Erotic Traveler,* ed. Edward Leigh (New York: G. P. Putnam's Sons, 1967). A new edition of the Burton-Arbuthnot translation of the *Kama Sutra* was issued jointly by George Allen and Unwin of London and G. P. Putnam's Sons of New York in 1963, with an introduction by W. G. Archer.

58. George Allgrove, *Love in the East* (London: Anthony Gibbs and Phillips, 1962), p. 12.

59. Important new scholarly translations of the *Kama Sutra* have been produced by Alain Danielou and Wendy Doniger and Sudhir Kakar. Among the many *Kama Sutra* titles are *The Complete Illustrated Kama Sutra, The Complete Idiot's Guide to the Kama Sutra, The Pop-up Kama Sutra, The Gay Man's Kama Sutra, The Women's Kama Sutra,* and *The Office Kama Sutra.*

60. Edward Rice, *Captain Sir Richard Francis Burton: The Secret Agent Who Made the Pilgrimage to Mecca, Discovered the Kama Sutra, and Brought the Arabian Nights to the West* (New York: Charles Scribner's Sons, 1990). The subtitle also reflects a renewed attention to the association between Burton and the Arabian world. Burton's personal sexual proclivities also have assumed a more central role in recent biographies. In addition to Rice, see Frank McLynn, *Burton: Snow upon the Desert* (London: John Murray, 1990), and Lovell, *A Rage to Live.*

61. Marcus Ardonne, ed. (pseud), *The Secret Sutras: The "Lost" Erotic Journals of Sir Richard Burton* (London: Hodder and Stoughton, 1996).

62. Lee Siegel, *Love in a Dead Language* (Chicago: University of Chicago Press, 1999), p. 16n6.

63. These include a new Modern Library edition published in 2001 with an introduction by A. S. Byatt. Even the Arabian Nights authority Robert Irwin, who has little good to say about Burton's translation, uses it in his *Arabian Nights: A Companion* (London: Penguin, 1994).

64. The auction announcement attracted the notice of the British popular press as well as anti-Semitic outlets such as David Irving's Action Report On-line.

65. Ondaatje, *Sindh Revisited,* pp. 150. This Sindhi translation is *Sindu 'ain Sindh-u mathr-i'a men rathandaru quam-un* (Milanaajohandu: Sindhi Adab-I Bord jo Buk, 1976).

66. Ralph E. Drake-Brockman, *British Somaliland* (London: Hurst and Blackett, 1912), p. 25.

67. I. M. Lewis, *A Modern History of Somali: Nation and State in the Horn of*

Africa, rev. ed. (Boulder, Colo.: Westview, 1988), p. 36. I am grateful to Laura Tabili for bringing this reference and the following one to my attention.

68. Farrax M. J. Cawl, *Ignorance Is the Enemy of Love*, trans. B. W. Andrzejewski (London: Zed, 1982), pp. 15–16.

Acknowledgements

This book can be seen as a belated attempt to practice what I preached nearly a decade ago, when I wrote a rather polemical essay urging historians to find a middle way between a theoretically challenged historiography on British imperialism and an empirically challenged body of literature known as postcolonial theory ("Imperial History and Post-Colonial Theory," *Journal of Imperial and Commonwealth History*, 24, no. 3 [September 1996]: 345–363). One of the few advantages of taking so long to act on my own exhortation is that I have been able to benefit from the wealth of new scholarship that has appeared in the interim, much of it responsive to the challenge I originally referred to. My delay also has allowed me to draw on the advice and assistance of far more people than would have been the case had the project proceeded more quickly and smoothly.

I started the research for this book when I was on the faculty of the University of Nebraska, Lincoln, where I was sustained by the support of some outstanding colleagues. I want to thank in particular David Cahan, Parks Coble, Jessica Coope, Tim Mahoney, Pete Mazlowski, Ben Rader, Alan Steinweis, Ken Winkle, and John Wunder, many of them members of a nineteenth-century studies group that read early drafts of several chapters. I am equally fortunate to find myself among such a remarkably congenial and intellectually vibrant group of colleagues at George Washington University, among them Muriel Atkin, Bill Becker, Ed Berkowitz, Nemata Blyden, Emmet Kennedy, Dina Khoury, Peter Klaren, Kirk Larsen, Linda Levy Peck, Ron Spector, and Andrew Zimmerman. I am grateful to Pradeep Barua for inviting me to try out some early arguments about Burton in a lecture at the University of Nebraska at Kearney, and to Oliver Pollak and the History Department at the University of Nebraska at Omaha, who invited me to deliver their fourth annual Richard Dean Winchell Lecture. Wm. Roger Louis and Tom Metcalf hosted the New Imperial History Conference at the University of Texas at Austin, where a draft of Chapter 5 benefited from their comments and those of the other participants. Drafts of other chapters were delivered as papers at sessions of the Association of Asian Studies, the Pacific Coast Conference on British Studies, and the Anglo-American Conference in London, as well as at an imperial history workshop organized in honor of Peter Marshall at King's College, London. It is impossible to specify the various ways panelists and members of the audience at these gatherings have aided this project, but I would be negligent if I didn't acknowledge the fact that they made useful contributions. A number of people have supplied me with references, translations, clarifications, and other forms of assistance: thanks to Muriel Atkin, Burke Casari, Eric Cline, David Gilmartin, Deana Heath, Alan Jutzi, the late Quentin Keynes, Dina Khoury, Peter Mellini, Paul Nurse, Doug Peers, Michael Saler, Laura Tabili, and John Wunder. Elizabeth Shaw and Michael Wright shared their home and hospitality during several stays in London. The following friends and colleagues took the time and trouble to read and comment on portions of the manuscript: Hibba Abugideiri, Nemata Blyden, Antoinette Burton, Burke Casari, Michael Fisher, Richard Price, Heather Sharkey, Lynn Zastoupil, and Andrew Zimmerman. My editors, Joyce Seltzer and Nancy Clemente, also gave the manuscript a close and helpful reading. I am very grateful to each of them for giving me such shrewd advice and saving me from some egregious blunders. For those that remain, the stock phrase still applies: I alone am to blame.

Institutional support has been equally important to the completion of this project. Early on a Fletcher Jones Fellowship from the Huntington Library allowed me to spend several months working through its superb Burton holdings. More recently I had the good fortune to receive a fellowship from the John Simon Guggenheim Foundation, which gave me the time to complete the book without interruption. Both George Washington University and the University of Nebraska at Lincoln were generous in their sabbatical and travel support. An early version of Chapter VII appeared in *The Journal of British Studies,* published by the University of Chicago Press, under the title "Captain Burton's Oriental Muck-Heap" (©2000 by the North American Conference on British Studies; all rights reserved).

Finally, Marty has my love and thanks for her continued advice, support, and example.

Index